A timely, seminal work on ethical responsibility for a post-digital world. This valuable guide could only come from a person with Wally Snyder's unique communication industry experience, legal background and sensibilities. This book, plus Wally's ethics certification program through his Institute of Advertising Ethics at the American Advertising Federation in partnership with the University of Missouri, are paving the way for greater responsibility and accountability at this time when content is increasingly created by individuals.

Tim Love, Former Vice Chair, Omnicom, USA

Wally Snyder's book, *Ethics in Advertising*, provides us an excellent blueprint on the role and value of ethical standards as an essential ingredient of business and advertising practices. This comprehensive review demonstrates how such standards are a direct benefit to the business community and to the consuming public.

Howard H. Bell, President Emeritus, American Advertising Federation, USA

I can't think of any person better qualified to literally write the book on ethics in advertising than Wally Snyder. The combination of Wally's experience, integrity, passion and industry influence gives him the unique ability to both espouse new standards and to tell us how to practically incorporate them into our businesses.

Linda Thomas Brooks, President and CEO, MPA—The Association of Magazine Media, USA

Usually, we preach that actions matter far more than words, but Snyder's words offer great insights into how reputations are built over time and how quickly they can crumble. Like the brands represented by our company, those who consistently invest in a purposeful, ethical, and positive mission will prosper most in society and in this industry.

John Osborn, CEO, BBDO New York, USA

ETHICS IN ADVERTISING

This book provides students and practitioners with a comprehensive overview of the rules and principles associated with ethical advertising practices. With extensive research, and a variety of case studies, and expert opinions, it discusses why advertising ethics is important both to the consumer and the professional.

The author presents the rules of ethical conduct recommended by the Institute for Advertising Ethics and demonstrates how these are applied in practice, examining why ethics is important; what the ethical dilemmas the industry faces are; and how to motivate better practices among professionals. The book uses real life stories of "native advertising," marketing to children, and diversity in advertising to show how professionals can be inspired to "do the right thing" for consumers and their companies. Readers will learn how they can solve ethical dilemmas to their personal satisfaction in the competitive work environment.

This balanced perspective to the ethical issues that arise in the advertising industry is sure to resonate with students of advertising and marketing.

Wally Snyder serves as Distinguished Visiting Professor at the University of Missouri, Professor and Senior Advisor for Advertising Ethics at Michigan State University, and Chair of the National Advertising Review Board, USA.

ETHICS IN ADVERTISING

Making the case for doing the right thing

Wally Snyder

Routledge
Taylor & Francis Group

NEW YORK AND LONDON

First published 2017
by Routledge
711 Third Avenue, New York, NY 10017

and by Routledge
2 Park Square, Milton Park, Abingdon, Oxon OX14 4RN

Routledge is an imprint of the Taylor & Francis Group, an informa business

Library of Congress Cataloging in Publication Data
A catalog record for this book has been requested

ISBN: 978-1-138-18898-3 (hbk)
ISBN: 978-1-138-18899-0 (pbk)
ISBN: 978-1-315-64194-2 (ebk)

Typeset in Bembo
by Taylor & Francis Books

To my wife, Jean Snyder
To our sons, Charlie and Steve
who always love and encourage me in my life and ethics
A special note of thanks to Jean for helping me proof
the text.

CONTENTS

Foreword		*xiii*
Preface		*xv*
1	The business and personal cases for enhanced advertising ethics	1
2	"Do the Right Thing" for consumers: The law and rising above it	14
3	Advertise to children fairly and appropriately	50
4	"Native Advertising": Transparency of advertising content	84
5	"Behavioral advertising": Protecting consumer privacy	103
6	The ethics of multicultural advertising and diversity	115
7	Ethical dilemmas we face in our business transactions	131
8	Inspiring and achieving enhanced advertising ethics	146
Index		*176*

I believe that advertising, news and editorial should alike serve the best interests of readers; that a single standard of helpful truth and cleanness should prevail for all.

The Journalist Creed by Walter Williams, Dean, School of Journalism,
University of Missouri 1908–1935

Trust is the Currency of our Business and Ethics is the Engine of Trust.

David Bell, Former Chair, IPG

FOREWORD

The "hot" term in business today is Corporate Social Responsibility (CSR), but no matter what you call it, ethics in business has never garnered so much public attention. With the grand ethical lapses that led to Volkswagen's desperate struggle for survival, and the similar faulty judgments that led to a rash of recalls for General Motors just a couple of years before that, the problems in just the automotive industry stand as iconic of the need for ethics training in business. I point to those two companies because they so clearly illustrate that good ethics is good business, and ethical voids are likely to lead to financial disasters. That really is the subtext of this book, and it can be taken as a primer in avoiding such missteps, at least in the area of advertising.

Wally Snyder is the perfect author for a book of this sort. Early in his career his role was that of a leading industry Inquisitor, a regulator of the advertising field, when he worked for the Federal Trade Commission (FTC). But, then, he transitioned to a role more akin to Chief Defender of Advertising, when serving for many years as the head of the American Advertising Federation (AAF). As such, he truly has seen both sides, appreciating both the arguments and counter-arguments surrounding ethical (and, of course, regulatory) considerations regarding advertising.

His more recent roles, as both Executive Director of the Institute for Advertising Ethics (IAE) and Chairman of the National Advertising Review Board (NARB), land him in precisely the right spot to demonstrate his unique insights into the ethical considerations affecting the practice of advertising. To the best of my knowledge, there is no one on this planet with the range of experience and perspectives on advertising ethics that could even put them in the same ballpark with Wally Snyder.

Business ethics is often perceived as anti-business, or as implying a demand for diminished profits in service of the "public good." I suspect that when he moved from the FTC to his role at the AAF, some critics of advertising saw Wally as jumping to the dark side. But what I've observed is that Wally always saw the value of advertising to our economy, and that belief is clearly front and center in this book. He reconciles those disparate, and sometimes opposite, perspectives by recognizing that both views have merit.

In this book he artfully treads that fine line between pro and con by framing it within the Business Case and the Personal Case for ethical decision-making, illustrating how ethical practices benefit not just the "public" but *everyone*, without need to push those standards to an excess that undermines the inherent value of advertisements. He is all about pursuing the "win-win" scenario, where the best ethical practices benefit business as much as the consumer.

The book takes us through some of the hottest topics in the profession today, from selling to children, native advertising, and privacy, to pharmaceutical promotions. In a case by case approach, he illustrates how ethical standards can be applied to achieve that win-win, in several cases showing real-world examples he gathered from industry leaders. Rather than lay out the abstract ethical ideals and then leave it to the reader to figure out how those ideals fit in their own lives, as so many ethics books do, Wally makes it tangible and easily comprehensible.

Wally Snyder shows that even someone who has spent years defending the advertising industry, and who sits in the Advertising Hall of Fame, can have a strong moral and ethical compass by which he has led his life. And following that compass, he is leading the rest of the industry down the high road. His mantra throughout this book is "Do the right thing." And he does.

Jef I. Richards
Professor and Chair
Department of Advertising and Public Relations
Michigan State University

PREFACE

When counseling on advertising ethics I engage in the "Why, What and How" of enhanced advertising ethics. Using research, case studies and expert opinions we first discuss why advertising ethics is important to both the consumer and the professional. Then, the discussion details the current ethical dilemmas our professionals are confronting daily in both ad and PR content and in their business interactions within and among clients agencies, media and services. The book documents with real life stories how our professionals can be inspired to "Do the right thing" for consumers, their companies, and how they can solve ethical dilemmas to their personal satisfaction in a very competitive work environment.

"Do the right thing." This is my basic definition of what it means to practice enhanced ethics. It has been one of the basic tenets for personal and business ethics over the centuries. We need to understand and appreciate from the outset that doing the right thing includes doing, and often rising above, what the law requires, and our ethical dilemmas will engage us in "gray areas" of the ad business that are not easy to resolve, including treating children fairly and avoiding ad content that is offensive.

A fair question directed to me is why am I so interested in the practice of enhanced advertising ethics? When did my interest in doing the right thing begin, and what do I, as a lawyer, have to contribute to motivating our industry to do so?

My commitment to business law and ethics commenced with my graduation from law school and move to Washington, DC, over forty years ago. I joined the Federal Trade Commission, as a trial lawyer, at the very time "consumer protection" was ignited by Ralph Nader; the regulation of national advertising became a major federal mission. In the early years of my government career, the FTC ruled that advertisers must have a "prior reasonable basis" for their ad claims, and I served as a trial attorney in several ad cases involving major advertisers and their agencies.

The increased governmental activity was prompted by a belief in the importance of truthful advertising to the economic welfare of consumers. In fact, the Supreme Court ruled for the first time that truthful advertising was protected by the First Amendment to the U.S. Constitution, stating that oftentimes commercial information is more important to the public than political speech. In addition to bringing cases against false advertising, the FTC and Justice Department brought cases against the American Medical Association and other professional groups that had prohibited their members from advertising.

In addition to believing in the importance of truthful advertising, I realized as a practicing attorney that government could only do so much in advancing the consumer's interest. There are only so many cases and investigations that can be conducted. Also, government was not—and should not be—involved in the ethical dilemmas arising above the law. While government plays an important role in setting legal standards, it is up to the industry, and its professionals, "To Do The Right Thing" for consumers. Therefore, I was heartened by the industry's advertising self-regulation program begun in the early 1970s. Howard Bell, as president of the American Advertising Federation (AAF), played a major role in creating the Advertising Self-Regulation Review Council (ASRC), and I was privileged to often attend ad industry conferences as a representative of the FTC. Howard became a mentor to me on the importance of the industry, itself, encouraging its professionals to practice truthful and honest advertising. Today, I am honored to be the Chair of the National Advertising Review Board, the appellate body of the industry's self-regulatory program.

After I joined the AAF, first in government relations, and then as president, I worked on major national issues, including the taxation of advertising and the First Amendment protection of the advertising of controversial products that, as I discuss, demanded my ethical thinking.

I also got the opportunity at the time to meet and learn from many ad professionals who demonstrated their belief in the importance of advertising and their commitment to high personal ethics. These included David Bell, Chairman of the Inter-Public Group of agencies; Dave Park, president of DDB Los Angeles; Keith Reinhardt, Chairman of DDB; John Osborn, president of BBDO New York; Janet Robinson, president of the New York Times; Carla Michelotti, General Counsel, Leo Burnett; Tim Love, Vice Chair of Omnicom; Linda Thomas Brooks, President and CEO, MPA; and many other national leaders.

I also had the opportunity to meet outstanding local ad leaders through AAF's local ad federations, as well as college students and leading academics from our college chapter network. It was from twenty-three years of representing the ad industry and serving as its counselor that I honed my belief in the critical importance ethics plays in our business and in the professional and personal lives of our professionals.

During the past seven years I have had the opportunity to engage in dialogue and learning about ad ethics with the academic community. Serving as visiting professor at the Missouri School of Journalism, and as professor, senior ethics advisor, at Michigan State University, I have interacted with students and professors, including Jef Richards, Chair of the Advertising and PR Department at Michigan State, and Margaret Duffy, Chair of the Communications Department at the Missouri School of Journalism, in teaching and learning the depth and breadth of ad ethics. They have become my mentors and partners in advancing ad ethics. This has included presenting ethics classes on campus and overseeing student research on the importance of ad ethics to consumers and professionals, and videoing the students in breakout sessions where they grappled with tough ethical dilemmas. My on-campus dialogues have inspired me, as I witness the students' commitment to enhanced ethics and to becoming "professionals" in the finest sense of the word.

Ten years ago I wrote my first article on the critical role enhanced ethics plays in the advertising industry. "Ethics in Advertising: The Players, the Rules and the Scorecard" was published in the University of Florida's *Business and Professional Ethics Journal.* Looking back we can see that our industry is still grappling today with many of the same ethical dilemmas. A focus is taken in this book on consumer privacy, treating children fairly in advertising directed to them, and promoting diversity and fairness in multicultural marketing. Also, time is taken to discuss the needed ethical response to advertising controversial products including prescription drugs and E-cigarettes.

In addition, two ethical dilemmas have emerged as major consumer issues that the government demands be resolved: the blurring of the line between advertising and news/editorial (that can occur in "native advertising"), and the lack of transparency in consumer blogs and other forms of endorsements. This book explores these ethical dilemmas, provides the most recent guidelines from the federal agencies charged with regulating them, and contains illustrations of how they have been resolved, often to the benefit of the client and agency.

On the positive side of the scorecard, we have underway an industry effort to educate ad professionals as to the importance of enhanced ethics and to inspire its practice. Under the banner of the Institute for Advertising Ethics (IAE)—a partnership between the American Advertising Federation and the Missouri School of Journalism—Principles for Advertising Ethics with commentary has been published on the AAF website (www.aaf.org). Also, with AAF we are conducting classes at conferences, college campuses, and online, where professionals and students are earning Certificates for the Practice of Enhanced Advertising Ethics. And, with the AAF we have initiated online ethics discussions, including Twitter Chats.

Also, on the plus side of the ledger is the inspiration I have felt from professionals who are practicing enhanced advertising ethics in their daily business lives. "Tell your stories to your professionals." That's what David Bell urges. Let them "feel" how important it was when you resolved ethical dilemmas. During my career I have learned just how important this personal case is in the inspiration of enhanced ad ethics. Many of these stories are set out in my book for your reading and feeling.

As a counselor to the advertising industry, I always have believed in our industry's importance to our consumers and our economy, but I have learned that the benefits only flow from honest and ethical advertising. This book is dedicated to the belief that with the awareness and practice of enhanced advertising ethics, we will benefit: first, as an industry that needs to be trusted in order to do our job of building band loyalty and corporate trust; and second, as professionals who want "To Do The Right Thing" for our business and our personal fulfillment.

1

THE BUSINESS AND PERSONAL CASES FOR ENHANCED ADVERTISING ETHICS

Advertising, public relations, marketing communications, news and editorial all share a common objective of truth and high ethical standards in serving the public.

Institution of Advertising Ethics Principle 1

Advertising, public relations, and all marketing communication professionals have an obligation to exercise the highest personal ethics in the creation and dissemination of commercial information to consumers.

IAE Principle 2

Ethics in Advertising plays a critical role in the success of our businesses and our professionals. As we look back in recent history, and up to the present time, we find companies and their leaders and employees that have prospered, or suffered, from the consequences of doing, or not doing, the right thing for their customers and shareholders. Perhaps the greatest illustration of failure in this century is Enron and its accounting firm, Arthur Andersen.

Enron began as an oil pipeline company that grew rapidly by acquiring and dealing with other companies—such as energy producing entities—that Enron used to inflate its profits and share price. For example, it acquired an energy producing plant in California, and ordered it to shut down production for a period of time to cause Enron's energy prices to go up. It constantly pushed its employees to continue to come up with growth proposals, even of questionable legal and ethical status, to push its profits. This included considering aggressive moves into businesses other than energy.

Its stock prices rose dramatically because of the way in which it calculated profits—not as current—but as "expected" future profits. While accounting firms are valued for independence in critical decisions, such as the stock reporting method, Arthur Andersen totally went along with Enron's illegal orders to do so.

Arthur Andersen was the first accounting firm in history to be convicted, in 2002, of a felony for its part in covering up what its client, Enron, was being investigated for by the Securities and Exchange Commission. The court found that Andersen professionals had destroyed documents critical to the investigation and that an Andersen lawyer sent an email suggesting changing a memo relating to earnings advice that had been given to the client. Enron's legal problems involved conflicts of interest and false reporting of profits for its off-balance-sheet partnerships. Enron's reported total assets in 2000 were $66 billion. The company had to restate those assets several times as the government investigation continued. "Enron's downward spiral continued and on 2 December 2001, Enron filed for protection from creditors and became the largest corporate bankruptcy in U.S. history."[1]

I begin my book on *Ethics in Advertising* with this vivid account of perhaps unparalleled ethical and legal failure, because I believe it provides the foundation for the study and conduct of modern business ethics in America. Enron conducted its many businesses in violation of known laws and regulations, and demanded that its professionals also strive for business "success" at any cost. The company and its accounting firm's lack of transparency violated the law and destroyed the very trust necessary for a corporation from its shareholders and Wall Street. The instances of employees being ordered to conduct unethical—and illegal—activities must have been enormous. And, yes, the negative results were overwhelming: Enron's share price collapsing to $1, thousands of employees retiring without retirement funds, and the end of Arthur Andersen, one of the industry's largest and most powerful accounting firms. The disaster also spurred the study and writing on ethical dilemmas occurring in business, and led to ethics courses in university MBA programs.

I believe Kurt Eichenwald, in his 700-page book on the downfall of Enron, captures the essence of the ethics failure: "Ultimately, it was Enron's tragedy to be filled with people smart enough to know how to maneuver around the rules, but not wise enough to understand why the rules had been written in the first place."[2]

The premise of this book is the importance of *knowing* why it is necessary and appropriate to do the right thing in the powerful and important world of advertising, and then having the moral courage to do so. Our clients, agencies, media companies and suppliers—as well as our professionals—face important ethical dilemmas daily. They include the need for honesty and transparency in our advertising and marketing to our consumers, as well as in our business dealings between our clients and agencies and media suppliers. This includes accuracy and fairness in charging for our services. Also, what do we do when our client or our boss wants us to do something unethical? And, how do we advertise to special audiences, including children, or for special products, including prescription drugs and e-cigarettes? We will deal with all of the major ethical dilemmas we encounter, and importantly, how they can be understood and resolved.

There are four key propositions I hope to prove to readers of my book. The first is that companies practicing ethics in their advertising and PR, i.e., doing the right thing for consumers, will do better for their businesses: "The Business Case." One such example you will read later in the book is the positive action taken by James Burke, Chairman of Johnson & Johnson, in the Tylenol crisis of 1985. Faced with the dilemma of whether to recall all Tylenol capsules, after it had been found that some had been poisoned, he chose to do so even at a cost of $100 million. He recognized this to be a problem greater than Tylenol; rather it was a "Johnson and Johnson" problem. The result was acceptance by consumers that Johnson and Johnson had done the right thing, and the company continued to flourish. We will consider how other companies facing difficult situations can, or will, succeed by adopting ethical solutions. For instance, how will Volkswagen respond to its consumers, the government and public, to correct the allegation that it engineered its diesel autos to cheat on emissions tests worldwide?

The second proposition is that ethics in advertising is best achieved by professionals "feeling" the need to do the right thing: "The Personal Case." The Institute for Advertising Ethics' *Principles and Practices for Advertising Ethics* is directed to the professional, and the professional teams, who decide ethical dilemmas at all levels in the company, as well as to the advertising students who will move into the business. This includes the executive leadership, the account managers, the creative teams, and the media representatives. It is not enough just to know the rules, you have to know "why" they are important, "how" to apply them to ethical dilemmas, and to "want" to do so as a personal mandate.

My third proposition relates to competition in the marketplace. Yes, the advertising business is one of the most competitive businesses on the American landscape. Clients compete against clients for business; agencies compete to win and hold accounts; media companies compete online and in traditional media to win business; and third party suppliers stand in line to provide needed services. I have had the opportunity to visit with many ad professionals and to hear from them just how competitive they find their business lives. For example, I worked with a seasoned creative director from the Detroit market on supervising student teams at Michigan State University in their design of a PSA campaign for a national charity. After we had worked together for several days and gained trust, I asked him one evening, "How do you feel about ethics in advertising?" He paused for a minute or two while continuing to work on his laptop; I think he may have been looking up "Wally Snyder and Advertising Ethics." Then, he said, "I've worked for some of the most ethical and some of the most unethical people in the business." He paused again, and then said, "They are going to be afraid that if they are ethical they won't be able to compete against those cheating."

My answer, and proposition, to my advertising colleague, and to you, is that being ethical does not make one less competitive. To the contrary, if you are doing the right thing you will connect with your clients and customers in a powerful and positive sense. My favorite quote on this comes from Phil Nike, inducted into the Advertising Hall of Fame, when he said, "Play by the rules, but be ferocious!" This powerful statement resonated with me, as a trial attorney, whose goal was to win the case and to follow the extensive ethical rules regarding transparency of your arguments and the evidence you were relying upon.

The fourth proposition is that, because of the recent power consumers have achieved in the digital world of communications, including the power to block ads from their devices, those companies practicing enhanced advertising ethics will be the winners, the only winners. As I document throughout my book, those to whom we advertise now possess "Consumer Information Power" that allows them to learn everything—good and bad—about a company, its products, and advertising. For instance, go on YouTube and look up "offensive advertising." Or Google "Volkswagen" and/or "diesel emissions tests" and you can read all the news articles about the government's latest investigation into emission testing "cheating."

This information power is now coupled with the ability of consumers to block some or all advertisements on any website they explore. Apple's decision to accommodate consumer choice on whether they want to view ads when seeking original or editorial information on a site is a "game changer" for our industry. Within but a short time, 16% had blocked ads resulting in a loss of ad revenue and money needed by the websites to produce the original content. It is now in the hands of the consumer to make the choice if he or she wants ads, and indirectly, whether the financial model for paying for the production of online information through advertising will continue to work. Fortunately, consumers can "whitelist" a site to continue to receive its advertisements. This choice will be based on how those ads are presented in terms of their attractiveness, usefulness, and the ethical manner in which they are delivered. This will be discussed more in Chapters 4 and 5.

Making the business and personal cases for ethics in advertising

There are two strong cases to be made for why the teaching and practice of enhanced advertising ethics is critical in today's marketplace. When I began my proposals for enhanced ad ethics, I focused on making a business case to influence individual companies as to the commercial benefits flowing from high ethics. This remains an important argument. Then, over the years, I came to realize that the personal case is what drives our professionals to practice enhanced ethics, and they are the ones upon whom the responsibility rests for the company, as they daily encounter ethical dilemmas. The two cases are related: our professionals can be motivated by knowing how important ethics is to driving a successful business, and their personal desires to do the right thing lead to ethical behavior from which the business benefits.

The two cases are also related in practice. Companies that want to build their businesses by winning over consumers who value enhanced ethics will establish ethical goals and structures to enable their professionals. And their professionals are the ones being called on daily to exercise enhanced ethics for the company. The Principles for Advertising Ethics, adopted by the Institute for Advertising Ethics, call upon companies to fully support and post them for their professionals, and the principles, themselves, are directed to individual professionals for their implementation.

The importance of advertising and its purpose

We begin with a fundamental proposition that I have come to believe as a counselor to the business of advertising, but that is not always understood within the business: advertising is important, as a business and profession, because it advances the social and economic welfare of America. This is a view understood by economists and business advisors. Gene Ahner in his book on business ethics states, "Six services are considered critical in a global economy: accounting, advertising, banking, insurance, law and management consulting."[3]

Ahner also urges that business entities need to establish a business purpose that "will eventually come to making some contribution to the general welfare of society. And that is what can inspire and motivate dedication to the core values of the company."[4]

As one who has spent his entire career in the competitive field of advertising, here is my statement as to our industry's core business purpose. Advertising:

- Provides consumers with commercial information on product, service and organization in making purchase decisions. Advertising is central to our capitalist economic system in spurring consumer purchase through awareness of products and services and their attributes.
- Provides a vehicle for price competition and product innovation. After all, if you could not comparatively advertise, there would be little reason for improving your product or engaging in price competition. The government agreed with cases striking down prohibitions by professional associations against their members advertising their services (e.g., doctors and dentists). The legal support climaxed in 1976 in the *Virginia Pharmacy Board* case when the Supreme Court for the first time ruled that truthful advertising is protected under the First Amendment to the United States Constitution. Justice Blackmun, speaking for the majority of the Court, stated that truthful commercial information is as important to the public as political speech.[5]
- Pays for the entertainment we get offline and increasingly online. Beginning with print, and moving through radio and television, the American economic model has relied upon advertising to provide public news and entertainment. Even with cable and satellite platforms, advertising remains important in reducing consumer costs to view. Advertising models are being developed and tested in the growing online content market that will continue to provide consumers with the choice of receiving free content at the "expense" of viewing paid content.

Gene Ahner's independent assessment of the importance of our advertising profession should have a major impact on us. If we believe that our advertising industry is critical to our economy and our consumers we should want to do the best job we can in our ad businesses. When we are doing important work, we want to do it well.

This is the view of many of the ad professionals I meet across the country, such as Adam Werbach, a member of the Advertising Hall of Achievement, who states: "As new professionals enter the advertising world it is imperative they are aware of the importance of high ethics to their consumers and careers." This concurs with the belief of a young creative I talked with at Sander/Wingo in Austin, who told me, "Because advertising is so important, I want to be ethical."

The importance of the advertising industry to the economy and the public is expressed in the first Principle for Advertising Ethics adopted by the Institute for Advertising Ethics:

> Advertising, public relations, marketing communications, news and editorial all share a common objective of truth and high ethical standards in serving the public.

This principle is based upon the Journalist Creed, enunciated by Walter Williams, first Dean of the Missouri School of Journalism. Mike Fancher—a veteran journalist from the *Seattle Times*—has done in-depth research regarding the Journalist Creed. He concluded that Walter Williams believed both journalists and people on the business side of the public journal share the responsibility to serve the public, and both must respect each other's important contributions.

The business case for advertising ethics—building consumer trust

The Business Case for enhanced advertising ethics rests on the importance to consumers of ethics and the positive relationship of enhanced ethics to building consumer trust. Ethics and values are very important to building strong and positive business relationships. For example, research reported in the *Wall Street Journal* showed that consumers think highly enough about ethics that they are willing to pay more for an ethically produced product.[6]

Ad ethics research conducted at the Missouri School of Journalism

During the Spring Semester 2009 four Capstone student teams conducted primary and secondary research into the importance and stature of ethics in advertising. Collectively the groups studied the beliefs of consumers, marketers, and advertising majors. The primary research, which is summarized here, consisted of online surveys with follow-up interviews. While not nationally representative, the work shows beliefs and attitudes that are consistent and worthy of follow-up surveys.[7]

All three groups—consumers, marketing professionals and advertising students—believed ethics in advertising to be very important for consumers and the advertising profession; advertising students held the highest level of belief in its importance. The groups also concurred in the belief that advertising is not as ethical as it should be. The students and consumer groups felt most strongly, with marketers concurring that "it could use more improvement." "Hot Button" issues to work on included: advertising to children; advertising of unhealthy or harmful products; advertising that is invasive to privacy; political advertising; and direct to consumer prescription drug advertising (DTCA). Solutions to advancing ethics in advertising included an industry-wide code, drafted with care, and an enhanced advertising ethics curriculum on campus.

The importance of ethics in advertising

Consumers, marketers and advertising majors all ranked the importance of advertising ethics as very high. Out of the 214 consumers surveyed, 44.3% believe advertisers should be punished for producing unethical ads. The top three aspects that would make a company ethical are honesty, fairness and trust. Most of the interviewed consumers also claimed they would be more likely to buy the products featured in ads if the company was ethical. Also, honest advertising was the top ranked aspect that would make a company ethical (89.1%), followed by socially responsible (80.1%), and environmentally friendly (58.8%).[8]

Of the marketers surveyed, 53% believed ethics is "very important" to professionals in the ad industry and 43% believed it is "somewhat important." "Building consumer trust" was seen by 42% of the sample as the greatest benefit from advertising ethics.[9]

Of the advertising majors surveyed an overwhelming 86.4% said advertising ethics was important to them and important to consumers. Reasons given included that people will pay more for an ethically produced product, will boycott an unethical one, and it is easy to access information on the Internet.[10]

How ethical is advertising?

Advertising received low marks from consumers, marketers and advertising majors. The majority of consumers surveyed (33.2%) did not trust advertising or believe it to be honest. With regard to consumer perception of prescription drug advertising (DTCA) the majority of respondents (61%) do not trust the information presented in the ads, and 44% have also viewed a DTCA ad that they knew was incorrect, misleading, or had left out information.[11]

Most marketers expressed the current state of ethics in the advertising industry as "it could use more improvement." Phrases like "secondary issue" and "not as good as it could be" were used to describe the current state along with concern that a declining economy and recession could cause more problems. On a scale of

1 to 10—with 1 being completely unethical and 10 being completely ethical—advertising majors provided a mean response of 5.86. "The average shows the poor image the advertising industry has" (comment of Student Team).

Advertising issues to tackle ("hot buttons")

From the marketers' point of view, political advertising (more than half), the targeting of children and the elderly, and tobacco were seen as the most pressing ethical issues in advertising. Multicultural and behavioral targeting were not seen as significant problems.

The three ethical issues most prevalent to the advertising majors are advertising to children, advertising of unhealthy or harmful products, and advertising that is invasive to privacy—they collectively accounted for over 75% of the responses. Notable also were "stealth marketing," such as product placement, or other advertising that is hard for the customer to identify as advertising, and unlike the marketers, advertising with sensitivity to minority or gender groups ("Stereotyping").

Other than expressing the top three general issues that would make a company ethical (honesty, fairness and trust), "Consumers don't really understand what it means to be ethical." However, individual answers to open-ended questions did include PETA and Dolce and Gabbana ads where women were displayed in sexual situations. Also, the high percentage of consumers surveyed who did not trust DTCA ads (61%) would indicate that this is a major area of ethical concern, to be discussed in the next chapter.

Solutions to advance advertising ethics

Of the consumers surveyed, 75.6% believed that advertising should have standards or a code for ethical advertising. In the follow-up phone interviews of marketing professionals, "All agreed that a blanket code would be a step in the right direction; however it was noted that much forethought is needed, and that those who ignore ethics would also ignore the code." Healthcare professionals interviewed in the DTCA survey said DTCA ads should be held to different ethical standards than other advertised products. Of the advertising majors surveyed, 81.8% concluded that an Ethics in Advertising class would be useful for their education and knowledge of the industry.

The importance of ethics in building consumer trust

The student research concluded that marketing professionals believe "Trust" is the key to building brand and corporate loyalty from consumers, and that enhanced ethics builds consumer trust. The Capstone research found that a majority of marketing professionals said that ethics is "very important," and that "Building Consumer Trust" was seen by 42% of the sample as the greatest benefit from advertising ethics. This also is the view of advertising leaders in our industry going back to Leo Burnett, who believed: "Ethics is at the center of how we express a brand," up unto the present when David Bell, Chair Emeritus, IPG, believes: "Trust is the currency of our Business and Ethics is the engine of trust."

Consumer information power

The online explosion of communications has placed consumers in control of the commercial information they want and how they wish to receive it. This includes the power to share ads they like—and dislike—because of ethical implications. An impactful illustration is the website created by EnviroMedia where consumers go to rate the credibility of green marketing claims. Hundreds of ads have been available to rate, and some have received very high—and some have received very low—ratings. Take the billboard ad in Pennsylvania that touted coal as a clean energy source. It received a very poor rating.[12]

Also, consumers share daily their likes and dislikes on social media, including YouTube, Facebook and Twitter.

An impactful illustration is the 2014 marketing by Urban Outfitters of a blood-covered sweatshirt featuring Kent State University. It was condemned by Kent State University and on social sites for poor taste and trivializing the deaths of four students in 1970 anti-war protests. Commentary published on September 15, 2014, on YouTube concluded: "In a tasteless move, the retailer auctioned off a 'vintage' Kent State University sweatshirt, complete with faux blood stains and tattered edges. The company says they had no intention of alluding to the tragic events of the Kent State Massacre."[13]

A 2011 Super Bowl ad for Groupon.com that offended many consumers is still being featured on YouTube with a recent count of 583,158 views. Groupon is a website that focuses in distributing coupons to consumers in local markets across the nation. The spot featured actor Timothy Hutton in what appeared to be a public service advertisement (PSA) to aid hurting Tibetans when he stated, "The people of Tibet are in trouble, their very culture is in jeopardy." Then, without a pause, he went on, "But they still whip up an amazing fish curry, and since 200 of us bought at Groupon.com, we're each getting $30 worth of Tibetan food for just $15 at Himalayan Restaurant in Chicago."[14]

The ad immediately was attacked by thousands of consumers for making light of Tibetans' hardships on social networking sites across the Internet. Groupon CEO Andrew Mason pulled the ad five days later. "'We thought we were poking fun at ourselves, but clearly the execution was off and the joke didn't come through,' Mason said in a blog Thursday. 'I personally take responsibility; although we worked with a professional ad agency, in the end, it was my decision to run the ads.'"[15]

In fact, it is the role of the ad agency to develop trust for the brand. That trust, however, cannot be built by advertising that is viewed as improper or unethical by the consumer. As noted earlier in this chapter, the Capstone student research found that marketing professionals believed that the greatest benefit from advertising ethics is in "building consumer trust."

From a positive perspective a multiracial family Cheerios ad made its Super Bowl debut in 2014. Camille Gibson, General Mills VP of Marketing, said, "The big game provided another opportunity to tell another story about family love."[16]

The personal case for advertising ethics—"ethics of achievement"

Turning now to the personal case for advertising ethics, I believe it is as important as the business case. In fact, the mission of the Institute for Advertising Ethics to build the awareness and practice of enhanced advertising ethics is directed to advertising professionals. IAE Principle 2 urges:

> Advertising, public relations, and all marketing communications professionals have an obligation to exercise the highest personal ethics in the creation and dissemination of commercial information to consumers.

The business case is based on principles, laws and rules, all of which are important to why we need to practice advertising ethics. This chapter has detailed the importance of building trust with consumers and our Institute for Advertising Ethics' Principles for Advertising Ethics provides guidance for specific ethical dilemmas. Gene Ahner, in his book on *Business Ethics*, calls this "Ethics of Compliance" and it is ruled by our external actions, and we might say controlled by our brain.[17]

The personal case for ethics—what Ahner terms "Ethics of Achievement"—is based upon our internal feelings, or we might say what our heart dictates. Feelings are very personal and subjective and yet very powerful in determining our actions. In fact, advertising itself is designed and directed toward connecting with the feelings of our customers. When we choose a brand, and repeat its purchase, whether it is an automobile or article of clothing, the feelings we have for the brand play a critical role.

With respect to ethics, Ahner puts it this way: "An ethics of compliance basically forbids us from doing things while an ethics of achievement demands our engagement. A person or a business becomes moral not by 'not doing things' but by doing things rightly. An ethics of achievement calls out the best in us: have courage, be creative, find a way."[18]

Rushworth Kidder, an ethicist whom I follow and often quote, describes those following the personal case in achieving ethics: "Those are the people, after all, whom we often think of as 'good' people. They are good, we say, because they seem to have some conscious sense of vision, some deep core of ethical values, that gives them the courage to stand up to the tough choices."[19]

Rushworth Kidder also has written an entire book on moral courage and its powerful impact on the practical application of ethics. He states, "'The courage to do the right thing' is about as concise a definition of moral courage as you can find." In further defining its importance, he states: "Moral courage is not only about facing physical challenges that could harm your body—it's about facing mental challenges that could wreck your reputation and emotional well-being, your adherence to conscience, your self-esteem, your bank account, your health. Simply put, moral courage is the courage to be moral. And by moral ... we tend to mean whatever adheres to the five core moral values of honesty, respect, responsibility, fairness and compassion."[20]

Many advertising and PR professionals believe and practice the personal and moral case for ethics. John Osborn, president of BBDO New York, says they talk about "Soul Works" at BBDO and want their professionals to be passionate about what they give back—to be energized and happy to come to work every day. I haven't found anybody who puts it better than Scott McAfee at Sanders/Wingo, who in a meeting with ten of his professionals that I attended said, "When we face ethical dilemmas we have to default to our higher judgment."

And then, we can rely upon the beliefs of one of the greatest ad professionals of all time, Leo Burnett, who urged: "Cling like wildcats to the only realities we can swear we have hold of—our own sacred and individual integrities."[21]

The personal case is particularly important in those ethical dilemmas that ethicists define as "right versus right" situations. In these cases strong claims can be made on both sides of the equation. We will be discussing many "right versus right" conflicts as we consider the major ethical dilemmas professionals are encountering in today's advertising and marketing. One concerns the hiring and firing of our professionals. For example, what do we do when we learn that one of our senior professionals, who is revered by a major client, has been cheating on his time and travel forms in clear violation of company policy? On one hand, his lying and false statements clearly undercut company rules and values, and his actions have become known by many on staff. On the other, we may lose the client's business, which accounts for far more income and money.

The decision will turn mainly on a personal case for ethics displayed by the manager making the decision as to what to do. Joseph Badaracco, in his book on ethics, *Defining Moments*, puts forth the questions that will help when considering the decision. First, how do my feelings define the "right versus right" conflict? What do my feelings tell me? He adds, "The heart has its reasons that reason does not know." Next, how deep are the moral roots of the values in the conflict? Understanding the values, and where they come from, defines my moral identity. Finally, how will this shape my future value system as I decide this right versus right ethical demand?[22]

I believe the business case—doing what consumers want and expect in building trust—and the personal case of wanting to achieve high ethics—are related and complementary. The government laws on advertising and the ethical dilemmas presented for discussion in this book, and the IAE Principles for Advertising Ethics, along with case studies, provide guidance for those wishing to achieve the personal case of being ethical.

Again quoting Rushworth Kidder in the practice of enhanced ethics: "You've got to think about it, reason it through, get the mind in gear and grapple with the tough issues. In other words, you've got to be mentally engaged. What's more, you've got to care, to be committed through the feelings as well as through the intellect."[23]

Questions and reflection

1. The author begins with a discussion of the business practices of Enron and its accounting firm, Arthur Andersen, over a decade and a half ago. How does that experience make you feel about the importance of ethics?
2. The author quotes ethicist Gene Ahner as placing advertising as one of the six essential businesses in a global economy. Why is advertising's inclusion important as to the manner in which we practice ethics in the ad world?
3. Ahner also urges that we establish a "business purpose" that will include making some contribution to the general welfare of society. Why is this important to our professionals?
4. What is the author's three-part statement as to the business purpose of advertising? What would you add?
5. The author provides a "business case" and a "personal case" for the practice of enhanced advertising ethics. In the business case what is the relationship between ethics and building consumer trust for our brands and corporations?
6. Why is the building of "trust" for the consumer, and our business partners, so important in the business of advertising?
7. Research conducted by Capstone Student Teams at the Missouri School of Journalism is cited on the importance of advertising ethics to consumers, advertising professionals, and advertising students. Which group held the importance of ethics at the highest level and why?
8. What was the benefit most of the advertising professionals cited for ethics?
9. The author uses the phrase "Consumer Information Power" as a strong basis for the business case. What is this power and what is its impact on our ethical decision-making?
10. How would you define a "Right versus Right" ethical dilemma?
11. The author cites Rushwood Kidder for his definition of moral courage. What is his definition and how does it relate to solving ethical dilemmas in advertising?
12. The "business case" for ethics is based on principles and giving the consumer what he/she wants, while the "personal case" is based on the professional wanting to do what she/he feels is the right thing to do. Which case is stronger for you? Why? Can the two cases work together?

Notes

1 Smith, N. Craig and Quirk, Michelle, "From Grace to Disgrace: the Rise & Fall of Arthur Andersen," London Business School, *Journal of Business Ethics Education*, 2004, 1(1): 91–130.
2 Eichenwald, Kurt, *Conspiracy of Fools*, New York: Broadway Books, 2005, p. 1.
3 Ahner, Gene, *Business Ethics, Making a Life, Not Just a Living*, Maryknoll, NY: Orbis Books, 2007, p. 51.
4 Ahner, *Business Ethics*.
5 Virginia Pharmacy Board v. Virginia Consumer Council, Docket No. 74–895, 425 U.S. 748 (1976).
6 "Corporate Reputation: Does it Pay?," *Wall Street Journal*, May 12, 2008.
7 Capstone Student Research, Missouri School of Journalism, 2009, conducted for IAE as senior class consumer research requirement.
8 Consumer research: Online survey on Survey Monkey followed by 13 personal interviews with open-ended questions. Demographics across all ages, but the majority of survey respondents were 21–30 years old.
9 Marketers: Online survey with advertising executives obtained from Missouri School of Journalism alumni; follow-up phone interviews with interested professionals to clarify and speak more personally. There were 21 survey respondents from 16 different cities. Most prevalent respondents were account executives (6) and chief executives (6). The median of years spent in the field was 24.5 and the mean years spent was 22.1 years.
10 Advertising Majors: Online survey directed to Advertising Students in the Missouri School of Journalism, Strategic Communications Majors—freshmen to recent graduates, male and female.
11 DTCA Research: Online survey with 23 consumer respondents.
12 Greenwashing Index, Help Keep Advertising Honest, http://greenwashingindex.com/coal-penn-clean-energy/.
13 "Urban Outfitters sorry for Kent State sweatshirt," *USA Today*, www.usatoday.com/story/news/nation-now/2014/09/15/kent-state-university-blood-sweatshirt/15659799/.
14 "Groupon Super Bowl Ad/Save the Money—Tibet," *Sportstrib*, www.youtube.com/watch?v=vVkFT2yjk0A.
15 Gross, Doug, CNN Wire Staff, February 11, 2011, "Groupon Axes Controversial Ad Campaign", www.cnn.com/2011/TECH/web/02/11/groupon.ad/.
16 Picchi, Aimee, January 29, 2014, "Cheerios to bring back biracial family for Super Bowl ad," *CBS Moneywatch*, www.cbsnews.com/news/cheerios-to-bring-back-biracial-family-for-super-bowl-ad/.
17 Ahner, op. cit., p. 84.
18 Ahner, op. cit., p. 90.
19 Kidder, Rushwood, *How Good People Make Tough Choices*, New York: HarperCollins, 1995, p. 13.
20 Kidder, Rushwood, *Moral Courage*, New York: HarperCollins, 2005, pp. 9–10, 24.
21 *100 Leos—Wit and Wisdom from Leo Burnett*, #85, Chicago, IL: Leo Burnett Company, Inc.
22 Badaracco, Joseph, *Defining Moments, When Managers Must Choose between Right and Right*, Boston, MA: Harvard Business School Press, 1997, pp. 71–73, 77.
23 Kidder, *How Good People Make Tough Choices*, p. 5.

2

"DO THE RIGHT THING" FOR CONSUMERS

The law and rising above it

Advertisers should follow federal, state and local laws, and cooperate with industry self-regulatory programs for the resolution of advertising practices.

IAE Principle 7

Advertisers should treat consumers fairly based on the nature of the audience to whom the ads are directed and the nature of the product or service advertised.

IAE Principle 5

When exploring ethics during the past and up to the present, the definition that stands out for me is "Do the Right Thing." When I wrote my first article on advertising ethics in 2003 I followed this definition. I quoted Carter McNamara's ethical standard: "Learning what is right or wrong, and then doing the right thing." He states, "Many ethicists assert there's always a right thing to do based on moral principle, and others believe the right thing to do depends on the situation— ultimately it's up to the individual." McNamara extends this definition. "Business ethics," he says, "is generally coming to know what is right or wrong in the workplace and doing what's right."[1]

We face two challenges in our ethical decisions: first, questions concerning the content and dissemination of advertising and public relations; and second, in our business transactions with our clients, as well as sub-contractors and partners, and between our own professionals. This chapter deals with how we treat content and claims.

My definition of doing the right thing for consumers in creating and disseminating advertising has three components:

1.   Truth. Claims should be fully substantiated and should not mislead the consumer by misrepresentation. Incomplete or omitted information,

resulting in "half-truths," can be as damaging as outright false statements. This is often a clear-cut area in which violators risk government restraining orders and fines, as well as loss of credibility with consumers.

2.   Fairness. In my definition, ethics also includes treating consumers "fairly" depending on the nature of the audience and the product advertised. Children are a prime example that will be discussed in the next chapter. I believe products that require special attention when advertised fairly include alcoholic beverages, prescription drugs and e-cigarettes. (Government may be involved in "fairness" determination, but clear-cut standards may be difficult to formulate. See discussion in Chapter 3 regarding FTC regulation of children's advertising.)

3.   Avoid advertising that offends the customer. This can include stereotypes of race, gender, and age, and depiction of violence, including directed against women. Government is not involved in this area, nor should it be. Nevertheless, the industry has an important ethical duty to self-regulate in an area very important to consumers.

Truth in advertising

The federal government is highly involved in the regulation of advertising because of its importance to the economy and consumers. Beginning with federal court cases striking down prohibitions by professional associations against their members advertising their services (e.g., doctors and dentists) the case was made and recognized that truthful advertising benefited consumers. The legal support climaxed in 1976 in the *Virginia Pharmacy* case when the Supreme Court for the first time ruled that truthful advertising is protected under the First Amendment to the United States Constitution. Justice Blackmun, speaking for the majority of the Court, stated that truthful commercial information is as important to the public as political speech.[2]

The *Virginia Pharmacy* case came in 1976 and the decision was critical to the advertising industry, the economy and the consumer. Up until this time states and even professional associations could prohibit truthful advertising. This never seemed appropriate to me, as an attorney at the Federal Trade Commission, where we had the burden of establishing that the advertising to be prohibited was false and deceptive. While the FTC may ban "Unfair" advertising, as we shall see in Chapter 3, it has a strict factual burden to prove.

What was involved in the *Virginia Pharmacy* case was both a competitive and ethical issue concerning price advertising. The focus in banning it was not on whether the claim is truthful, but whether some felt it appropriate to engage in price advertising. For them the question was not whether patients or consumers would benefit. The pharmacy association with support from the State of Virginia suppressed truthful commercial information on the basis of its "professional" code. This basis ended in the 1970s when government and the courts focused on "consumer protection." More specifically, the Court in *Virginia Pharmacy* found that the interests of the pharmacy organizations in suppressing price ads "did not outweigh the petitioner's right to disseminate the information and the public's right to receive it."[3]

The case and the Court's reasoning became the basis for protecting truthful commercial information because it benefited the consumer and the economy. Legal historians Kenneth Plevan and Miriam Siroky find the Court's holding rested on three principles:

1. Commercial speech is not "so removed from any 'exposition of ideas' and from 'truth, morality, and arts'" that it lacks all protection.
2. The speaker's economic motivation does not disqualify him from protection under the first amendment since advertising, like speech related to labor disputes, is necessary to a widespread system of marketing and the proper allocation of society's economic resources.
3. The consumer's interest in receiving commercial information is at least as great as his interest in the "most urgent political debate."[4]

The Court became even more specific in subsequent cases: advertising serves to reduce retail prices and to "aid the new competitor in penetrating the market."[5]

The Court's pronouncements in the *Virginia Pharmacy* case and subsequent rulings gave a major boost to the importance of truthful advertising to the U.S. economy and its citizens. The importance of commercial speech became equal to that of political speech, in terms of the Constitution, as long as it was truthful.

A second major Constitutional case, *Central Hudson*, held that truthful commercial speech could be regulated if the government satisfied the following criteria:

1. the government has a substantial interest in regulating the speech;
2. the government interest is directly advanced by the regulation; and
3. the regulation is no more extensive than necessary to serve the interest, i.e., the regulation is the least restrictive alternative available.[6]

Under *Central Hudson*, and subsequent cases, the Court authorized government to prohibit truthful commercial speech, but in a limited fashion. In *Central Hudson* the state argued the interest was to discourage electricity consumption, but the Court found the restriction banned all forms of advertising, including about other electrical devices and services.

Central Hudson gave Constitutional support for the "Unfairness" section of the Federal Trade Commission's Section 5 authority to regulate advertising. Section 5 provides such authority to "prohibit deceptive and unfair" acts or practices. As we shall cover in detail in Chapter 3, the unfairness authority was the primary basis for the FTC staff's proposal in 1978 to ban advertising for sugared products directed to children based on health considerations. Also, to be discussed is the Commission's FTC Policy Statement on Unfairness provided to Congress in 1980.

The Supreme Court's rulings and support for truthful advertising as a benefit to the consumer complemented the drive during the 1970s by Ralph Nader and other activists to create the consumer protection movement. Once the Court rulings encouraged advertising as a benefit to the consumer and economy, emphasis was placed upon insuring its accuracy. The Federal Trade Commission emerged from a rather docile regulatory period to become the center for regulatory activism. New FTC Chair Miles Kirkpatrick and Bureau of Consumer Protection head Bob Pitofsky led a rebirth of national ad regulation with the new Division of National Advertising tripling in legal strength to over thirty attorneys, of which I was one. National advertising cases were brought against major companies, including those that I worked on: Ford Motor Company, Warner-Lambert, and Sun Oil Company.

Ralph Nader kept his eye upon the FTC, as it grew in regulatory strength, and in the early 1970s filed a petition for Commission consideration. The petition recommended that the FTC establish a process to allow companies to voluntarily submit their proof of ad claims to the FTC for review and approval in advance of disseminating them. While an admirable proposal, it would have been impossible for the FTC's limited legal and paralegal staff to have been able to review scientific data in a timely manner for an unlimited number of companies. Yet, the idea of companies developing adequate scientific data for their claims in advance of delivering them to the public had ethical and practical applications. This became the "Prior Substantiation Doctrine."

In the *Pfizer* case, a landmark ruling in 1972, the Federal Trade Commission held that companies must possess and rely upon a prior "reasonable basis" of fact for their advertising claims.[7] It was up to the FTC to prove that the challenged claim had been made. This ruling changed national advertising requirements in profound ways both ethically and administratively. Now, a company would develop its scientific basis for claims prior to making them, including limiting them in significant ways.

Prior to the *Pfizer* case companies could simply make a claim and continue it until the government proved it false, after the fact. While I am certain many companies developed and reviewed scientific data prior to making claims, now that became the law: advertising claims without a prior reasonable basis in science and fact were deemed "deceptive" under Section 5 of the Federal Trade Commission Act. The FTC staff has the burden of showing by a preponderance of evidence that the challenged claims were made, and that the basis presented by the company in support of the claims is not a reasonable scientific basis.

In regulating commerce, both in its antitrust and consumer protection mandates, the Commission engages in strong public policy analysis, including economic input, to insure that its involvement will benefit consumers. This includes reviewing the scope of its orders and determining whether to investigate, including using its subpoena power. Occasionally, economic analysis is required to justify interaction. The question is how will the action and proposed order impact the public? Much internal discussion takes place before formal action is taken.

Most Federal Trade Commission cases begin as investigations by the staff, as it monitors ad campaigns. As we will discuss in the next section regarding advertising self-regulation, the FTC also reviews cases from the industry's program: the National Advertising Division (NAD), National Advertising Review Board (NARB) and the Children's Advertising Review Unit (CARU) when companies refuse to voluntarily make the recommended changes. All FTC investigations are private with no public comment until the FTC Commission has ruled. This is, of course, ethical and helps advance resolution with the advertisers on a voluntary basis.

Once the staff has completed its investigation and made its recommendation, the Commission can issue a Part II complaint and consent order prohibiting the legal violations if agreed to by the advertiser. Where agreement does not occur, the Commission can issue a formal Part III Complaint where the case is tried before an Administrative Law Judge. At that point, the staff can have no further contact with the Commissioners nor their staff. The judge's final order can be appealed to the FTC Commission. After the Commissioners sitting as a review board hear and issue a final order, the defendant company can appeal through the federal court system. The Commission relies on Federal District Courts to enforce its orders with money damages.

The Federal Trade Commission is an independent government agency whose power to regulate is based totally on federal law with Congressional oversight. The Federal Trade Commission Act proscribes the authority the agency has to regulate, including to prohibit "unfair and deceptive acts or practices in commerce." Also, Congress provides ongoing power to the agency through "Reauthorizations" that may limit its authority in certain areas. While the President appoints the Chair and Commissioners, the Executive Branch has no further power over the FTC, as an independent regulatory agency. The FTC shares authority with other federal agencies over certain practices, such as on children's advertising on television, with the Federal Communications Commission. With respect to the Food and Drug Administration, FTC has authority for "over-the-counter" (OTC) drug advertising, and thr FDA for prescription drug advertising (DTC). During my time at the FTC I served as liaison officer with the FDA.

Deception includes false claims, as well as demonstrations that do not support the claim, and claims that require disclosures so as to avoid misleading the consumer ("deception by half truth"). Disclaimers are required to be presented in a "clear and prominent" manner. The FTC provides industry with legal guidelines through its cases, guides and public hearings, all reported on its website.[8]

The *Sun Oil Company* case that I tried while at the Federal Trade Commission charged that Sunoco gasoline was not more powerful than competing brands as advertised. Sunoco gasoline did have a higher octane rating than competing brands (Ultra 93.5 and 94), but experts testified that this did not make the gasoline produce more engine power or acceleration. Also, the TV ads contained demonstrations to convey the power claim. One showed a car fueled by Sunoco Premium pulling a railroad car, and another showed an auto pulling a trailer up a ramp superimposed on the rising seats in a sports arena. An Administrative Law Judge (ALJ) upheld the charges in litigation, and the company ultimately agreed to a consent order prohibiting such power claims in the future without an adequate and scientific basis.[9]

The *Warner-Lambert* Listerine case tried and argued in the decade of the 1970s was another instance where the Commission's authority was expanded, in this case to require "Corrective Advertising" to dispel false beliefs caused by long-term cold and sore throat advertising benefits for the mouthwash. I served as junior counsel on this case and handled the advertising charges and corrective advertising remedy. In this case we did not use prior substantiation doctrine to prove the claims false, but relied on medical doctors and scientists to affirmatively prove false the claim that "Listerine prevents colds and sore throats and reduces their severity." The concern was that ending the false claims would not end the problem for Listerine users, who would continue to believe the cold claims, even after they ceased by Commission order. Our evidence was based upon expert testimony that "beliefs," such as Listerine will prevent colds and sore throats, are based on "behavior," such as using Listerine for the prevention of colds and sore throats, and that the belief would not change unless and until corrected in future advertising. The ALJ agreed and in his order required the first $10 million of Listerine's future advertising to contain the disclosure: "Contrary to past advertising Listerine will not prevent colds or sore throats or lessen their severity." I argued the case on Warner-Lambert's appeal to the Commission and the charges and order were sustained. The company appealed the case to the Court of Appeals for the D.C. Circuit, which upheld the findings and the authority of the FTC to require "corrective advertising," but struck the introductory phrase, "Contrary to past advertising," as punitive and beyond the FTC's authority to require.[10]

In a 2014 case the FTC charged home security company ADT with deceptively advertising that paid endorsements from safety and technology experts were independent reviews. The complaint alleged that ADT paid spokespeople to demonstrate and review the ADT Pulse on NBC's Today Show, and on 40 other television and radio programs nationwide, as well as on posted blogs and material online. ADT set up the interviews for the endorsers—often providing reporters and news anchors with suggested interview questions and background video—leaving the consumer to believe they were impartial, expert reviewers of the products.

Jessica Rich, Director of the Bureau of Consumer Protection, stated: "It's hard for consumers to make good buying decisions when they think they're getting independent expert advice as part of an impartial news segment and have no way of knowing they are actually watching a sales pitch." She added, "When a paid endorser appears in a news or talk show segment with the host of that program, the relationship with the advertiser must be clearly disclosed."[11]

In another 2014 case the FTC prohibited Sony Computer Entertainment America from engaging in false and misleading claims. This case also required Sony to provide refunds to consumers, and it joined the advertising agency in the complaint.

The Commission charged that Sony "deceived consumers with false advertising claims about the 'game changing' technological features of its PlayStation Vita handheld gaming console." Sony agreed to provide notice via email to consumers eligible for refunds. Bureau Director Jessica Rich stated, "The FTC will not hesitate to act on behalf of consumers when companies or advertisers make false product claims."[12]

Sony's advertising agency was also joined in the investigation and agreed to a consent settlement that impacts marketing on social media, in this case Twitter. The Commission charged that Deutsch LA "knew or should have known"—the legal standard for joining ad agencies—that the advertisement it produced contained misleading claims about the console's capabilities. Also, in a precedent-setting charge the Commission alleged that Deutsch further "misled consumers by urging its employees to create awareness and excitement about the (product) on Twitter, without instructing employees to disclose their connection to the advertising agency or its then-client Sony." Under a separate consent order the agency is barred from such conduct in the future.[13]

Truthful advertising under industry self-regulation

The advertising industry's well recognized self-regulation program also provides guidance for how to create ads ethically and truthfully. The efforts by its legal and professional staff in reviewing ads, recommending changes and deletions, publishing the final results and holding conferences to educate the industry demonstrate an outstanding industry ethical mission that complements government ad regulatory action. The advantages of the self-regulation program include speed in resolving disputes, as well as the expertise professionals bring to the table in voluntarily resolving questions as to truth and accuracy. Former FTC Chair Bob Pitofsky saluted the program as "the best self-regulatory system of any industry in this country."[14]

The commencement of the advertising industry's self-regulation programming began in 1971 when the federal government sharpened its focus on the industry and the Federal Trade Commission significantly increased its advertising regulation. Howard Bell, then President of the American Advertising Federation, led a major commitment of AAF with the other two national advertising associations, the 4A's and the Association of National Advertising, to build a national program that is complementary to the federal regulation. Its mission was, and is, to conduct voluntary ad review, and appropriate changes to questionable advertising, to reduce the need of formal government regulation.

The program today is conducted by lawyers and other professionals and is administered by the Council of Better Business with active oversight by the Advertising Self-Regulation Council, consisting of CBBB and the three founding members: AAF, ANA and the 4A's. The program is funded by contributions from the advertising industry.

The National Advertising Division (NAD) and the Children's Advertising Review Unit (CARU) are the two self-regulation units responsible for independently monitoring and reviewing national advertising for truthfulness and accuracy. CARU is responsible for national ads primarily directed to children 12 years of age and under. They both receive complaints from industry members and the public, and initiate their own investigations into ad claims. Upon notice to the parties the NAD and CARU can rely upon outside experts.

After a complaint is made the advertiser submits a written response to which the challenger promptly files its response. After the advertiser files its response to the challenger, the NAD/CARU staff may meet with the parties to discuss the issues, and then staff will formulate its decision as to the truth and accuracy of the claims at issue. If it is determined that some or all of the advertising claims are not substantiated the advertiser may either submit a notice that it will correspondingly modify its claims or that it will appeal the decision to the National Advertising Review Board (NARB), the self-regulation appellate body. All filings are required within specified time periods laid out in the Policy and Procedures for NAD, CARU, and NARB.[15]

The advertiser has an absolute right to file an appeal to the NARB. The challenger may file a request for an appeal to the NAD/CARU decision and it is up to the Chairman of the NARB to determine whether to grant the challenger's appeal based on the likelihood of a review panel changing the decision of the NAD. During the process the NARB Chair may also be asked to determine if the appellants are raising new issues or introducing new evidence that will not be considered by the review panel. The NARB Chair then appoints a panel of five qualified NARB members, and designates the panel member who will serve as panel chair. I have had the honor of serving as NARB Chair since January 2015, after appointment by the ASRC Board.

Upon a panel ruling affirming all or part of the NAD/CARU recommendations that the advertising be modified, the advertiser has the choice of whether to comply with the changes. If it chooses to do so, the NARB Chair approves the statement issued to the public by the advertiser. If it determines not to do so the NAD/CARU may refer the file to the appropriate government agency for its review.

At the conclusion of the self-regulation process the facts and holdings are published by NAD/CARU as part of its Case Reports distributed throughout the year. This provides the industry with the conclusions and reasoning of the NAD/CARU for the guidance of the industry. Conferences also are prepared and held by each group to educate the industry as to recent trends and decisions.

During the year 2014 the NAD reviewed over 80 challenges to advertising claims. The focus has been on whether or not there is sufficient substantiation for claims made by advertisers and whether disclosures are clear and conspicuous— the key areas investigated by the Federal Trade Commission in determining if ads are free from deception.

The 2014 case involving Euro-Pro Operating claims for its Shark brand vacuum cleaners brought by challenger Dyson, Inc. is illustrative of the NAD investigative and self-regulation process. The claims in challenge included the claim that Shark vacuum cleaners are "America's Most Recommended Vacuum Brand." Dyson challenged, and the NAD and NARB panel agreed, that the "advertiser's evidence was insufficiently reliable or robust to provide a reasonable basis for the claim."

Dyson's substantiation rested upon aggregated consumer reviews from several marketing websites. NAD, while acknowledging that online comments and reviews by consumers are relevant, found several defects with the survey research: in most cases the online reviews could not be verified as from actual users or owners of the vacuum; verifications by the sites were not adequate to prevent unreliable and false reviews; and the data was not clear as to whether the newer models were adequately represented in the reviews utilized. The NAD conclusion, upheld by the NARB, was that the aggregated online review data relied upon by the advertiser did not represent American upright vacuum cleaner consumers.[16]

In another 2014 NAD case, which the NARB upheld, BP Lubricants USA was recommended to discontinue challenged "stronger" claims, made for the companys' Castrol EDGE motor oil, that were based on a "torture test." NAD concluded that the claims made in television commercials, and on BP's website, YouTube, and Facebook pages conveyed that its torture test results were relevant to consumer's normal driving conditions, when in fact the results did not support that superiority claim. ExxonMobil Corporation originally challenged the BP motor oil claims at the NAD. While not agreeing with the conclusion, BP noted that nevertheless it "respects the self-regulatory process and will take the panel's decision into consideration in future advertising."[17]

For guidance we can also turn to Britain's Advertising Standards Authority. L'Oreal agreed to the Authority's request to remove a print ad for Maybelline featuring actress Christy Turlington, because it received "excessive airbrushing and digital manipulation techniques" to enhance the photo. The company admitted that the image had been digitally retouched and agreed to pull the ads though it contended that the enhancement did not make a material difference.[18]

This could be a difficult case for the Federal Trade Commission to prove a material deception, but was it ethical for the company to enhance the very cosmetic features that were advertised? We know that ad agencies routinely "photo shop" ads to enhance their image. However, here the company enhanced the facial features the ad promised to help eliminate—"Crow's feet", "Fine lines", and "Dark circles"—without disclosure to consumers. The facts were put online and millions of consumers became aware of what the company did. This will not help to build credibility and trust.

Also, ethics rises above truthfulness, and this is the next section we will cover.

Fairness in advertising due to the nature of the product

Truth is the foundation upon which ethical ads are constructed. But, ethics rises above being truthful and not misleading. It requires us to take into consideration both the consumers to whom we are advertising, as well as the characteristics of the products and services. Our Institute for Advertising Ethics Principle 5 urges:

> Advertisers should treat consumers fairly based on the nature of the audience to whom the ads are directed and the nature of the product or service advertised.

The key "audience" of concern is children to whom the entire next chapter is devoted. In this chapter we shall look at the nature of products I believe require "fairness" in advertising, including prescription drugs, alcoholic beverages, cigarettes and e-cigarettes.

Prescription drug advertising

Prescription drug advertising directed to consumers (DTC) is a prime example of advertising requiring high ethics. This is a major category of television, print and online advertising that is getting considerable attention and debate as to its appropriateness and benefits. In fact, DTC advertising was not permitted in the U.S. until the 1980s and it is still forbidden in many countries. And in late 2015 the American Medical Association urged that it be once again "banned" because of the argument that it raises consumer prices for prescription drugs. It also has been suggested that medical doctors do not appreciate their patients repeatedly asking them for DTC medicines they have seen advertised on TV.

Countering this argument in a classic "Right versus Right" ethical discussion is that DTC has major benefits for consumers as patients. After all, it can provide specific information about medical products and procedures available to treat the major illnesses we face. Further, the Food and Drug Administration (FDA) has regulatory authority and requires that all appropriate warnings be provided in the particular advertising. Concerns are raised that because of the advertising, consumers may request and receive drugs that they do not need. In balance, however, I believe from an ethics point we should want and support fully informed patients.

During my time at the Federal Trade Commission I came to believe in the value of truthful DTC, and during my time at AAF I continued to make the case and testify on its behalf. Under federal law the FTC has jurisdiction over the advertising of over-the-counter drugs, and the Food and Drug Administration (FDA) has jurisdiction for prescription drug advertising (DTC). In the 1970s the FDA did not permit any advertising of DTC to consumers. The Federal Trade Commission believed that the truthful advertising of DTC products would be of value to consumers. As liaison to the FDA, I carried that message to my counterpart. Interest was expressed, but not activated.

After I moved to the American Advertising Federation in 1985, as SVP for Government Relations, I continued to make the case for the advertising industry. We learned that Congressional approval, at least informally, would be necessary. We proposed a test case with consumer advertising for a particular prescription drug with follow-up consumer research as to its impact. The FDA agreed, but a letter from the Chair of the House Commerce Committee ended the effort. Finally, in the late 1980s the FDA gave approval for print advertising requiring a full page of warnings, and later to television with the elaborate audio and video warnings we witness today.

During my tenure as president of AAF, I testified before the FDA on behalf of truthful DTC. One argument I made was that if done fairly it has the ability to provide poorer consumers with important health information not otherwise available to them. The illustration I used was based on DTC TV ads to treat asthma, a major illness then at a crisis stage in children in poorer communities. In contrast to me, also diagnosed with asthma, they had little information coming from medical specialists about the latest medical drugs. The FDA panel conducting the hearing showed interest in my statement, and they questioned how more advertising could be directed to the poorer communities. My suggestion was for the FDA to encourage the pharmaceutical industry, including companies selling asthma DTC medicines, to do so.

The other three panelists testifying that day all were opposed to DTC with arguments ranging from excessive costs to dangerous side effects. One of the opponents was a young professional from the advertising community, whose husband had committed suicide when using a prescription anti-depressant. The debate continues strongly to the present. For instance, Kurt Strange, Professor of Family Medicine and Community Health, Case Western Reserve University, argues that DTC should be banned. He argues: "There is no evidence that consumer ads improve treatment quality or result in earlier provision of needed care. Research has shown that the ads convey an unbalanced picture with benefits and emotional appeals given far greater weight than risks."[19]

Consumers have raised considerable concerns about this advertising, including a lack of trust. For example, in 2015 "Almost half of Americans (47%) say pharmaceutical firms are less trustworthy than other large companies."[20]

At the Institute for Advertising Ethics forum in 2009 at the Missouri School of Journalism, Professor Glen Cameron urged that DTC ads must be allowed to be seen and heard. At first, he said, there will be healthy skepticism, but over time there will be a move to relevance. He also pointed out the importance of this advertising by referring to a study in North Carolina showing that a high percentage of consumers first learned of cervical cancer from DTC advertisements.

The consumer concerns appear to be beyond the truthfulness of the claims. The serious side effects of the DTC products require that the advertising be done in a serious manner. For instance, ads for anti-depressants carry very strong warnings, including the danger of suicide. It may be that these very necessary disclosures as to the potential negative effects arouse concerns in members of the public not impacted by the disease or malady: "Why are they making these negative statements on television?" Specific targeting to the audiences with specific maladies could be received with higher relevance and acceptance. This is difficult with mass marketing advertising, but ads with links to websites for more specific information are being used.

Professional and industry DTC input

As noted at the beginning of this section, the American Medical Association (AMA) does not favor the advertising of prescription drugs directly to consumers, and in a November 17, 2015 statement urged that it be banned. The main argument made was that the advertising contributed to the high prices of DTC medicines. "Today's vote in support of an advertising ban reflects concerns among physicians about the negative impact of commercially-driven promotions and the role that marketing costs play in fueling escalating drug prices," said AMA Board Chair-elect Patricia A. Harris, M.D., M.A. "Direct-to-consumers advertising also inflates demand for new and more expensive drugs, even when these drugs may not be appropriate."[21]

The high price of prescription drugs is a major concern. The AMA statement cites a study showing that prescription drugs "have steadily risen and experienced a 4.7% spike in 2015."[22]

While I respect the AMA position and am concerned by the high prices of prescription drugs, I come down on the other side of the ethical question: the right and importance of patients/consumers receiving truthful information about products and services important to them. But, it is critical that the information be presented in an appropriate way to consumers, or their loved ones, who are suffering from serious medical issues. Consideration must be given to not overstating benefits and placing the use of the medicine in the context of what may be serious side effects. This is necessary in order to build consumer/patient trust in the marketing of these products directly to consumers.

We turn now to a review of industry input and activity, including by the Coalition for Healthcare Communication (CHC) and the Pharmaceutical Research and Manufacturers of America's (PhRMA) voluntary advertising principles.

Coalition for Healthcare Communication (CHC)

CHC states its role as "First, to defend the rights of medical professionals and consumers to receive appropriate healthcare information, and second, to act to prevent or reverse actions interfering with the free flow of healthcare information." The pro-DTC organization, which lists as its members the American Academy of Family Physicians, as well as business entities, including ad agencies, media companies and the Association for Medical Media, states that it "proactively explores ways to break down barriers" whenever DTC communications of pharmaceutical or medical products are obstructed.

The organization formulates positions on behalf of DTC members. Its website also posts relevant news stories on pharmaceutical advertising.[23]

A 2015 posting covers recent research by the National Bureau of Economic Research (NBER) that was reported to have found that "While DTC advertising increases the number of drug prescriptions, it also boosts the number of people being treated for commonly undertreated conditions and improves drug adherence." The NBER study, "Prescription Drug Advertising and Drug Utilization: The Role of Medicare Part D," discusses "the dramatic rise in advertising that occurred over the last two decades" and states that "per-capita spending on prescription drugs increased five-fold between 1990 and 2010, following decades of little spending growth." John Kamp, Executive Director for the Coalition of Healthcare Communication, stated in the article: "This study underscores that there are tremendous health benefits of DTC advertising. Reaching the underserved and encouraging drug adherence are powerful outcomes of DTC ads." The article also notes that "The Pharmaceutical Research and Manufacturers of America (PhRMA) recently stated that DTC advertising encourages discussions between doctors and patients, another sound benefit."[24]

We next turn to the pro-DTC activities of the leading pharmaceutical marketing association, PhRMA, and regulation by the Food and Drug Administration.

PhRMA support for DTC and FDA regulation

PhRMA's case for the ethics of DTC rests upon the premise of patients wanting information about their medical problems so they can better understand their treatment options and more effectively communicate with their physicians. This includes educating patients about diseases and treatment options, and "increasing the likelihood that patients will receive appropriate care for conditions that are frequently under-diagnosed and under-treated."[25] This relates to my concern in my testimony before the FDA that the caregivers and parents of children in our poorer communities were not receiving adequate information about asthma medications. My main information about my treatment options was mostly coming from my medical doctor, a specialist in pulmonary medicine. People in poorer communities rely on DTC information instead of medical specialists.

PhRMA argues in its Preamble that "We know that DTC communications, particularly DTC television advertising, can be a powerful tool for reaching and educating millions of people, and we are committed to ensuring that our DTC communications provide, accessible and useful health information to patients and consumers ... DTC advertising of such important and powerful products as prescription drugs should be responsibly designed to achieve these goals and to encourage the appropriate use of these products."[26]

We now turn to how the pharmaceutical industry is assisting and ensuring that its members' DTC advertising for "such important and powerful products" is being done responsibly and appropriately. This includes its relationship with the FDA.

"First and foremost," PhRMA states, "We have a responsibility to ensure that our DTC communications comply with the regulations of the Food and Drug Administration (FDA)." In general, according to PhRMA, the FDA requires all DTC information to:

- be accurate and not misleading;
- make claims only when supported by substantial evidence;
- reflect balance between risks and benefits; and
- be consistent with FDA-approved labeling.[27]

Clearly, FDA pronouncements and rules regarding DTC are important, and in particular, regarding the disclosures required that must be in both audio and video formats. The Preamble encourages pharmaceutical companies to discuss claims and labeling with the FDA on a one-on-one basis.

The FDA's Office of Prescription Drug Promotion (OPDP) of the FDA's Center for Drug Evaluation and Research (CDER) conducts research and enforces FDA rules on advertising. Its staff will discuss questions with the pharmaceutical companies, but does not provide advance approval, nor can it require that ads be submitted in advance of broadcast or print. If concerns are raised the OPDP sends letters of enquiry to the advertiser after the claims are made. The FDA requires the DTC ad contain at least one FDA approved use for the drug; the generic name of the drug; and all the risks of using the drug. Also, as to design of the ad, it must meet the "fair balance" requirement that the side effect information be presented in a manner similar to that used for the benefit information. Type size, bulleting, amount of white space, and headlines can affect the fair balance requirement. FDA does not require that DTC ads contain cost information, if there is a cheaper generic version, if there is a similar drug with fewer or different risks or how quickly the drug works.[28]

In addition to urging that DTC advertising follow all FDA rules and regulations, PhRMA provides an extensive list of eighteen guidelines, including, "In accordance with FDA regulations, all DTC information should be accurate and not misleading, should make claims only when supported by substantial evidence, should reflect balance between risks and benefits, and should be consistent with FDA approved labeling" (Guide 2). The guides also urge that new DTC television ads should be submitted to the FDA before using them (Guide 8). This differs substantially from FTC regulation of OTC drugs where all review is after the fact. Another suggestion, not required by the FDA, is that DTC ads should discuss options other than drugs, including diet and lifestyle changes where appropriate (Guide 12). The guides also urge a balanced presentation of both the benefits and risks of the medicine and the manner in which they are presented in the ad (Guide 14).[29]

The need for complementary self-regulation

PhRMA has published a substantial and substantive voluntary code for the advertising of DTC. This is commendable. However, the pharmaceutical industry has not developed a self-regulation program to implement the values and guidelines of its code, nor to act as a complementary force to the FDA to assure consumer benefits from DTC advertising. I believe it would carry more credibility if enforced by an independent third party, such as the Advertising Self-Regulatory Council (ASRC) that administers the National Advertising Division (NAD), the Children's Advertising Review Unit (CARU) and the National Advertising Review Board (NARB).

PhRMA's "accountability" for its Guiding Principles includes distributing them to pharmaceutical companies and urging their adoption of the principles; this results in a signed certification by companies' top officials that they "commit to abide" by the principles. PhRMA also receives comments about DTC from the public and healthcare professionals and "provides to the signatory company at issue any comment that is reasonably related to compliance with the Principles." It also issues "periodic reports to the public regarding the nature of the comments and the signatory companies' responses, and provides a copy of each report to the FDA."[30]

While useful, such accountability does not provide the necessary oversight and self-regulation that would both benefit consumers/patients relying upon DTC and build needed credibility for DTC advertising with consumers and healthcare professionals. The industry needs to address the question of "why" consumers and doctors remain skeptical of DTC advertising even after all of the oversight by

FDA, stiff regulations requiring extensive disclosures and proven value of their marketing. An ethical response by the DTC industry on behalf of the consumer could well build confidence and credibility. My suggestion would be for the implementation of a self-regulation program that is conducted independently of PhRMA and pharmaceutical companies. Its accountability in its professional conduct and appropriate actions would be to the Advertising Self-Regulation Council (ASRC), as that organization oversees an ERSP staff that investigates and negotiates changes to direct response advertising. The mission would be to self-enforce the PhRMA Guiding Principles for DTC advertisements, which are well written, but would gain in credibility.

The self-regulatory unit would be funded by PhRMA and would be dedicated to the self-enforcement of appropriate and effective DTC advertising. This would build credibility for DTC, enhance its importance to the consumer, and serve as a complementary self-regulatory force with the Food and Drug Administration in its regulatory mandate to assure truthful DTC with appropriate balance of claims with important warnings. This will prove to offer much support to the FDA in its regulatory mandate. Proof of that fact comes from the manner in which our National Advertising Division and Children's Review Unit support federal regulation of over-the-counter drug claims, with the decisions often based on FTC case law. The Federal Trade Commission counts on self-regulation to help it carry out its important mandate to insure that truthful advertising benefits the consumer. The complementary nature and success is emphasized in that under the National Advertising Division and Children's Advertising Review Unit's self-regulatory codes if a final voluntary solution cannot be achieved after investigation, negotiation, decision and review by our appellate unit, the matter is forwarded to the Federal Trade Commission for its review and action.

Prescription Drug Advertising (DTC) remains one of the most important, and yet contested, forms of advertising to the American Consumer. I believe it is ethical when presented fairly and appropriately taking into consideration its important health information and consequences, the need to target adult audiences, and create a beneficial dialogue between patient and doctor. With current opposition from the medical community, as well as from some consumers, it is time to build credibility with a strong consumer self-regulation program.

Alcoholic beverages

The alcoholic beverage industry (beer, wine and distilled spirits) takes great care in urging that their respective products are marketed and advertised in an appropriate and ethical manner. For instance the Beer Institute Advertising and Marketing Code provides that "Brewers strongly oppose abuse or inappropriate consumption of their products." The advertising guidelines specify that advertising should not depict "excessive" consumption, nor persons "lacking control" after its consumption.

The beer advertising code also emphasizes that ads not encourage under-age consumption. For instance, models and actors employed in beers ads "should be a minimum of 25 years old, substantiated by proper identification, and should reasonably appear to be over 21 years of age." Significantly, care is taken to only place ads in media directed to adult audiences: "Placements made ... in magazines, newspapers, on television, on radio, and in digital media ... may only be made where at least 71.6% of the audience is expected to be adults of legal drinking age."[31]

The Distilled Spirits Council of the United States (DISCUS), representing over 70% of distilled spirits brands in the United States, also promulgated a Code of Responsible Practices and Digital/Social Media Code of Responsible Practices. This includes a Code Review Board that issues semi-annual reports on complaint decisions and the advertisers' response.

According to the Code, "The overriding principle of our Code is to market our products to adults of legal purchase age in a responsible and appropriate manner ... DISCUS members encourage responsible decision-making regarding drinking, or not drinking, by adults of legal purchase age, and discourage abusive consumption of their products." A Code Review Board provides a mechanism for complaints or inquiries regarding marketing material subject to the code.[32]

As in the Beer Institute code emphasis is placed on marketing to adult audiences through broadcast, cable, radio, print, and Internet/digital communications "only where at least 71.6% of the audience is reasonably expected to be of legal purchase age." It is urged that electronic and print composition data be reviewed on a regular basis to assure accurate audience composition. Also, the Code states that alcohol products should not be advertised in college or university newspapers, nor placed on any outdoor stationary location within five hundred feet of an established place of worship, an elementary school or secondary school except on a licensed premise.[33]

The Code provides extensive provisions regarding not using content, such as cartoons, that would appeal to those under the legal drinking age; not placing ads on the comic pages of publications; not depicting social situations where alcohol is being consumed excessively; not making therapeutic claims; not encouraging or condoning driving while intoxicated; not disseminating ads that stereotype or degrade the image of women, men or any ethnic, minority, sexually-oriented, religious or other group; not using lewd or indecent language; not depicting sexual prowess and sexual success. The Code also urges that any product placement of alcoholic beverages in any measured media be consistent with the responsible placement provisions protecting against viewing by underage audiences.[34]

DISCUS has developed and implemented a strong Code Review Process that facilitates the review of complaints against the advertising of distilled spirits by its members or non-members. A response by the advertiser is expected "forthwith" and the Code Review Board then convenes and renders a decision, which could include urging the advertiser to revise or withdraw the challenged ad as not in compliance with the Discus Code. The Code Board is available to answer questions or assist with compliance. The Code Review Board's decision and the advertiser's response are summarized in the Semi-Annual Code Report.[35]

The publishing of the complaint, decision and the response of the advertiser enhances the likelihood that there will be compliance with the Code Review Board's decision. In reviewing annual reports one finds a clear statement of the complaint, the review boards finding as to whether there is a violation of the voluntary code, the advertiser's response, and importantly, whether it will agree to change the challenged ad. The DISCUS review and compliance procedure is stronger than other industry review programs, such as that just discussed in this book regarding the PhRMA process for complying with its guides for DTC prescription drug advertising. Still, the independent self-regulation by a third party industry group, such as under the Advertising Self-Regulation Council, as I recommended for DTC claims, would strengthen the process.

Cigarettes and e-cigarettes

The cigarette industry has a long history of selling its products under strict government regulations. Congress prohibited television and radio advertising of the products beginning in 1970, and print advertising requires rotating health warnings expressing the product's unique health consequences. Regulated by the Federal Trade Commission and now by the Food and Drug Administration, regulatory action has continued to strengthen the warnings of the product.

The sale and marketing of e-cigarettes, some brands of which are now owned by tobacco companies, is getting much regulatory attention. States are considering banning their consumption in restaurants, just as cigarette smoking is banned.[36] The major concern for these products is the health implications. Norman Edelman, MD, chief medical officer, American Lung Association, stated: "We are concerned about the potential for addiction and abuse of these products. We don't want the public to perceive them as a safer alternative to cigarettes."[37]

The Food and Drug Administration proposed in 2014 that the sale and marketing of e-cigarettes would be covered under its authority to regulate tobacco products. Those rules are now final and include prohibiting the sale of the product to anyone under 18, the use of vending machines, and putting health warnings on the labels.[38] I believe it would be unethical to advertise e-cigarettes to children or adolescents in a manner or in any medium that will draw their attention.

Because of the potential similarity of cigarettes and e-cigarettes, as far as addiction and perhaps health issues are concerned, an exploration of the government's regulation of tobacco products—and the industry's continuous opposition—will provide a useful background should the rapidly growing vaping industry challenge the new FDA rules.

Major regulation began in 1964 with the Surgeon General's report affirmatively linking cigarette smoking to lung cancer. The Federal Trade Commission under its Section 5 authority immediately proposed a new and stronger warning: "CAUTION: cigarette smoking is dangerous to your health and may cause death from cancer and other diseases." Congress intervened, a result that has occurred several times over the years, and required a weaker warning. Then in 1965 Congress passed the *Federal Cigarette Labeling and Advertising Act*, requiring the following health warnings on all cigarette packs: "Caution: Cigarette Smoking May be Hazardous to Your Health." In 1970, the *Public Health Cigarette Smoking* act banned cigarette ads on radio and television.

The 1965 Act also required the Federal Trade Commission to transmit a report to Congress annually on the effectiveness of cigarette labeling, current cigarette advertising practices and the need for additional legislation.[39]

We now turn to the 1980 staff report to the FTC laying out the results of a comprehensive investigation into cigarette advertising practices, consumer injury and legal and remedial recommendations. I believe this document, which I approved for submission to the Commission, covers the essence of the legal, ethical and public policy issues involved in the regulation of cigarette sales and advertising. Many of those issues may be relevant to the regulation of e-cigarettes. We will review excerpts of the summary of the staff report to the Commission:

Staff Report on the Cigarette Advertising Investigation—May 1981[40]

Summary of Findings

The past efforts of the Commission plus the efforts of Congress and other governmental agencies and private organizations to increase the amount of health information available to consumers have had an important impact. Many more consumers now are aware that smoking is hazardous to their health than in 1964.

The percentage of Americans who smoke has declined significantly over the same period, and a substantially larger number of those who do smoke now smoke cigarettes with lower levels of "tar" and nicotine.

Nonetheless, the problems which prompted the Commission to act in the past still exist. While most Americans are generally aware that smoking is hazardous, some consumers, especially smokers, do not know this basic fact. However, even if it is assumed that every consumer is aware that smoking is hazardous, the evidence indicates that many consumers do not have enough information about the health risks of smoking in order to know how dangerous smoking is, i.e., what is the nature and extent of the health risk of smoking. Many consumers also do not know whether the general health risks of smoking have any personal relevance to themselves or whether they are among those groups of people who may be uniquely vulnerable to these health hazards. Finally, without more specific, concrete information, consumers have a more difficult time remembering and are less likely to consider health information at all in making their smoking decision.

More specifically, the data discussed in Chapter III suggest that many consumers do not know enough about the health effects of smoking to know how dangerous smoking is and indeed desire more information about the specific hazards of smoking. For example, the data indicate that many do not know about what diseases are smoking related. Over 30% of the public is unaware of the relationship between smoking and heart disease.

Nearly 50% of all women do not know that smoking during pregnancy increases the risk of stillbirth and miscarriage. Approximately 30% of those polled do not know about the relationship between smoking, birth control pills and the risk of heart attack.

The data also indicate that substantial numbers of consumers seriously misunderstand and underestimate the increased risk of suffering these health problems as the result of smoking. And many more consumers seriously underestimate the severity of increased dying from these smoking-related illnesses. The survey data indicate that a large number of people do not believe they will personally suffer the health consequences of smoking.

The importance of the fact that many consumers do not know about the health effects of smoking is heightened by the following. The Medical evidence gathered over the past two decades indicates that cigarette smoking is far more dangerous to health than was thought in 1964. Smoking causes more than 300,000 deaths annually (one out of seven of all deaths) in this country. In 1978, 54 million Americans smoked a total of 615 billion cigarettes. Many of those smokers are uninformed about the serious health effects of smoking.

Summary of Recommendations

Based upon the evidence obtained in this investigation, staff is concerned that current cigarette advertising practices may mislead consumers by omitting material facts about the health risks of smoking. Staff has also tentatively concluded that additional action designed to provide consumers with more information about the health consequences of smoking is necessary. In Chapter V the staff has considered a number of remedial options, including: (a) educational efforts of other governmental and private organizations; (b) voluntary industry self-regulation; (c) alteration of the size and shape of the warning; (d) replacement of the current warning with a single new, more specific warning; (e) replacement of the current warning with a rotational warning system; (f) placement of limitations on the use of imagery in cigarette advertising, known as "tombstone advertising"; and (g) disclosure of carbon monoxide levels.

Of the options explored, staff, at this preliminary stage believes the following are likely to be most effective: (a) additional funding for expanded educational efforts, such as public service announcements; (b) changing the shape and increasing the size of the current warning; and (c) replacing the current warning with a system of short rotational warnings.

Expanded educational efforts, such as public service announcements broadcast during prime viewing hours, would reach millions of consumers. Changing the size and shape of the warning would improve its noticeability, but would not provide consumers with the additional necessary health information. Replacing the current warning with a more specific, single new warning would be an improvement; however, having more than a single warning would allow greater information to be available to the public and, thereby, decrease the possibility of deception. Rotating the various health warnings would also assist in maintaining their noticeability over an extended period, and would effectively communicate a substantial amount of specific health information about which millions of consumers are uninformed. To be effective these changes should involve the warning both on cigarette packages and in cigarette advertisements. While the adoption of any one of these remedial options by itself would not eliminate the problems discussed in this report, the adoption of the three options staff tentatively believes to be most effective as part of an overall educational effort would provide the public with additional health information and remedy any possible deception in cigarette advertising.

In light of the findings, conclusions and recommendations in this report, the staff recommends that: (a) copies of the staff report should be released to Congress for its consideration, (b) the report should be released for public comment, (c) the Commission should continue its investigation, while working with Congress, members of the industry and appropriate governmental and private organizations to coordinate and determine what action should be taken by whom; and (d) after the close of the comment period, the staff should report back to the Commission with an analysis of the information obtained from public comments and a further recommendation as to whether additional or formal Commission action is necessary and appropriate.

Legal Basis for Proposed Remedies

A number of options to remedy the problems discussed in the report have been presented in this Chapter. If at any time the Commission decides to take some action, it is necessary to examine the legal implications of each remedial option it is likely to seriously consider.

Proposed Remedies are Reasonably Related to the Elimination of the Deceptive Practices.

The Commission has broad remedial authority to enforce Section 5 of the Federal Trade Commission Act. In recognition of the agency's special competence in dealing with trade practice problems, Congress delegated primary responsibility for fashioning remedial orders to the Commission,[41] and gave it wide latitude in choosing among alternative remedies to redress violations of its Act,[42] as long as its solutions are reasonably related to the removal or prevention of an unlawful practice.[43]

Affirmative disclosures have repeatedly been found reasonable and necessary to cure violations stemming from the failure of advertisements to reveal material facts.[44]

Moreover, the Commission has indicated that affirmative disclosures are "especially appropriate" in cases, such as this one, involving public health and safety.[45] In fact, affirmative disclosures, such as detailed health warnings, have been required in numerous instances in which the Commission has found advertisements deceptive for containing misleading health and safety claims or for failing to reveal health and safety related facts regarding product use.[46]

In this case, staff has made great efforts to ensure that the remedies discussed are "reasonably related" to any deception in cigarette advertising. Staff has reviewed the existing data concerning consumer knowledge of the health hazards of smoking, and has commissioned studies of its own to assess consumer knowledge. Based on this accumulated data, the single warning and rotational warnings discussed were carefully tailored to remedy the important gaps in consumer knowledge of the health effect of smoking. In addition, staff has tested various warning messages and shapes for both effectiveness in communicating information and understandability, see, Ch. V, Sec. II, supra. It has consulted with social scientists and marketing experts in this regard. Finally, an advertising agency has worked closely with staff to insure that the informational remedies discussed in this report are feasible, effective, and can be implemented at minimal cost and burden to the industry.

In sum, the informational remedies discussed are directly related to the ineffectiveness of the current warning and the consumers' lack of specific knowledge concerning the health hazards of smoking. As such, they are "reasonably related" to the possible deception in current cigarette advertising, and the Commission has the legal authority to require them.[47]

Proposed Remedies are Consistent with the First Amendment

Government regulation designed to cure deceptive advertising is consistent with the First Amendment to the Constitution. In fact, warnings and affirmative disclosures such as those proposed by staff further the First Amendment interest in increasing the amount of truthful information available to consumers.

Several recent Supreme Court cases illustrate these principles. In the landmark case, Virginia State Board of Pharmacy v. Citizens Consumer Council, Inc., 425 U.S. 748 (1976), the Court stated:

… (Much) commercial speech is not provably false, or even wholly false, but only deceptive or misleading. We foresee no obstacle to a state's dealing effectively with this problem. The First Amendment, as we construe it today, does not prohibit the State from insuring that the stream of commercial information flow *cleanly as well as freely*. 425 U.S. at 771–772 (emphasis added)

In a significant footnote, the Court added that:

... (it may be) appropriate to require that a commercial message appear in such a form, *or include such additional information, warnings, and disclaimers, as are necessary to prevent its being deceptive.*[48]

In Bates v. State Bar of Arizona, 433 U.S. 350 (1977), the Court also made clear that requiring affirmative disclosures to cure advertising deception does not offend the First Amendment. In overturning a prohibition on advertising by attorneys, the Court pledged that the state bar "retains the power to correct omissions that have the effect of presenting an inaccurate picture," and emphasized that "the preferred remedy is more disclosure, rather than less".[49] Again, the Court was careful to note that warnings or disclaimers could be required if necessary to assure that the consumer is not misled.[50]

Most recently, in Central Hudson Gas and Electric Corporation v. Public Service Commission, 447 U.S. 557 (1980), the Court confirmed that government regulation of potentially deceptive advertising is not prohibited by the First Amendment. The Court wrote:

The First Amendment's concern for commercial speech is based on the *informational function* of advertising. [Citation omitted.] Consequently, there can be no constitutional objection to the suppression of commercial messages that do not accurately inform the public about lawful activity. The government may ban forms of communication more likely to deceive the public than inform it....[51]

Thus, the Supreme Court has concluded that misleading commercial speech is not entitled to First Amendment protection. In this case the proposed remedies solely seek to remedy the potential deception in cigarette advertising. None of the proposed remedies in anyway restricts the right of the cigarette industry to exercise its First Amendment right to disseminate truthful information about cigarettes.

Conclusion of Staff Report on Cigarette Advertising Investigation

Based upon its review of these remedial options, the staff has tentatively concluded that there are remedial options available that appear to be capable of providing consumers with the material health information necessary to remedy the possible deception in cigarette advertising. Of the options explored, staff believes the following are likely to be most effective: (a) additional funding for expanded educational efforts, such as public service announcements, (b) changing the shape and increasing the size of the current warning; and (c) replacing the current warning with a system of short, specific rotational warnings.

Expanded educational efforts, such as public service announcements broadcast during prime viewing hours, would reach millions of consumers. Changing the size and shape of the warning would improve its noticeability, but would not provide consumers with the additional health information.

Replacing the current warning with a more specific single new warning would be an improvement, but having more than a single warning would allow greater information to be available to the public. Rotating the various health warnings would also assist in maintaining their noticeability over an extended period, and would more effectively communicate a substantial amount of specific health information about which millions of consumers are uninformed. To be most effective these changes should involve the warnings both on cigarette packages and in cigarette advertisements. While the adoption any one of these remedial options by itself will not eliminate the problems discussed in this report, the adoption of these remedial actions as part of an overall educational effort by Congress, the Commission or other relevant organizations appears to offer the most effective way of informing the public about significant health risks of smoking and eliminating any possible deception in cigarette advertising.

During the 1980s the FTC continued to investigate and bring cases against cigarette companies for deceptive advertising claims. For instance, I supervised a case against Brown & Williamson Tobacco Company (B&W) charging the company with making false claims that their cigarettes were lower in tar than competing brands. The claims made for Barclay cigarettes were that the brand was "Ultra Low" in Tar, 99% tar free, and tested as just 1% tar. The case went through the court system to the Federal appellate court in the District of Columbia. The court affirmed the FTC prohibition on the 1% tar tested claim, but remanded on the other claims. The court affirmed FTC jurisdiction under its Deception authority and that the First Amendment did not protect deceptive ad claims.[52]

The Food and Drug Administration issued the "FDA Rule" in 1996 that claimed jurisdiction over cigarette advertising and published proposed regulations to reduce tobacco use by children. These included the types of promotions that will be relevant to the marketing of e-cigarettes, including no face-to-face sales of the products to children, no outdoor advertising near schools or playgrounds, no brand name sponsorships, and more stringent ad regulations. The tobacco industry successfully sued in 2000 and the Supreme Court ruled that Congress had not given the FDA authority over tobacco and tobacco marketing (FDA v. Brown & Williamson Tobacco Corp.). Congress acted in 2009 to give FDA substantial authority to regulate tobacco.

Family Smoking Prevention and Tobacco Control Act

This major legislation made a clear turning point in government regulation of tobacco legislation. It gave the FDA a strong and clear mandate to regulate as it does for pharmaceuticals and foods. The provisions or those that are similar may well cover how FDA regulates e-cigarettes with those provisions now under consideration by the FDA and Administration. Much of the legislation in the Act is targeted specifically at cigarettes and smokeless tobacco products. The FDA is given power to:

- require tobacco companies to submit a list of ingredients in their products;
- require tobacco companies to make public the nicotine content of their products;
- enlarge warnings on tobacco packaging to take up 50% of the front and back panels;
- regulate with standards the use of terms such as "mild" and "light";
- create a scientific advisory committee to help the FDA on tobacco issues.

Under the last provision the Center for Tobacco Products (CTP) was established at the FDA with eight divisions, each charged with some aspect of public health. The main duties are as follows:

- Establish and set performance standards.
- Review applicants for new and modified risk tobacco products before they reach the market.
- Require and control warning labels.
- Establish and enforce advertising restrictions.

The Family Smoking Prevention and Tobacco Control Act also mandated a ban on the sale or distribution of flavored tobacco products, other than menthol, which was implemented by the FDA on September 22, 2009.

The act also mandated the creation of a Tobacco Products Scientific Advisory Committee (TPSAC) to assess health and safety issues concerning tobacco products and provide advice to the Commissioner of Food and Drugs based on their findings. One responsibility is to consider whether there is a certain level below which nicotine does not produce addiction, an issue that would be relevant for e-cigarettes. The Commissioner appoints the committee of 12 members, 9 of whom come from the medical community with voting power, and non-voting members from the tobacco industry.

The tobacco industry filed a lawsuit against the United States in opposition to the legislation and against the FDA for policies decided under the act by the Center for Tobacco Control. A U.S. District Court ruled that a full ban of graphics and colors on all advertisements and packaging does not infringe on the First Amendment rights of the tobacco companies to communicate to adult audiences while limiting the effect on youths. The judge also ruled that requiring enlarged warning on packaging is reasonable because it serves to better alert the public. (Philip Morris, the largest tobacco company, did not join the lawsuit and did not oppose FDA regulation, and spoke in favor of the legislation on its website as being tough but reasonable.) On March 19, 2012, the Court of Appeals for the Sixth Circuit found many parts of the TCA legally valid, including the larger warning labels, but held that a ban on color and graphics on labels and advertising violated the First Amendment. However, the Washington D.C. Court of Appeal ruled on August 24, 2012 that the required graphic warning labels violate the tobacco companies' First Amendment rights. The Supreme Court declined to review the court's decision. The FDA must now develop a second set of proposed labels and make them available for public comment.[53]

FDA regulation of e-cigarette marketing and advertising

The advertising of e-cigarettes has become a major ethical and legal issue. As noted at the beginning of this section the FDA has taken responsibility for the regulation under its authority over tobacco advertising. Concerns expressed initially link to the impact of the marketing on teens, adolescents and children. The final rules include not distributing free samples, prohibit implied claims of reduced health risk, require health warnings, and restrictions to prevent sales to underage youth.[54]

According to news report the sale of e-cigarettes and other vapor devices is expected to reach $3.5 billion in 2015. "Vaporizers use heat to release active ingredients in a liquid or plant without combustion. The market is expected to expand to $10 billion by end of 2018, but an extension of regulatory power of the Food and Drug Administration could effectively slow that growth."[55]

The article reports that "An extension of authority proposed by the FDA in April 2014 would allow the agency to require manufacturers of e-cigarettes ... to obtain its approval before going to market." This would result in "retroactive premarket review," or intensive scientific study and other measures which could cost companies "millions and millions" says Gregory Conley, president of the American Vaping Association, a nonprofit trade organization. Conley estimates that more than 99% of e-cigarette products currently on the market would be banned for their inability to meet the approval requirement. He adds that vaping products have been effective in helping smokers quit tobacco cigarettes. Companies would have two years from the effective date of the regulations to comply or be taken off the market. A spokesman for the FDA says the purpose of the proposal is "to protect Americans from tobacco-related disease and death in today's rapidly evolving industry."[56] The FDA will require approval of all e-cigarettes under its new regulations.[57]

With the regulation of tobacco advertising as a model, it may take a considerable amount of time to resolve the federal and state regulatory issues. The ethical dilemma involved in the advertising of e-cigarettes should be addressed now. To me, how or whether we advertise these products turns on both the nature of the product and the nature of the audience that may be exposed to the marketing. To "do the right thing" ethically requires that consumers be "treated fairly" because of both the nature of the product's potential health consequences and the nature of the audience (youth and children) that might be attracted to the ads.

We can view the ethical dilemma from a "right versus right" perspective. On the side of the industry, Cynthia Cabrera, executive director of the Smoke-Free Alternatives Trade Association, the largest industry trade group, said in a statement, "These new regulations create an enormously cost-prohibitive regulatory process for manufacturers to market their products to adult smokers and vapers." She also stated, "It also limits access to the 40 million adult smokers in the U.S. yet to make the switch to vaping and cripples a multi-billion dollar, job-creating industry, the majority of which are made of small businesses."[58]

On the other side of the ethical dilemma we have first, the nature of the product's health consequences. As noted earlier, Normal Edelman, MD, chief medical officer, American Lung Association, stated: "We are concerned about the potential for addiction and abuse of these products. We don't want the public to perceive them as a safer alternative to cigarettes."[59]

While e-cigarettes don't contain tobacco, they do contain nicotine and additive chemicals, and little is known about their long-term effects, according to a Harvard T.H. Chan School of Public Health study released in October 2015. There are also concerns that the devices will popularize smoking in public places. To this can be added the quote above from the FDA spokesman saying the purpose of the FDA regulation is "to protect Americans from tobacco-related disease and death in today's rapidly evolving industry."[60]

According to the Centers for Disease Control and Prevention (CDC), in 2015 about 5.3% of middle school children used e-cigarettes in a thirty day period, and the figure for high school students had risen to 16%. According to FDA and CDC, in 2015, 3 million high school and middle school students reported using e-cigarettes. "As cigarette smoking among those under 18 has fallen, the use of other nicotine products, including e-cigarettes, has taken a drastic leap," said Sylvia Matthews Burwell, secretary of health and human services, in announcing the rules. "All of this is creating a new generation of Americans who are at risk of addiction."[61]

The potential health concerns, for me, weigh heavily in favor of not allowing these products to be advertised unless they meet the new FDA standards for safety and for the nature of the ways in which they can be advertised. The proposal already is a bit of a compromise because it would permit e-cigarettes to be marketed for two years from the effective date of the regulation as the companies complete and submit their data for FDA approval.

Then, there is the fairness and care to be taken regarding how and to whom these products are advertised. Of paramount concern is that teenagers, youth and children are not exposed to marketing for e-cigarettes. Here, regulation and self-regulation should be similar to those for the advertising of cigarettes. More specifically, not distributing free samples, no outdoor advertising close to schools, and other restrictions to limit exposure to the underage population, as used for cigarettes.

The nature of the potential health concerns also impacts my views as to regulations required for advertising to an adult audience. This would include future warnings that the FDA might require, as well as what can be said about these products other than taste. I note that the president of the industry association argues that e-cigarettes "have been effective in helping smokers quit tobacco products."[62] On the other hand, concerns might be raised that their use will lead former smokers, as well as youth, into smoking tobacco products. Research on this issue would be most helpful.

Because of the nature of the product and the need to avoid attracting an underage market, I believe ethics calls for fairness in the ways in which e-cigarettes are marketed. This is paramount during the time it takes for the FDA to implement its final regulations and they are upheld in the courts. Then, ethics will require that marketers follow the law.

Avoiding advertising that offends the consumer

To "do the right thing", in addition to being truthful and fair with our consumers, we should not communicate in ways that are offensive or demeaning. This includes humor, language or physical depictions that consumers find repellent or repulsive. The government has taken no role in this ethical mandate, nor, in my opinion, should it. It is up to our industry to show restraint.

This is one of the most difficult areas of advertising ethics. Clear-cut standards cannot be generated to regulate these factors in advertising, but we must be very sensitive to these issues and respect concerns. It is wise for advertisers to heed these concerns because they risk alienating major market groups. With regard to guidelines, certain things should be avoided:

- utilization of stereotypes of race, gender, or age;
- exploitation of the human form;
- expletives and vulgarity;
- violent or morbid images;
- sacrilege; and
- humor at the expense of the physically or mentally challenged.

Unfortunately, it is all too easy to find illustrations of ads that have offended consumers. One can go on YouTube to find "Six Most Offensive Banned and Rejected Ads."[63]

In this book I am focusing on two areas of advertising and marketing that consumers find offensive and objectionable: ads and programing that demean multicultural consumers because of the unfair depiction of people of color, and the use of violence in advertising.

Unfair depictions of people of color

Chapter 7 is dedicated to the ethics of the manner in which we deal with multicultural advertising. The positive work of the American Advertising Federation's Mosaic Council is detailed as it covers hiring of professionals of color and the positive manner of creating effective advertising to multicultural audiences. A major section also counters the current unfair depiction of people of color in reality TV and other programming. The latter ethical dilemma needs immediate attention by the producers, writers and actors—and supporting advertisers—of the programs with unfair depictions.

Offensive advertising, including unfair racial depictions and violence, will not be resolved by the government, whose authority is focused on product safety and avoiding deception. In fact, as will be detailed, the Supreme Court has ruled efforts to avoid violence in children's advertising as a violation of the First Amendment. It is up to the industry to "do the right thing" in the area of unfair depictions of people of color and with respect to violence in advertising. A right versus right analysis, for me, comes down heavily on the side of care and restraint. Producers, and advertisers, of the reality TV shows might argue that this is what their audience wants and ratings might support this. However, on the other side is that the depictions, such as overwhelmingly depicting black men as violent, counter the ethical goal of our country in practicing fairness, objectivity and equality in our racial relations. Also, concern must be felt with regard to how these depictions might affect young people of color as they grow and become citizens of America. Will they believe they have no opportunity to advance as they view these unfair depictions?

Chapter 7 deals with the ethics of multicultural marketing and programming in detail with solutions presented from knowledgeable and concerned professionals and citizens.

We turn in detail, now, to the ethical problem of the depiction of violence in advertising, including its negative impact on women and children in our society.

Violence in advertising

Allow me to say at the outset that I am indebted to the extensive work that others have done in conducting research and presenting illustrations of, and solutions to, the ethical problem of violence in advertising. This includes the recent and comprehensive, *Advertising and Violence: Concepts and Perspectives*, edited by Nora J. Rifon, Marla B. Royne, and Les Carson.[64] I was honored to write the Foreword to this important academic work, in which I stated that the book provides the essential compendium and collection of academic research, conclusions, and recommendations on "violence in advertising."

As I noted in the Foreword, the ethical dilemmas presented by any amount of violent advertising and the possible impact it may have on children, women, and vulnerable audiences, need to be addressed for the benefit of the public. And, the issue for further discussion is not about the political correctness of the depiction of violence in advertising. The research findings and conclusions in the book *Advertising and Violence* provide a strong foundation for discussing two issues with the industry: (1) the communication intent and usefulness in using violent depictions and (2) the ethical dilemmas presented with violent depictions in both adult and children's advertising. Whether the particular ad is ethical and responsible depends on already determined factors, including the nature of the audience, as well as the purpose of the acts of violence, such as to prevent actual harm in the real world.

A major assertion made in *Advertising and Violence* relates to the impact of violence in advertising and in the media upon aggression:

> Bushman and Anderson (2001) indicate, despite opinions to the contrary, that there is no longer any need for further debate on the relation between exposure to violence in the media (which, of course, includes advertising) and a detrimental outcome—that is, aggression. Rather, literature reviews and media-analyses, of the conjunction of aggression and media violence all point to the same conclusion. Specifically, Bushman and Anderson (2001) note that based on numerous studies since the mid-1970s, there is a positive link between depictions of media violence and aggression. Moreover the magnitude of this relation has increased over time, not decreased. Perhaps even more important, the significance of the correlation between violence and aggression across studies is second only to the relation between smoking and lung cancer, and even supersedes the magnitude of correlations between more "obvious" relationships such as calcium consumption and increases in bone mass.[65]

The book makes clear that the government, while interested in the impact of violence in advertising, is not in a strong position to prevent its use or reduce its negative impact. As I believe this book makes clear, the First Amendment to the U.S. Constitution protects truthful commercial speech. That can include violent depictions or content in ads unless a "real" threat of violence is proved. As I noted in my Foreword to *Advertising and Violence*, the Federal Trade Commission remains interested in violence in advertising aimed at children and holds hearings and publishes reports to Congress and the public on the self-regulatory actions of the music, film and video-game industries.

Any change in the current amount and type of violence in advertising is being left up to the industry. Without the legal support provided, change can only come about through action taken voluntarily, including through industry self-regulation. The ethical premise of "doing the right thing" provides the basis for real discussions between academia and industry with support from government leaders. The fact that it has been proven that violence in media and advertising results in aggression should provide the support needed for a careful analysis of when it is appropriate and when it is not.

The ad industry's self-regulatory group, the Children's Advertising Review Unit (CARU), investigates advertising addressed to children and recommends change. This includes ads containing violent content. It has published guidelines relating to "Inappropriate Advertising" and that "only age appropriate videos, films and interactive software are advertised to children" and that "advertising should not portray or encourage behavior inappropriate for children," and that "Advertising should not portray or encourage behavior inappropriate for children (e.g., violence or sexuality) or include material that could unduly frighten or provoke anxiety in children; nor should advertisers targeting children display or knowingly link pages of a website that portrays such behavior or materials."[66]

Other than using violence in advertising or media as part of an ethical platform to discourage violence, one has to ask what is its purpose. Some have suggested that it is to draw attention and build brand awareness; but at what cost? Also, while a particular audience, perhaps young men, might be attracted to the ad, it might well have a negative impact on other consumers. As I noted in Chapter 1, advertisers must acknowledge and deal with "Consumer Information Power." Ads that offend get much negative attention online at the expense of the advertiser. While the total number of violent ads may be relatively small in comparison to the vast amount of other advertising, violent ads often stand out and receive much consumer attention—favorable and unfavorable—in online discussions. Some might believe that the controversy such advertising generates builds brand awareness. But is it worth the negativity often engendered by the violent depictions? This is one of the major issues raised in *Advertising and Violence*, and should be addressed in discussions within and between the academic and ad professional networks.

It must be noted, as I did in *Advertising and Violence*, that those offended by the violence depicted often are part of the audience targeted by the advertiser. Consider the public service campaign with the noble purpose of getting young, first-time voters to vote in the presidential election. Titled "Do Not Silence Yourself," the campaign relied upon graphic depictions of silent young people. One ad showed a young woman, bound and gagged with black duct tape, with a look conveying great fear.

When I asked the opinions of ad students, including those in creative classes, women almost universally condemned the ad as depicting violence against women. As one stated, "I will never respond favorably to an ad that shows violence against women." The ad also received considerable online negative attention. It appears that the PSA offended much of its target audience.

In addition to unfair stereotyping of people of color, and violence in advertising, there are other forms of advertising that are offensive to the public.

A major ethical concern is the way women are stereotyped in advertising as sex objects. The infamous Dolce and Gabbana print ad showing five men hovering over a scantily clothed woman lying on her back is one such illustration. In 2016 one ad agency began a mission to urge ad agencies and marketers to stop objectifying women in their ads to sell products. Madonna Badger, co-founder of Badger & Winters, in honor of her daughters, produced a two and a half minute video called "We Are #WomenNotObjects" that has been passed around on the Internet. It features a collection of ads from big brands that show women with little clothing on in provocative poses. The goal is to raise awareness about the issue in the hope of getting it stopped.[67]

Another offensive illustration is the TV spot for Groupon that appeared in the 2011 Super Bowl and that was featured on YouTube. Groupon, which focuses on giving consumers good deals, used a television spot featuring actor Timothy Hutton in what appeared to be a PSA to aid hurting Tibetans where he states: "The people of Tibet are in trouble, their very culture is in jeopardy." Then, without a pause, he goes on: "But they still whip up an amazing fish curry, and since 200 of us bought at Groupon.com, we're each getting $30 worth of Tibetan food for just $15 at Himalayan Restaurant in Chicago." The ad was quickly attacked for making light of Tibetans' hardships on social networking sites across the Internet. The Groupon CEO pulled the ad five days later, but after many had commented negatively.[68]

Advertising Age reported on a 2014 marketing tactic by Urban Outfitters "that riled the pubic with a sweatshirt that looked to many as if it showed splotches of blood over the crest of Kent State University, where four students were shot to death at a 1970 anti-war protest." The article quoted Urban Outfitters as saying the red spots are simply part of the vintage look of the shirt, but predictably it touched off an enraged wave of criticism. Kent State wrote in a statement on its website: "This item is beyond poor taste and trivializes a loss of life that still hurts the Kent State Community today." The company apologized and removed the shirt from its website, but users took to Twitter, mostly to express condemnation or pledges to avoid the store.[69]

As we have covered in this chapter, "Doing the Right Thing for Consumers" includes being truthful and not offensive in our advertising and PR. Also, we should treat consumers "fairly" depending upon the nature of the product, as we have discussed. We also should act fairly depending upon the nature of the "audience," for instance the manner in which we direct ads to children. This will be addressed in the next chapter.

Questions and reflection

1. The author uses "Do the Right Thing" as the standard for practicing ethical advertising. What are his three components for doing the right thing?
2. In the *Virginia Pharmacy* and *Bates* Supreme Court cases, the Court ruled that truthful advertising is protected under the First Amendment to the Constitution. What are the financial benefits upon which the Court based its decision?

3. What are the two FTC requirements needed to avoid deceptive advertising?
4. In the FTC case involving Sony, the ad agency was also charged with deception. What are the requirements for an agency to discuss favorably its clients' products in Tweets or other social media?
5. Under the *Central Hudson* case, the Supreme Court ruled that government can prohibit truthful advertising if it meets a three part test. What are the components of the test?
6. The ad industry's advertising self-regulation program is complementary to the FTC's legal regulatory requirements. If an advertiser does not voluntarily agree to the changes requested, what options are available?
7. To be ethical ads must be truthful, but "ethics rises above truth." The author believes that advertisers must treat consumers "fairly" because of the nature of the products being advertised. What are examples of such products?
8. The author provides a "right versus right" ethical discussion for the advertising of prescription drugs to consumers. What are the major ethical arguments on each side of this debate between the prescription industry and the American Medical Association? Would having a third party review and self-regulate the industry's ethical guidelines assist in building consumer trust?
9. A "right versus right" ethical discussion is also provided for the advertising of e-cigarettes, along with medical and industry viewpoints; government regulations regarding cigarette and new FDA advertising regulations for e-cigarettes are set out. What are the major ethical arguments on each side, and where do you come out on the ethics of advertising e-cigarettes?
10. With regard to "violence in advertising" what are the concerns raised with respect to its impact on actual violence, as well as its negative impact on effectively reaching the consumer?
11. Concerning the stereotyping or objectifying of women in advertising what are the arguments from the business case and personal case against this unethical practice?

Notes

1 McNamara, Charles, *The Complete Guide to Ethics Management: An Ethics Tool Kit for Managers*, http://www.managementhelp.org/ethics/ethxgde.htm.
2 Virginia Pharmacy Board v. Virginia Citizens Consumer Council, Docket No. 74–895, 425 U.S. 748 (1976).
3 Virginia Pharmacy Board, ibid., p. 770.
4 *Advertising Compliance Handbook*, New York: Practicing Law Institute, 1988, pp. 312–313.
5 Bates v. State Bar, 433 U.S. 350, 377–78 (1977).
6 Central Hudson Gas & Electric Corporation v. Public Service Commission of New York, 477 U.S. 557 (1980).
7 Pfizer, Inc., 3 Trade Reg. 20,056, July 11, 1972.
8 www.ftc.gov.

9 In the Matter of Sun Oil Company, Inc., Docket C-3381, 1992, http://caselaw.findla
   w.com/pa-superior-court/1074894.html.
10 Warner-Lambert v. FTC, 562 F.2d 749 (D.C. Cir. 1977), https://h2o.law.harvard.
   edu/cases/4969.
11 ADT Pulse, FTC Press Release, June 24, 2014, www.ftc.gov/news-events/press-relea
   ses/2014/06/ftc-approves-final-consent-settling-charges-home-security-company.
12 Sony Computer Entertainment America, Press Release, November 25, 2014, www.ftc.
   gov/news-events/press-releases/2014/11/sony-computer-entertainment-ameria-provide-c
   onsumer-refunds.
13 Sony Press Release, ibid.,
14 Pitofsky, Robert, FTC Chairman, "FTC support, recognition for advertising industry self-
   regulation," October 1998, www.ftc.gov/sites/default/files/documents/public_statem
   ents/helping-ftc-help-you-effective-self-regulation-better-business/050926selfreg.pdf.
15 "The Advertising Industry's Process of Voluntary Self-Regulation," January 1, 2014,
   www.asrcreviews.org/wp-content/uploads/2012/04/NAD-CARU-NARB-Procedur
   es-revised-1-1-141.pdf.
16 Euro-Pro, Press Release, October 14, 2014, http://www.asrcreviews.org/narb-finds-a
   ggregated-reviews-across-retail-sites-do-not-serve-to-support-claim-that-euro-pros-sha
   rk-vacuums-are-americas-most-recommended-2/.
17 BP Lubricants USA, Press Release, June 19, 2014, http://www.asrcreviews.org/na
   rb-panel-recommends-bp-lubricants-discontinue-stronger-claims-based-on-companys-
   torture-test/.
18 Moss, Hilary, July 27, 2011, "Julia Roberts & Christy Turlington L'Oreal Ads Banned
   in U.K.," http://www.huffingtonpost.com/2011/07/27/julia-roberts-loreal-ad-ban_
   n_910587.html.
19 "Consumer Drug Advertising Should be Banned," *New York Times*, December 16,
   2013, www.nytimes.com.
20 "What Americans Think About Business - New Polling Data for 2015," Public Affairs
   Pulse Survey, July 6–20, 2015, by Princeton Survey Research Associates International,
   http://pac.org/pulse/?p=480.
21 "AMA Calls for Ban on Direct to Consumer Advertising of Prescription Drugs and
   Medical Devices," November 17, 2015, http://www.ama-assn.org/ama/pub/news/
   news/2015/2015-11-17-ban-consumer-prescription-drug-advertising.page.
22 Ibid.
23 Coalition for Healthcare Communications, www.cohealthcom.org.
24 "NBER: DTC Ads Increase Treatment of the Undertreated and Underdiagnosed,
   Improve Drug Adherence," December 7, 2015, www.cohealthcom.org.
25 "PhRMA Guiding Principles—Direct to Consumer Advertisements About Prescription Drugs," http://phrma.org/sites/default/files/pdf/phrmaguidingprinciplesdec08fina
   l.pdf.
26 "PhRMA Guiding Principles."
27 "PhRMA Guiding Principles."
28 FDA Office of Prescription Drug Promotion (ODPD), http://www.fda.gov/downloa
   ds/Drugs/DevelopmentApprovalProcess/SmallBusinessAssistance/UCM361326.pdf.
29 "PhRMA Guiding Principles."
30 "PhRMA Guiding Principles."
31 Beer Institute Advertising and Marketing Code, http://www.beerinstitute.org/assets/
   uploads/general-upload/2015-Beer-Ad-Code-Brochure.pdf. An example of an ad
   suggesting moderation in consumption is a "Heineken 'Moderate Drinkers Wanted'
   spot by Publicis Italy featuring a woman wandering through a bar singing Bonnie
   Tyler's 'I Need a Hero' as the men around them fall down drunk. The ad ends with a
   woman eyeing a more sophisticated guy who declines another bottle of Heineken."
   Business Insider; AAF Smart Brief, January 13, 2016, www2.smartbrief.com.

32 "Code of Responsible Practices for Beverage Alcohol Advertising and Marketing," http://www.discus.org/responsibility/code/.
33 "Code of Responsible Practices for Beverage Alcohol Advertising and Marketing."
34 "Code of Responsible Practices for Beverage Alcohol Advertising and Marketing."
35 "DISCUS Semi-Annual Code Report," http://www.discus.org/assets/1/7/2010-Jan-Jun.pdf.
36 "Lawmakers taking a Closer Look E-Cigarette Ban," http://wivb.com/2015/01/25/lawmakers-taking-a-closer-look-e-cigarette-ban/.
37 WebMD, http://www.webmd.com/smoking-cessation/news/20140507/e-cigarette-vapor-contains-potentially-harmful-particles-review.
38 McGinley, Laurie, and Dennis, Bradley, May 6, 2016, "FDA Launches Rules for Hot E-cigarette Industry; Minors banned from buying; products must win government approval," *The Washington Post.*
39 Federal Cigarette Labelling and Advertising Act, 15 U.S.C. 1331 (1965).
40 Staff Report on the Advertising Investigation, May 1981, by Matthew Myers, Program Advisor; approved, Collot Guerard, Deputy Assistant Director, Division of Advertising Practices; Wallace S. Snyder, Assistant Director, Division of Advertising Practices; concur, James H. Sneed, Director, Bureau of Consumer Protection.
41 "The Commission is the expert body to determine what remedy is necessary to eliminate the unfair or deceptive trade practices ...," Jacob Siegel Co. v. FTC, 327 U.S. 608, 612 (1946).
42 FTC v. Ruberoid Co., 343 U.S. 470, 473 (1952); see, e.g., FTC v. Cement Institute, 333 U.S. 683, 726 (1948).
43 E.g., Jacob Siegel Co. v. FTC, 327 U.S. at 613.
44 Warner-Lambert Co. v. FTC, 562 F.2d 749 (D.C. Cir. 1977), Cert. Denied, 433 U.S. 950 (1978); J.B. Williams Co. v. FTC, 381 F.d 28, 32 (7th Cir. 1963), Cert. Denied, 375 U.S. 944 (1963).
45 See Firestone Tire and Rubber Co., 81 FTC 398, 451–452 (1972), aff'd 481 F.d 246 (6th Cir. 1973), cert. denied, 414 U.S. 1112 (1973); American Home Products Corp., 70 FTC 1524, 1695 (1966); Kirchner v. FTC, 337 F.d 751, 753 (9th Cir. 1964); Moretrench Corp v. FTC, 127 F.d 782, 795 (2d Cir. 1942); 1964 Cigarette Rule at 8354.
46 Positive Products Co., 33 FTC 1327, 1335, aff'd sub nom. Aronberg v. FTC, 132.Fd 165 (7th Cir. 1942); American Medical Products Inc., 32 FTC 1376, aff'd, 136 Fd 426 (9th Cir. 1943); Warner-Lambert Co. v. FTC, 562 Fd 749 (D.C. Cir. 1977); see also the discussion in Firestone Tire and Rubber Co., 81 FTC at 462–74.
47 The "reasonable relation to deception" is applicable whether the Commission proceeds via adjudication or rulemaking. See section 18(a)(1)(b) of the Magnuson-Moss Warranty-FTC Improvements Act, 15 U.S.C. Section 2031, et Seq.
48 Ibid., Virginia State Board of Pharmacy, 425 U.S. at p. 772, note 4, emphasis added.
49 Ibid., Bates, 433 U.S. at p. 375.
50 Ibid., Bates, footnote 84, at 5–45 & 46.
51 Ibid., Central Hudson, 447 U.S. at p. 563.
52 FTC v. Brown & Williamson Tobacco Corporation, 778 F2 35 (DC Cir. 1985). Named cases can be found at www.law.justia.com.
53 Family Smoking Prevention and Tobacco Control Act, www.changelabsolutions.org.
54 "FDA Launches Rules for Hot E-Cigarette Industry," May 6, 2016, *The Washington Post.*
55 "The FDA may soon be able to vaporize e-cigarette products," November 13, 2015, www.marketwatch.com/story/the-fda-may-soon-be-able-to-vaporize-e-cigarette-products-2015-11-13.
56 "The FDA may soon be able to vaporize."

57 "FDA Launches Rules for Hot E-Cigarette Industry," May 6, 2016, *The Washington Post*.

58 "FDA Launches Rules for Hot E-Cigarette Industry," May 6, 2016, *The Washington Post*.

59 WebMD, http://www.webmd.com/smoking-cessation/news/20140507/e-cigarette-vapor-contains-potentially-harmful-particles-review.

60 "The FDA may soon be able to vaporize."

61 "FDA Launches Rules for Hot E-Cigarette Industry," May 6, 2016, *The Washington Post*.

62 "The FDA may soon be able to vaporize."

63 "6 Most Offensive Banned and Rejected Ads," https://www.youtube.com/watch?v=8jveB3dTB3A.

64 *Advertising and Violence: Concepts and Perspectives*, edited by Nora Rifon, Marla B. Royne, and Les Carson, 2014, Armonk, NY and London: M.E. Sharpe, Inc.

65 Rifon et al., *Advertising and Violence*, pp. 3–4, referring to Bushman, B.J., and Anderson, C.A. (2001) Media violence and the American public: Scientific facts versus media misinformation," *American Psychologist*, 56, 477–489.

66 Self-Regulatory Program for Children's Advertising, "Unsafe and Inappropriate Advertising to Children," Part II (D) (2)(I).

67 Vranica, Suzanne, "Ad agency swears off crafting ads that objectify women," *Wall Street Journal*, January 25, 2016, http://wsj.com/news/author/1556.

68 "crazycommercials4you," 176,701 views, www.youtube.com/watch?v=pOwJOcp-Mxk.

69 "With Kent State shirt, did Urban Outfitters go too far?" *Advertising Age*, September 15, 2015.

3

ADVERTISE TO CHILDREN FAIRLY AND APPROPRIATELY

> Advertisers should treat consumers fairly depending upon the nature of the audience to whom the ads are directed and the nature of the product or service advertised.
>
> *IAE Principle 5*

Advertising to children—defined by government as 12 and under—raises very important ethical, as well as legal, questions. Perhaps there is a no more vulnerable audience in America that receives the amount of advertising both online and in traditional media. Advertising to children is prohibited in a growing number of countries and has been under scrutiny and attack by consumer groups in America over the past fifty years. The Federal Trade Commission has investigated and regulated children's advertising over that period of time, and the advertising industry has committed major resources, through the Children's Advertising Review Unit (CARU), and Children's Food and Beverage Initiative (CFBI), to self-regulating advertising to this targeted audience.

Companies advertising to children spend annually in the millions of dollars and place ads on traditional media—television, radio and print—as well as increasingly online and in new media, including Internet, apps, DVDs, and mobile. This includes when playing computer games and video games on company websites where the products are featured. In addition, in-store advertising, promotions and event sponsorships are used. Products advertised include toys, fast foods, cereals and beverages, games and clothing.

The question of whether or not it is ethical to advertise to children age 12 and under began in the 1970s and continues until today. This chapter explores the historical record of government investigation, often directly impacted by Congressional oversight; action taken on a case-by-case approach by government enforcement and industry self-regulation; and the legal and ethical options available as we move forward in "doing the right thing" for children. This must be a candid and thorough review and evaluation, taking into consideration what child experts, the medical community and the government and industry urge and believe. We will explore what we have learned over the years in addressing this "right versus right" ethical dilemma.

Government has not banned advertising directed to children 12 and under in the United States, in part because Congressional action has not allowed the federal regulators to use their authority to do so. This will be discussed in the next section of this chapter covering in detail the FTC's Children's Advertising Rulemaking in 1978. This has focused regulation on a case-by-case approach that depends on whether the ad is deceptive and on self-regulation initiatives by the advertising industry.

In determining if it is appropriate to advertise, in general, to children, or with respect to certain products and services, and if so what limitations should be applied, we consider two central issues. The first is children's limited cognitive ability to understand the persuasive nature of advertising, as well as the impact from the ways in which ads are directed to them. The basic ethical tenet is that the audience must understand that the content directed to them is advertising. "There is a great deal of research that shows children don't distinguish between content and advertising," said Kathryn Montgomery, a professor of communications at American University and an advocate of children's media protections.[1]

The second issue is the nature of the product or service that is being advertised to them. There is agreement that adult products, such as tobacco and alcoholic beverages, are inappropriate and care is taken to minimize advertising of adult products in programming frequented by children. Also, as discussed in the last chapter, children's advertisements should not contain violent or sexual depictions. On the other hand, a major area of controversy involves the advertising of food and beverage products contributing to childhood obesity in the United States. As we will discuss, British legislators and regulators are now considering banning food and beverage ads in the UK because of what they consider to be a childhood obesity crisis.

First, we will study in detail what the government has learned over the years in its investigations bearing on the appropriateness of advertising to children, based on the nature of the audience and the nature of products advertised. We will focus on the FTC Children's Advertising Rule of 1978 that produced a watershed of scientific evidence, intense opposition to the proposed staff ban of advertising, and unprecedented political involvement and control. In order to assess the important information learned and contested, I will excerpt sections of the staff report that I hereby note was supervised and approved by me.

Then, we will cover current FTC case-by-case legal requirements, and the review and guidelines of the industry's well organized and supported Children's Advertising Review Unit (CARU). The chapter will conclude with a discussion on the current focus on children's food advertising and its impact on childhood obesity.

Federal Trade Commission's Children's Advertising Rulemaking Proceeding 1978

The FTC initiated this heavily contested rulemaking proceeding, based upon recommendations by consumer groups, including Action for Children's Television (ACT). After an extensive review of the petitions submitted, and the underlying allegations and studies on the inability of young children to understand the persuasive nature of advertising, legal staff in the Division of Advertising Practices under my direction as Assistant Director, recommended the commencement of a rulemaking proceeding to determine if advertising directed to children for highly sugared products should be banned. The health concern was impact on children's dental caries. Today, the medical issue has shifted to the advertising of foods and beverages' impact on childhood obesity:[2]

FTC Staff Report on Television Advertising to Children[3]

I Introduction and Staff Recommendation

This Report addresses the large volume of current television advertising which is directed to children. Many young children—including an apparent majority of those under the age of eight—are so naive that, as this Commission and the Federal Communications Commission (FCC) have previously recognized, they cannot perceive the selling purpose of television advertising or otherwise comprehend or evaluate it and tend, as the FCC has observed, to view commercials simply as a form of "informational programming." The youngest children tend to be even more naive and thus even less capable of comprehending the influence which television advertising exerts over them. For example, it appears that a large proportion of pre-schoolers think that the persons or animated figures on television are addressing them personally, and that the animated figures are "real" and in some sense appropriate objects for emulation. Apparently the youngest pre-schoolers think that there are "real little people" inside the set.

The largest single part of the television advertising addressed specifically to children is for sugared foods, consumption of which poses a threat to the children's dental health, and possibly to other aspects of their health as well.

The Commission now has pending before it two petitions on this subject, both of which urge that a major portion of the advertising to children for such sugared products is unfair and deceptive within the meaning of the FTC Act. Both petitions request that the Commission promulgate a trade regulation rule (1) banning what they describe as the worst of that advertising during hours when children are an especially large proportion of the audience, and (2) granting certain related relief.

The petitioners are Action for Children's Television ("ACT"), a non-profit Massachusetts corporation with 10,000 members which works to eliminate commercial abuses from television advertising addressed to children, and the Center for Science in the Public Interest ("CSPI"), a non-profit District of Columbia corporation with 4,000 members which works to improve domestic food policies. The petitions point out that sugar consumption, especially between meals, is commonly understood by experts to be a principal cause of tooth decay; that tooth decay is a disease that afflicts virtually every person (and more than half of all adult teeth) in the United States; that it is so widespread that at any given moment there are an estimated 1,000,000,000 unfilled cavities in American mouths; and that there is some medical evidence that excessive consumption of sugar probably contributes to obesity, and possibly contributes to heart disease.

The petitions also point out that the great volume of televised advertising which urges children to eat sugar is not balanced by any remotely comparable volume of advertising which urges them to consume other foods—or impresses on them the risks they take by eating the advertised products.

The petitions contend that the special naivete, suggestibility and vulnerability of children have long been recognized by the commission, so that advertising practices which might be neither unfair nor deceptive as to adults can be both unfair and deceptive to children.

ACT's petition, received on April 16, 1977, seeks a ban on "candy" advertising addressed to children. Specifically, ACT asks that such advertising be prohibited (a) before 9:05 p.m.; or (b) where the dominant appeal of the advertising is to children; or (c) during any periods when children make up at least half of the audience. ACT does not define the word "candy," but proposes that the Commission obtain the aid of an expert body such as the American Dental Association in arriving at an appropriate definition for regulatory purposes.

CSPI's Petition, received on April 26, 1977, seeks a ban, during any periods when children make up at least half of the audience, on televised advertising for between-meal snacks which derive more than 10% of their calories from added sugar. CSPI also seeks mandatory affirmative disclosure of the added sugar content of foods permitted to be advertised, as well as of the dental health risks posed by eating sugared products, during periods when children make up at least half of the audience.

Regulation of televised advertising of sugared products to children has obtained broad expert and public support. On December 1977, Dr. Donald Kennedy, Commissioner of Food and Drugs, wrote to Chairman Pertschuk of this Commission that:

"In view of the large amounts of advertising—particularly television advertising—that are directed to children urging them to consume a seemingly endless variety of sugared products and the substantial likelihood that children will be unable to appreciate the long-term risks to dental health that consumption of these products will create, I strongly support action by the Federal Trade Commission to regulate the advertising of these products directed to children."

Likewise, the Council on Dental Health of the American Dental Association has endorsed "the elimination of advertising of sugar-rich products on children's television." Similarly, the Council of Foods and Nutrition of the American Medical Association has characterized present televised food advertising to children as "most distressing," and as "counter-productive to the encouragement of sound (nutritional) habits."

On July 20, 1977, representatives of the following organizations met with Chairman Pertschuk to express their endorsement of the petitions: The American Academy of Pediatrics, the American Parents Committee, the Dental Health Section of the American Public Health Association, the Association for Childhood Education International, the Black Child Welfare League of America, the East Coast Migrant Head-Start Program, the Latino Media Task Force, the National Association for the Education of Young Children, the National Association of Elementary School Principals, the National Council of Negro Women, and the National Women's Political Caucus.

Significantly, too, the U.S. Department of Agriculture (USDA) has been exploring ways to curb the overpromotion to children of heavily sugared and otherwise nutritionally poor foods. USDA has proposed that the use of "formulated grain/fruit products" such as specially formulated doughnuts, cream-filled cakes, coffee cakes, oatmeal bars, and peanut butter cookies be prohibited in school breakfast programs. In explaining this proposal, USDA noted that "questions have been raised over the sugar and fat content of the products ... and their value in teaching good eating habits to children." USDA has also recently issued guidelines for that program "encourage(ing) the service of foods with relatively low sugar content."

Similarly, the Assistant Secretary for Health of the Department of Health, Education and Welfare, Julius Richmond, M.D., recently told the Senate Select Committee on Nutrition and Human Needs that "there is a need to change current [food] advertising directed to children." He commended this Commission for what he described as its present efforts "to bring a reasonable degree of regulatory control to bear on nutrition related advertising, particularly on television."

These experts and others believe that reform of children's television advertising is needed in part because that advertising induces children to take health risks which they are not equipped to assess. But the potential for health-related risks is not the only reason for such views. Many believe it is unfair to advertise any product on television, specifically to children who are so young (evidently below the age of 8) that they cannot understand the selling purpose of, or otherwise comprehend or evaluate, commercials and thus cannot discount them, as adults or older children can. That unfairness is exacerbated when television advertising is directed to the very youngest children who are even more naive. The abuse inherent in advertising directly to such an audience via a medium as powerful and pervasive as television is such that a committee established by the British Parliament has just recommended that "*no* advertisements should be shown within children's programmes." (Emphasis added.) The committee explained that:

"Children are inclined to believe that what they are told in a television programme is not only true, but the whole truth. How are they to distinguish between what they are told in a children's programme and what they are told in an advertisement? Yet in singing the praises, and the jingles, of a particular product, a child cannot be expected to know that other, less advertised products may be equally good ... That is why the majority of us believe that children should not be exposed during their own programmes to the blandishments and subtle persuasiveness of advertisements."[4]

That view has widespread support throughout the world. Of the major industrialized nations, the United States and Britain are part of only a handful that have ever allowed television advertising—for any product—to be directed specifically to pre-school children. The other members of that handful are Australia, Canada and Japan. And experience in those first two countries has led to authoritative proposals now pending to ban such advertising.

At least one advertiser of sugared products recognizes the need for fundamental change in televised advertising directed to children. On November 22, 1977, Kenneth Mason, President of the Quaker Oats Co., appeared as part of a panel of cereal industry representatives to discuss the televised advertising of that industry's products to children. Mr. Mason vigorously defended his company's products, but he conceded that:

"We do not believe any reasonable person can view a typical eight to twelve noon Saturday morning period on any of the major television networks and fail to recognize the need for fundamental change in the way our society is using its most powerful and pervasive medium of communication to entertain and enlighten the very young." Mr. Mason accordingly urged the Commission to hold thorough hearings on the present petitions.

In view of the breadth and importance of the issues raised in these petitions, staff has conducted its own extensive investigation of those and related issues. This is the report of that investigation.

Summary of FTC Staff Report

The Facts

In 1977, the average American child aged two through 11 was exposed to more than 20,000 television commercials. This came as a result of watching an average of 3–2/3 hours of television per day throughout the year. Those children who attended school spent, on the average, more time watching television over the course of the year than they did in the classroom. Moreover, the amount of time which children spend watching television has apparently increased by a full hour per day over the last 22 years, and is now almost double the amount of time that children spent listening to radio immediately before the advent of television.

Infants are attracted to television almost from the moment they first become aware of the world. Not only are they attracted to television, but they are more attracted to commercials than to programs. This is not surprising, given the resources and the accumulated experience of advertisers, and given the financial incentives they have to make every second count for the purpose of gaining and holding children's attention. By the early 1970s, $400 million was spent annually by the processed cereal industry alone. Joan Ganz Cooney, producer of the Children's Television Workshop, and producer of Sesame Street and The Electric Company, has explained that those educational programs were designed to resemble commercials because this allowed them to employ the same attention-getting devices that advertisers had perfected. Those devices, according to Dr. Kenneth O'Bryan, a child psychologist, are so potent that they make the 30-second commercial the most effective teaching device yet invented for implanting any relatively simple idea in a child's mind—including the idea that a product is desirable.

The effectiveness of television advertising in "teaching" children is especially great among those who are still too young to understand the selling purpose of that advertising. This category takes in an apparent majority of children under the age of eight. Even when children in this category understand that there is some difference between commercials and programming, they tend to explain that the difference is that commercials are "shorter," or "more funny," or to point to some other superficial distinction.

Among pre-school children, moreover, confusion about the nature and purpose of television advertising tends to be even greater than among elementary school children up to the age of eight. As we noted in the Introduction and Recommendations, the youngest children may think that there are actual people inside the television set; and even when they outgrow that illusion they may think that a person speaking from the set is specifically addressing them. Cartoon fantasy figures, such as elves, wizards and the like, tend to be perceived by such children as in some sense real and as appropriate figures to be imitated and learned from.

Very young children have trouble grasping what advertising is because they "believe that everything has a purpose and that such a purpose is built around them. Unlike the egocentric adult, who can take another person's point of view but doesn't, the child does not take another person's viewpoint because he simply cannot." In other words, the purpose of televised advertising is inherently beyond the child's comprehension. Thus, according to Dr. Richard Feinbloom, then acting medical director of the Family Health Care Program, Harvard Medical School, "an advertisement to a child has the quality of an order, not a suggestion."

In challenging the ads directed to young children the FTC staff emphasized the impact of the advertising of high sugar cereals on what they called a "pandemic" of tooth decay in the United States:

> Tooth decay commonly starts in early childhood and attacks most severely in adolescence. As Dr. Kennedy, the Commissioner of Food and Drugs, recently advised Chairman Pertschuk:
> "It seems clear that children are more vulnerable (than adults) to dental caries (tooth decay) and that the damage to the teeth resulting from tooth decay in childhood can have a substantial detrimental effect on dental health in later life."[5]

The staff also quoted Dr. Kennedy as pointing out that there is a "substantial likelihood that children will be unable to appreciate the long term risks to dental health that consumption of (the sugared products advertised to them on television) will create."[6]

Also, the FTC staff recognized and discussed the impact of sugared products on childhood obesity. This health issue is the concern raised today, again for the effects of advertising high sugar and high fat products to children. As we will cover later in this chapter, private organizations, such as the Yale Rudd Center, and government groups, including the Centers for Disease Control and Prevention (CDC), are researching the impact of these foods on children's health and have come to conclusions and recommendations similar to those advanced nearly 40 years ago by the FTC staff, as is now set out:

> Other reasons for concern with the amount of sugar promoted to children on television include evidence which suggests that at the present United States levels of consumption (more than a third of a pound of sugar per day for every man, woman, child, and infant) some persons are probably consuming so much sugar as to exclude from their diet essential nutrients, and that heavy consumption of sugar probably contributes to obesity and may contribute to heart disease and diabetes.
> Staff's investigation of the amount of television advertising being addressed to children for sugared products has yielded results similar to those obtained by others who have investigated this issue. We have found, for example, that on Saturday morning network television—a time of the week when children actually constitute a majority of the national audience—sugared cereals,

candies, snacks and drinks account for half or more of all the products advertised (except during the pre-Christmas season, when toy advertising is especially heavy). Further, these sugared products are advertised to children almost to the exclusion of any other foods—the principal apparent exception being fast-food restaurants whose products include such sugared items as desserts, "thick shakes," and carbonated soft drinks. On Saturday, September 24, 1977, when staff monitored all three networks from 8 a.m. until 1:30 p.m., sugar was promoted as many as four times per half hour on each network, and as many as seven times per half hour if fast-food advertising is taken into account. On ABC, 45 of the 59 food commercials (76%) were specifically for sugared products. On CBS, the corresponding figure was 41 out of 54 food commercials (76%), and on NBC, it was 43 out of 59 food commercials (73%).

A large proportion of the foods advertised to children on Saturday (or Sunday) daytime television are ready-to-eat cereals. Many of these are between 40 and 60% sugar. In the most extreme case, the sugar content exceeds 70%.

There is evidence not only that these food advertisers get the results they pay for, but also that, in the aggregate, their advertisements skew children's notions of "appropriate" things to eat toward highly sugared, relatively non-nutritious foods. Thus, in one study in which children were asked to specify "the kinds of foods you call snacks," 78% responded by naming the sugared products they saw advertised on television.

For this reason, among others, a number of prominent nutritionists, educators, other public health professionals, and parents have expressed concern that televised food advertising addressed to children is distorting nutritional habits, negating what little nutrition education takes place in the schools, and undermining the authority of parents in their own homes on matters of nutrition.

The law

The staff report concluded and argued, "It is both unfair and deceptive, within the meaning of Section 5 of the FTC Act, to address televised advertising for any product to young children who are still too young to understand the selling purpose of, or otherwise comprehend or evaluate, the advertising. This conclusion rests, in part, on legal precedents which hold that even adults—a group much less vulnerable than children—are not to be exposed to 'disguised' or 'hidden' advertising."[7] An illustration provided was the Federal Communications Commission prohibiting the broadcast of paid ads not clearly identified as such.

The report argued that "Unfairness also arises out of the striking imbalance of sophistication and power between well-financed adult advertisers, on the one hand, and children on the other, many of whom are too young even to appreciate what advertising is … In the present situation, it is ludicrous to suggest that any such balance exists between an advertiser who is willing to spend many thousands of dollars for a single 30-second instead trustingly believes that the spot merely provides advice about one of the good things in life."[8] This staff conclusion supported its proposed ban of "all television advertising for any product which is directed to, or seen by, audiences composed of a significant proportion of children who are too young to understand the purpose of, or otherwise comprehend or evaluate, the advertising."[9]

The staff argued, "It is unfair to address television advertising to children who may be aware of the selling purpose, when that advertising has the capacity to induce them to take health risks that they are incapable of evaluating for the purpose of deciding whether, on balance, the products that pose those risks are desirable."[10] This argument supported staff's proposal seeking a "ban on advertising directed to, or seen by, audiences composed of a significant proportion of older children for sugared products, the consumption of which poses the most serious dental health risks."[11]

Turning to the "Unfairness" basis of their recommendation, the staff argued that its proposed remedies were permissible under court legal determinations:

> The Supreme Court has characterized the Commission's powers in interpreting and enforcing the unfairness provision of Section 5 as those of a "court of equity," FTC v. Sperry & Hutchinson Co., 405 U.S. 233, 244 (1972), and has recognized that an especially broad definition of unfairness is in order where children are concerned because of their special naivete and vulnerability. FTC v. R.F. Keppel & Bro., 291 U.S. 304 (1934). Further, the Commission has recognized that the concept of unfairness should be defined most broadly of all where advertising induces consumers—especially children—to risk injury to their health, not just to their pocketbooks.[12]
>
> The most elaborate test stated by the Commission for determining unfairness—and one cited approvingly by the Supreme Court in S & H, supra, 405 U.S. at 244–45 n. 5—appears in the Cigarette Rule issued by the Commission in 1964. That test looks to three factors: first, whether the challenged practice, even if it has not previously been considered unlawful, "offends public policy" in the sense of being "within at least the penumbra of some common-law, statutory, or other established concept of unfairness"; second, "whether it is immoral, unethical, oppressive or unscrupulous"; and third, "whether it causes substantial injury to consumers (or competitors or other businessmen)." As the Court recognized in S & H, it is not necessary for a practice to be offensive under each of the three parts of the test in order for it to be unfair. Indeed, there have been instances since the Cigarette Rule where the Commission has found a practice to be unfair without specifically measuring it against any of the three parts. Moreover, the Commission itself has recognized that the Cigarette Rule test is not the exclusive test for

Section 5 unfairness. Notwithstanding, we will demonstrate that televised advertising of sugared foods to children is offensive under all three parts of the Cigarette Rule test.[13]

First, the report argued that the advertising sought to be prohibited offends public policy "to protect children from serious or lasting consequences of their own mistakes, and to protect them from adults who would profit from the disparity between their own sophistication and the naivete of children."[14] It was argued that the law protects children who do not yet have the capacity to appreciate the risks associated with the products advertised. Also, "Such advertising causes 'substantial injury' to children to the extent that it induces them to consume products which pose health risks and interferes with their education on matters of nutrition."[15]

The Federal Trade Commission, after the closing of the Children's Advertising rule and at the request of Congress, on December 17, 1980, issued its FTC Policy Statement on Unfairness. That document will be discussed in the conclusion to this chapter.

While violation of the FTC's Unfairness authority was the major argument for regulating ads for sugared products to children, a deception argument was also put forth:

Present televised advertising for sugared products to children is also "false," "misleading," and "deceptive" within the meaning of Sections 5, 12 and 15 of the FTC Act. These terms, like "unfairness," are to be construed especially broadly where children constitute the target audience and where personal health, as distinct from mere pecuniary interest, is at stake. The advertising at issue is deceptive in that it fails to state facts which are material, either in light of the claims made in the advertising, or in light of the customary or recommended use of the advertised products. All advertising for sugared products makes at least the implicit claim that consumption of the advertised products is desirable.

The material but unrevealed fact is that the products can also pose health risks.[16]

Staff argument in support of an advertising ban

The staff considered several remedies for dealing with the unfairness they concluded resulted from the advertising of sugared products to children. They recognized that affirmative disclosures within the ads dealing with dental and health risks were within the Commission's authority, but argued that "young children have trouble understanding (and sometimes even perceiving) such disclosures."[17] Also considered, were health disclosures presented outside the ads by food advertisers or other groups. Advertisers would fund such disclosures, and staff argued that the Commission had authority to impose this remedy. "Issues raised by this proposal concern its mechanics (e.g., how a funding system would work and who would control it) and would have to be explored in the context of rulemaking proceedings."[18]

The staff also considered "a rule which restricted the amount of television advertising for sugared products which could be broadcast per time unit of children's programming." But staff concluded: "(I)t might raise the price of time available for such advertising, or impose barriers to new entrants to the market or otherwise produce anti-competitive effects."[19]

The staff also considered restrictions on techniques (e.g. the use of "superheroes") and representations (e.g. "sweetness") in TV advertising for sugared products. It was felt that the Commission had clear authority, but "this solution is not likely to prove effective" because it would be difficult to identify the techniques and enforce the remedy in ongoing advertisements.[20]

The staff, having considered these remedies insufficient, then turned to imposing a ban on television advertising to children. "As we have noted, television advertising for any product directed to children who are too young to appreciate the selling purpose of, or otherwise comprehend or evaluate, the advertising is inherently unfair and deceptive. It is hard to cure this inherent unfairness and deceptiveness. Further, ACT and CSPI have urged that television advertising directed to children for the most cariogenic products be banned."[21]

In the report it is acknowledged "bans are remedies of last resort and are not to be imposed where less stringent remedies would suffice. But there are several factors which suggest the appropriateness of a ban here. And there is ample precedent establishing the Commission's authority to impose bans."[22]

The argument in favor of a ban on televised advertising of the most cariogenic sugared products to children is that products which pose the most severe dangers to health ought not to be presented via television advertising to children, a uniquely credulous and trusting audience. This is particularly so because children are much less able than adults to temper easily-aroused impulses with considerations of long-run harm or to understand the magnitude and nature of the specific risks which arise from the consumption of particularly cariogenic sugared products:

> The Commission in the past has not hesitated to ban advertising or marketing practices which pose risks of harm to children. Thus, for example, the practice found to be unfair in Keppel—inducing children to gamble with relatively trivial sums of money, rather than with their health—was banned outright; it was not permitted to continue on condition that the children be given affirmative disclosures about the risks involved. Additionally, the Commission has on several recent occasions recognized the need for bans on broadcast advertising that induces children to take health risks. In both 1968 and 1969, the Commission recommended to Congress that all broadcast

cigarette advertising be banned (not, again, that it be permitted to continue subject to affirmative disclosure requirements, or other conditions). Recently, in Hudson Pharmaceutical Co., the Commission obtained a consent order whose effect was to ban from children's programming any advertising for children's vitamins. This was the very form of relief which the National Association of Broadcasters had earlier determined to be appropriate as to such advertising. The Hudson case is similar to the present one in that consumption of the advertised product poses health risks which children may not be able to evaluate.

Another pertinent line of cases supporting the Commission's authority to impose a ban concerns prohibitions on the use of deceptive trade names. See, e.g., FTC v. Algoma Lumber Co, 291 U.S. 67 (1934). These cases have generally involved protecting adults against economic injuries, not children against risks to their health. Accordingly, the Commission's discretion in formulating an adequate remedy is, if anything, broader in the present case.

The foregoing remedies, of course, do not have to be considered in isolation from one another; some appropriate combination might be devised. On that point, the present practice in the Netherlands is instructive. There, advertisements for sugared foods are banned before 7:55 p.m. After 7:55 p.m., they can be broadcast, but they cannot be "clearly directed towards influencing children in favour of the recommended product," and during a portion of the commercial the advertiser must show a stylized toothbrush on the screen as a reminder of the health hazards of the product.[23]

Staff recommendations

We have concluded that the petitions are generally meritorious, that rule-making proceedings should be commenced under the Magnuson-Moss FTC Improvements Act and that the Commission should proceed to rulemaking to determine whether it should: (a) Ban all televised advertising for any product which is directed to, or seen by, audiences composed of a significant proportion of children who are too young to understand the selling purpose of, or otherwise comprehend or evaluate, the advertising (children younger than the age of 8); (b) Ban televised advertising directed to, or seen by, audiences composed of a significant proportion of older children for sugared products, the consumption of which poses the most serious dental health risks (children as old as 11 and as young as 8); (c) Require that televised advertising directed to, or seen by, audiences composed of a significant proportion of older children for sugared food products not included in paragraph (b) be balanced by nutritional and/or health disclosures funded by advertisers.

The remedy described in paragraph (a) follows from the conclusion that televised advertising directed to children too young to understand the selling purpose of, or otherwise comprehend or evaluate, commercials is inherently unfair and deceptive. The remedy described in paragraph (b) reflects the conclusion that the most cariogenic sugared products should not be advertised to children on television. The remedy described in (c) reflects the view that those products of lesser cariogenicity should be advertised to children only if balanced by nutritional and/or health disclosures addressed to that group.

The remedy in paragraph (a) must be implemented in a way that protects child audiences without unreasonably foreclosing the right of adults to receive otherwise protected commercial speech. Remedies (b) and (c) must be implemented in a manner which fairly differentiates among sugared products in terms of their relative cariogenicity, capturing the worst for remedy (b) and leaving the rest for remedy (c).

The reasons why these particular remedies have been proposed are set forth in Part VI of this Report, particularly at Sections B, C and F therein.[24]

The investigation and hearings lasted throughout 1978–79 and were hotly debated. In addition, extensive lobbying was conducted on Capitol Hill and ultimately the Commission was stripped of its authority to proceed with the rulemaking. The staff recommendation was predicated on the "Unfairness" authority contained in Section 5 of the Federal Trade Commission Act. As an independent regulatory agency, FTC authority is based totally on laws passed by Congress and on reauthorization on a periodic basis. In the 1979–80 Session Congress voted to reauthorize the FTC without its unfairness authority to be used in children's advertising rulemaking: "The Commission shall not have any authority to promulgate any rule in the children's advertising proceeding pending on the date of enactment of the Federal Trade Commission Improvements Act of 1980 or in any substantially similar proceeding on the basis of a determination by the Commission that such advertising constitutes an unfair act or practice in or affecting commerce."[25]

Since the proposed ban of Children's Advertising was predicated upon the Commission's unfairness authority, staff recommended closing the Children's Advertising Rule and the Commission agreed. Certainly this was a defeat for the government officials and the consumer groups urging Commission action against children's advertising they believed negatively impacted the health of children. Nevertheless, much was learned in the rulemaking hearings—discussed below— that I believe should be considered today in an ongoing effort to ethically advertise to this vulnerable group. We will conclude this chapter with a discussion of how what we have learned relates to a "right versus right" ethical determination.

Children's exposure to advertising has risen dramatically since the 1978 rulemaking proceeding. The trend toward increasing advertising to children in broadcast and cable programming and on children's websites and mobile devices has greatly expanded commercial messages. According to an American Psychological Association task force report in 2004, "It is estimated that advertisers spend more than $12 billion per year to reach the youth market and that children view more than 40,000 commercials each year."[26]

Current children's advertising regulation and self-regulation

As noted in the last chapter, the government and the industry have established strong programs to enhance the value of advertising to consumers, including to children. The Federal Trade Commission's mission is based on prohibiting deceptive advertising to children, including false claims and "half-truths" where disclosures are required. The industry's Children's Advertising Review Unit (CARU) plays a complementary role in protecting children from deceptive and unfair advertising. Indeed, when CARU recommends changes in its investigations that are not agreed to by the advertiser the case can be forwarded to the FTC for its investigation.

CARU has published guidelines for advertising to children under the age of 12 that include core principles and specific areas of concern. The principles focus on the limited knowledge and inexperience of children and urge that ads should not be deceptive or unfair and should be adequately substantiated under terms applied by the Federal Trade Commission; should use understandable disclosures to children; only use endorsements that are accurate and reflect actual experience; and should avoid blurring advertising and editorial/program content. Also, the principles urge that ads should avoid social stereotyping; and should avoid content inappropriate for children:

CARU Core Principles[27]
 The following Core Principles apply to all practices covered by the self-regulatory program.

1.   Advertisers have special responsibilities when advertising to children or collecting data from children online. They should take into account the limited knowledge, experience, sophistication and maturity of the audience to which the message is directed. They should recognize that younger children have a limited capacity to evaluate the credibility of information, may not understand the persuasive intent of advertising, and may not even understand that they are being subjected to advertising.
2.   Advertising should be neither deceptive nor unfair, as these terms are applied under the Federal Trade Commission Act, to the children to whom it is directed.

3. Advertisers should have adequate substantiation for objective advertising claims, as those claims are reasonably interpreted by the children to whom they are directed.

4. Advertising should not stimulate children's unreasonable expectations about product quality or performance.

5. Products and content inappropriate for children should not be advertised directly to them.

6. Advertisers should avoid social stereotyping and appeals to prejudice, and are encouraged to incorporate minority and other groups in advertisements and to present positive role models whenever possible.

7. Advertisers are encouraged to capitalize on the potential of advertising to serve an educational role and influence positive personal qualities and behaviors in children, e.g., being honest and respectful of others, taking safety precautions, engaging in physical activity.

8. Although there are many influences that affect a child's personal and social development, it remains the prime responsibility of the parents to provide guidance for children. Advertisers should contribute to this parent-child relationship in a constructive manner.

CARU guidelines[28]

The document emphasizes that the principles "aim to cover the myriad advertising practices in today's marketplace, as well as those that may emerge as technologies and advertising practices evolve." With regard to the guidelines, they "are designed to provide additional guidance to assist advertisers in applying these broad principles to their child-directed advertising and to help them deal sensitively and honestly with children ... Part I of the Guidelines offers general guidance on deception and other marketing practices that are inappropriate when directed to children, and encourages certain practices."

Part I: General Guidelines

a   Deception
    To assure that advertising directed to children is not deceptive:

   1. The "net impression" of the entire advertisement, considering, among other things, the express and implied claims, any material omissions, and the overall format, must not be misleading to the children to whom it is directed.

   2. Whether an advertisement leaves a misleading impression should be determined by assessing how reasonable children in the intended audience would interpret the message, taking into account their level of experience, sophistication, and maturity; limits

on their cognitive abilities; and their ability to evaluate the advertising claims.

b Product Presentations and Claims

To avoid deceptive and/or inappropriate advertising to children involving product presentations and claims:

1. Copy, sound and visual presentations should not mislead children about product or performance characteristics. Such characteristics may include, but are not limited to, speed, method of operation, color, sound, durability, nutritional benefits and similar characteristics.
2. The presentation should not mislead children about benefits from use of the product. Such benefits may include, but are not limited to, the acquisition of strength, status, popularity, growth, proficiency and intelligence.
3. Claims should not unduly exploit a child's imagination. While fantasy, using techniques such as animation and computer-generated imagery, is appropriate for both younger and older children, it should not create unattainable performance expectations nor exploit the younger child's difficulty in distinguishing between the real and the fanciful.
4. Advertisements should demonstrate the performance and use of a product in a way that can be duplicated by a child for whom the product is intended.
5. The advertisement should not mislead children about what is included in the initial purchase.
6. Advertising that compares the advertised product to another product should be based on real product attributes and be understandable to the child audience.
7. The amount of product featured should not be excessive or more than would be reasonable to acquire, use or consume by a person in the situation depicted. For example, if an advertisement depicts food being consumed by a person in the advertisement, or suggests that the food will be consumed, the quantity of food shown should not exceed the labeled serving size on the Nutrition Facts panel; where no such serving size is applicable, the quantity of food shown should not exceed a single serving size that would be appropriate for consumption by a person of the age depicted.
8. Advertising of food products should encourage responsible use of the product with a view toward healthy development of the child. For example, advertising of food products should not discourage or disparage healthy lifestyle choices or the consumption of fruits or vegetables, or other foods recommended for increased consumption by current USDA Dietary Guidelines for Americans and My Pyramid, as applicable to children under 12.

9. Advertisements for food products should clearly depict or describe the appropriate role of the product within the framework of the eating occasion depicted:

a Advertisements representing a mealtime should depict the food within the framework of a nutritionally balanced meal. (The guides elaborate upon acceptable ways to depict a balanced meal, including at least 3 of the 5 recommended food groups by the USDA Dietary Guidelines and My Pyramid (i.e., fruits, vegetables, fat-free or low-fat milk and milk products and whole grains). Also, the food should reflect reasonable portion sizes, and if a beverage is included, it should take into account its nutritional attributes and calories.)

b Snack foods should be clearly depicted as such, and not as substitutes for meals.

Guidelines 7, 8 and 9 affect and relate to food advertising to children, which is most contentious in the current debate over children's advertising. CARU is taking an active role in the self-regulation of such advertising. We will discuss CARU's food advertising self-regulation cases, and CARU's importance in the "right versus right" ethical debate now underway concerning the impact of children's food ads on childhood obesity.

a Material Disclosures and Disclaimers

1. All disclosures and disclaimers material to children should be under-standable to the children in the intended audience, taking into account their limited vocabularies and level of language skills. For young audiences, simple words should be chosen, e.g., "You have to put it together." Since children rely more on information presented in pictures than in words, demonstrative disclosures are encouraged.

2. These disclosures should be conspicuous in the advertising format and media used. e.g., online, advertisers should make disclosures clear and proximate to, and in the same format (i.e., audio or graphic) as, the claims to which they are related; in television, advertisers should use audio disclosures, unless disclosures in other formats are likely to be seen and understood by the intended audience.

Lee Peeler, President of the National Advertising Self-Regulation Council, which oversees the work of CARU, sums up the ethical care that should be taken to protect children:[29]

Tell the truth

- Don't exploit their vulnerability
- Show products used safely
- Don't blur ads and content
- Don't promise to make popular
- Protect privacy.

During 2014 CARU reviewed approximately 1,500 television commercials and 1190 magazine ads, and completed approximately 30 decisions. CARU also works with the MPAA to insure that ads for PG-13 films are not advertised during children's programs.

CARU examines content on both TV and online websites designed for children to insure that they understand the content to be advertising. This includes television ads that are structured like newscast segments. The concern, as in such ads directed to adults, is that the editorial format gives the ad a greater sense of objectivity and importance.

Take the print ad for "Tulip Glam-It-Up! Iron-on Crystals" marketed by Duncan Enterprises. This ad featured a young girl and the concern was that to children "this might be seen as an article about the girl as a fashion designer." CARU looked at the structure, content, and presentation of the ad. It recommended that the ad be clearly and conspicuously labeled as such, in a manner that children would understand, taking into account "their limited vocabularies and level of language skills."[30]

In its monitoring program CARU reviewed a television ad for Telebrands Phantom Saucer and concluded that the toy did perform the tricks and aerial movements depicted in the commercial. However, it recommended that the ads include an audio disclosure so that children would know the total cost of the toy, including shipping. The company agreed and implemented the audio disclosure for its broadcast ads.[31]

CARU and the FTC have brought food advertising cases that will be discussed in our next and last section of this chapter, dealing with the current ethical dilemma over the impact of children's food advertising on childhood obesity.

The current focus on food advertising to children

Childhood obesity, which has become an epidemic in the United States, has become the major concern regarding the advertising of foods and beverages to children under the age of twelve. In 2009 research findings were released regarding the advertising of sugared cereals to children with recommended government regulation going beyond even that envisioned by FTC staff in 1978. The Yale Rudd Center Report alleged that strong evidence shows that TV advertising influences food preferences for children under the age of twelve, and that the least nutritious cereals are advertised to children. The report urged that companies could only advertise the more nutritious products to children, based upon government standards established without involvement of industry.[32]

In 2012 the Yale Rudd Center updated its report on the advertising and consumption of cereals to children. Its summary conclusions and recommendations are:

> In 2009 the Rudd Center for Food Policy & Obesity at Yale University issued Cereal Facts. The report documented the nutritional quality and marketing of cereals to youth and found that cereal companies aggressively marketed their worst products to children as young as two years old. From 2008 to 2011, cereal companies improved the nutritional quality of most cereal marketed directly to children and reduced the advertising for some products.

But, according to the report, during this period, cereal companies increased advertising to children for many of their least nutritious products with the majority of cereal ads seen by children being for products consisting of one-third or more sugar. Findings also included that total media spending to promote child-targeted cereals increased by 34% with increases in Spanish-language TV, as well as Black children's exposure. Also, child visitors increased for 8 of 10 child-targeted websites.

The 2012 Yale Rudd Center Report urged that cereal companies expressing a commitment to be part of the solution to childhood obesity "do the right thing":

- significantly reduce the hundreds of advertisements for high-sugar cereals that children see every year; and
- use their substantial resources and creativity to find ways to encourage children to consume the healthful products in their portfolios.[33]

The government plays an important research, educational and regulatory role in combating the childhood obesity crisis in America. The Centers for Disease Control and Prevention (CDC) publish research findings and advice:

- Children who are obese are more likely to become obese adults.
- Adult obesity is associated with a number of serious health conditions including heart disease, diabetes, and cancer.
- If children are obese, obesity and disease risk factors in adulthood are likely to be more severe.

The CDC also describes the "Community Environment" contributing to childhood obesity, including advertising.

> American society has become characterized by environments that promote increased consumption of less healthy food and physical inactivity. It can be

difficult for children to make healthy choices and get enough physical activity when they are exposed to environments in their home, child care center, school, or community that are influenced by … advertising of less healthy foods. Nearly half of U.S. middle and high schools allow advertising of less healthy foods, which impacts students' ability to make healthy food choices. In addition, foods high in total calories, sugars, salt, and fat, and low in nutrients are highly advertised and marketed through media targeted to children and adolescents, while advertising for healthier foods is almost nonexistent in comparison.[34]

According to a *New York Times* article there is some good news regarding childhood obesity in America. "The obesity rate in children ages 6 to 11, after big increases, has now flat-lined, at 18 percent, and the rate of children ages 2 to 5 has fallen below 10 percent for the first time since the 1980s." The writer attributes this to "health advocates succeeding at what they set out to do," and uses the Robert Wood Johnson Foundation having spent $500 million since 2007 to fight childhood obesity as an illustration. That foundation, incidentally, helps fund the Yale Rudd Center that we just discussed. The theme of the article is that just as much effort should be spent on combating adult obesity that is at the level of 38%.[35]

The focus on combating childhood obesity appears to be strengthening in the United Kingdom, one of the few countries outside the U.S. that has permitted advertising to children. *The Guardian* reported that a committee of MPs has called for junk food ads to be banned in popular shows such as *The X Factor* as part of a tightening of UK rules to tackle the growing issue of childhood obesity. A House of Commons select committee has published a report into child obesity that makes a range of recommendations including a junk food ad ban across social media, the Internet, cinemas, in print, "advergame," and posters. The committee called for TV ad restrictions on products high in fat, sugar and salt to be extended to a complete ban before 9 pm. Current restrictions stop advertisers running commercials in programs that are likely to have more than a certain proportion of young people watching them. Dr. Sarah Wollaston MP, the chair of the health committee, was quoted:

> One third of children leaving primary school are overweight or obese, and the most deprived children are twice as likely to be obese than the least deprived. There are many causes and no one single or simplistic approach will provide the answer. We therefore urge the prime minister to make a positive and lasting difference to children's health and life chances through bold and wide-ranging measures within his childhood obesity strategy.[36]

The Advertising Association criticized the committee for not taking evidence from the industry and for the report having reflected a "narrow focus." The report concluded that consultation with the body responsible for implementing the law "should not be on whether it should be done, but on how it should be implemented following clear direction from the government within the childhood obesity strategy."[37]

Today, we face an ethical dilemma concerning advertising to children who are under the age of twelve. While the health crisis today is childhood obesity compared to childhood dental caries in 1978, many of the concerns and findings remain the same. Staff in 1978 argued that it was the advertising of sugared products that was contributing in a major way to the health issue, i.e., it was causing children to consume the advertised product in amounts that were unhealthy. Today, opponents of children's advertising of sugar and high fat products make similar arguments. For example, the Yale Rudd Center urges cereal companies to significantly reduce the hundreds of advertisements for high-sugar cereals that children see every year. And the government organization, the Center for Disease Control, finds that "Foods high in total calories, sugars, salt, and fat, and low in nutrients are highly advertised and marketed through media targeted to children and adolescents, while advertising for healthier foods is almost nonexistent in comparison."[38]

Based on nutritional and medical evidence, staff in 1978 argued that all children twelve and under were exposed to advertising for unhealthy products leading to dental caries. It argued that advertising for such products should be banned because of the health considerations.

Another major concern today that was addressed in the 1978 rulemaking was whether or not children could understand the persuasive nature of advertising. That is, could they distinguish advertising from editorial or entertainment content? Did they realize they were being advertised to? Based on scientific evidence, staff determined that children 8 and under were not likely to understand advertising, and that with regard to children 9–12 it would depend on the manner in which the ad was designed and disseminated.[39]

Staff in the 1978 Children's Advertising Rulemaking urged that the only remedy that would end the unfair practice under Section 5 of the FTC Act was an advertising ban. Due to children's cognitive limitations, staff in the rulemaking report proposed banning all TV advertising for any product when a significant proportion of the audience is too young to understand the persuasive intent. It also urged banning TV advertising to older children for sugared products posing the most serious dental risks, and requiring TV ads for less serious dental risks to be balanced with health disclosures.[40]

The Ad Ban remedy became the focus of the 1978 hearing and the successful lobbying by the industry to Congress. As noted earlier, in 1979–80 Congress amended the FTC Authorization to take away Unfairness authority for advertising regulation; that essentially eliminated the ad ban proposal. While the possibility existed for the FTC to proceed on a deception theory because children 8 and under could not understand the selling intent, staff concluded that there was no way consistent with Constitutional requirements to protect that group of children within the larger group of children understanding the selling intent. With our enforcement powers curtailed, the Commission accepted our staff recommendation to close the rulemaking proceeding.[41]

In 1980, the FTC, at the request of Congress, issued a new FTC Policy Statement on unfairness that governs the application of its statutory authority to prohibit unfair practices. Taking into consideration the First Amendment protection for certain truthful speech, the Commission stated the document: "delineates the Commission's views of the boundaries of its consumer unfairness jurisdiction" resulting "from an evolutionary process" beginning in 1964 when three factors became the basis of whether or not to apply the unfairness authority: (1) whether the practice injures consumers; (2) whether it violates established public policy; and (3) whether it is unethical or unscrupulous. The Commission points out that these three factors were quoted with apparent approval in the 1972 case of *Sperry & Hutchinson*, cited in the 1978 staff report.[42]

With respect to the consumer injury requirement, the Commission states it must satisfy three tests: it must be substantial; not outweighed by any countervailing benefits; and must be an injury that consumers could not reasonably have avoided. "Unwarranted health and safety risks may also support a finding of unfairness. Emotional impact and other more subjective types of harm, on the other hand, will not ordinarily make a practice unfair."

"Second, the injury must not be outweighed by any offsetting consumer or competitive benefits that the sales practice also produces ... The Commission also takes account of the various costs that a remedy would entail."

Finally, the injury must be one that consumers could not reasonably have avoided. Normally we expect the marketplace to be self-correcting, and we rely on consumer choice—the ability of individual consumers to make their own private purchasing decisions without regulatory intervention—to govern the market. However, it has long been recognized that certain types of sales techniques may prevent consumers from effectively making their own decisions, and that corrective action may then become necessary. Most of the Commission's unfairness matters are brought under these circumstances.

The second leg of the Commission's unfairness application asks whether the conduct violates public policy as it has been established by statute, common law, industry practice, or otherwise. While "public policy" is listed as a separate consideration, the Commission notes that usually it will be reviewed as "a means of providing additional evidence on the degree of consumer injury caused by specific practices ... The public policy should be one that is widely shared, and not the isolated decision of a single state or a single court."

As to the third consideration, "unethical or unscrupulous conduct," the Commission policy statement states, "this test has proven, however, to be largely duplicative. Conduct that is truly unethical or unscrupulous will almost always injure consumers or violate public policy as well." The Commission states it has never found unfairness solely on this basis, "and in the future it will act only on the basis of the first two."[43]

Complementary to the Unfairness Policy statement in 1980 was the *Central Hudson* Case where the Supreme Court held that truthful commercial speech could be regulated if the government met the following three criteria:

1. the government has a substantial interest in regulating the speech;
2. the government interest is directly advanced by the regulation; and
3. the regulation is no more extensive than necessary to serve the interest, i.e., the regulation is the least restrictive alternative available.[44]

Under *Central Hudson*, and subsequent cases, the Court authorized government to prohibit truthful commercial speech, but in a limited fashion. In *Central Hudson* the state argued the interest was to discourage electricity consumption, but the Court found the restriction banned all forms of advertising, including about other electrical devices and services.

Central Hudson provides Constitutional support for the Federal Trade Commission's authority to regulate truthful advertising under its Section 5 power to "prevent unfair acts or practices." Of course, Congress specifically prohibited the FTC in the same year, 1980, from using its unfairness authority in the promulgation of trade regulation rules concerning children's advertising. Still, it is useful to consider the FTC's unfairness authority in regulating future children's food advertising, assuming the Congress relents in its prohibition. Also, the criteria of both the Unfairness Policy Statement and *Central Hudson* are helpful in considering how we can treat consumers fairly based on the nature of the audience to whom the ads are directed and the nature of the product or service advertised (*IAE Principle 5*).

The first criterion of the FTC policy statement relates to whether the advertising would injure consumers. The Commission emphasizes that the injury must meet three tests: it must be substantial; not outweighed by any countervailing benefits; and must be an injury that consumers could not reasonably have avoided. These tests relate to *Central Hudson's* first tenet that the government has a substantial interest in regulating the speech. The Commission's second requirement is that the unfairness action is necessary because the speech violates public policy. The public policy requirement, the Commission concludes, relates to supporting action under the first criterion of showing substantial consumer injury.

The dental health problems concerned in the 1978 staff investigation, and certainly the childhood obesity crisis of the present day, make a strong case for justifying the showing of consumer injury necessary to apply the unfairness authority. The 1978 staff report sets out the injury in terms of children impacted. The severity of the current childhood obesity crisis is set out by the 2009 and 2012 Yale Rudd Reports, as well as the findings of the CDC.[45]

The major argument, today, turns on the second and third prong of *Central Hudson*: does the government regulation directly advance the government interest and is it no more extensive than necessary to serve the interest, i.e., the regulation is the least restrictive alternative available?

Howard Beales, former Director of the FTC's Bureau of Consumer Protection, has written an extensive critique of the 1978 Children's Advertising Rule in which he expresses extensive opposition to the staff investigation and findings, as well as to a similar action, today, to combat childhood obesity by banning children's food advertising for high calorie or high fat foods. His analysis is based upon the requirements the Supreme Court articulated in the *Central Hudson* case, which we have just reviewed. He states that the government would be able to meet the first prong of the three-part test because of the substantial government interest in protecting children's health.[46]

He believes the second and third part of the *Central Hudson* test would be "difficult and probably insurmountable obstacles." He argues that the government would have to submit evidence of a "link between food advertising and children's health, i.e., that the advertising itself (as opposed to time spent in front of the TV) leads to increased caloric consumption, which in turn leads to obesity."[47] This remains a central issue, today. As I document in this chapter, health organizations, such as the Yale Rudd Center and the government's Centers for Disease Control and Prevention (CDC), contend that the advertising of high calorie foods to children does have an impact on childhood obesity.

Professor Beales argues that the third prong of the *Central Hudson* test— whether the restrictions are no more extensive than necessary to serve the government's interest—"would be especially difficult to meet if there are other more effective less speech-restrictive means to protect children's health." He believes that remedies, such as more physical education in school, public nutrition education, and restrictions on the foods sold to children in schools, "are likely to prove more effective without our banning speech."[48]

While I respect Professor Beales' economic and policy arguments, I believe the 1978 Children's Advertising Rulemaking provided facts and policy arguments that are relevant, today, as we continue to address the ethical and legal issues surrounding advertising directed to children 12 and under. First, it became clear that children have cognitive and experiential limitations that must be taken into consideration if they are to understand the persuasive nature of advertising. Second, there are critical health implications involved in advertising to children. Today, the major concern is the impact of the advertising of foods and beverages on childhood obesity, a major health crisis in America. Third, because of the Congressional prohibition of the FTC use of unfairness in Children's Advertising Rulemaking, rather than attempts to ban advertising directed to children, the government focus was placed on prohibiting deceptive ads to children on a case-by-case basis, and for the industry to participate in a complementary manner through a strong self-regulatory program to guide advertisers to "do the right thing." That brings us to a discussion of the excellent self-regulatory programs that both investigate and bring self-regulatory cases and work with industry to set fair and appropriate standards for advertising food products to children.

The Children's Advertising Review Unit, whose principles were discussed earlier in this chapter, investigated and recommended that IHOP modify its website to better disclose advertising within one of its online games. The game featured "The Lorax," a character from the Dr. Seuss book and movie. Directions for the game stated that winning "would bring you closer to saving Truffula Valley and treating yourself and the Lorax to a delicious Lorax's breakfast at IHOP." NAD concluded that this was an ad for IHOP "delicious breakfasts."[49]

CARU cases show the importance and effectiveness of the industry's self-regulation program in resolving food ad claims in favor of protecting children. CARU's principles and guidelines are central to the issues surrounding the fairness of advertising food products in a manner that will be understood by children, still lacking the cognitive development and experience to deal with complex nutritional claims. This includes not using visual or copy that misleads children about nutritional benefits or encourages excessive consumption. Also, the claims are encouraged to be presented in the context of showing nutritionally balanced meals, and not to discourage the consumption of fruits and vegetables and other nutritious foods.

Equally impressive is the respect shown to CARU by children's advocacy groups, and importantly, the food industry. Food companies work closely with CARU staff to resolve the challenged issues, always in favor of "doing the right thing" on behalf of the children. Under the CARU charter challenged claims where the company does not agree to make the suggested changes will be forwarded to the Federal Trade Commission for its official resolution. However, that ultimate step is rarely needed, as food companies work with staff to resolve the challenged claims in favor of protecting the child audience.

Children's Food and Beverage Advertising Initiative (CFBAI)

The advertising industry in the U.S. also has taken on the obesity challenge through a strong voluntary program administered by the Council of Better Business Bureaus. Under the Children's Food and Beverage Advertising Initiative (CFBAI) eighteen major food and beverage companies, including American Licorice Company, Burger King Corp., Campbell Soup Company, The Coca-Cola Co., ConAgra Foods, Inc., General Mills, Inc., The Hershey Company, Kellogg Company, The Kraft Heinz Company, Mars Incorporated, McDonald's USA, Mondelez Global LLC, Nestle USA, PepsiCo Inc., Post Foods LLC, and Unilever United States, have made individual pledges to shift the mix of foods advertised to children under 12 to encourage healthier dietary choices and healthy lifestyles. They commit that "in any advertising primarily directed to children under age 12 ('Child-directed advertising'), they will feature only foods that meet CFBAI's uniform nutrition criteria."[50]

What "child-directed advertising" means under CFBAI

About CFBAI. An advertising self-regulation program, CFBAI works to shift the foods in advertising primarily directed to children under age 12 ("child-directed advertising") to healthier ones. Leading food companies and quick-serve restaurants, who are responsible for most food ads directed to children, agree to limit their "child-directed advertising" to foods that meet meaningful uniform nutrition criteria, or to not engage in such advertising. While not a CFBAI requirement, many also have a policy to not direct advertising to children under age 6.

What media are covered? CFBAI's requirements apply to child-directed ads on TV, print, radio, Internet, interactive games (including advergames), tablets, smartphones, video games, computer games, DVDs and word-of-mouth. Participants submit self-conducted compliance assessments to CFBAI, and CFBAI also independently assesses their compliance with CFBAI's requirements.

What is child-directed advertising? For measured media, such as TV which still dominates kids' media use, child-directed advertising generally means ads on programs where children under age 12 constitute at least 35% of the expected audience ("audience threshold") at the time ads are purchased. CFBAI permits participants to use an audience threshold lower than 35% and four do so … Those with policies to not direct ads to children under age 6 also use audience thresholds to meet this commitment. Some participants also use factors in addition to audience thresholds to determine what is child-directed measured media. Online media is generally considered primarily child-directed if at least 35% (or a lower percentage, as applicable) of the visitors are children under age 12. In the online world, however, visitor thresholds may not encompass all child-directed sites. Also, the percentage of child visitors may not be known because some sites do not receive enough visitors to be tracked by third-party services, and not all sites require visitors to register and give their ages. Accordingly, CFBAI uses a multi-faceted approach to determine whether an online destination is child-directed. Based on an assessment of the percentage of child visitors (if available), site content and where and how the site itself or the food on the site is otherwise advertised, CFBAI may consider a site child-directed even if child visitors represent less than 35% of all visitors or the percentage of child visitors is unknown.

Why focus on children under age 12? Historically, U.S. government regulation and self-regulation have focused on children under age 12. Although studies suggest various ages at which children begin to understand the persuasive intent of advertising, it is generally agreed that by age 12 children do have that ability. Because special protections are important for children, the Children's Advertising Review Unit (CARU), another BBB advertising self-regulation program, has promoted responsible advertising to children under age 12 through guidelines since 1974. Thus CFBAI's efforts also focus on this age group. CFBAI was created in 2006 to respond to Federal Trade Commission (FTC) and Institute of Medicine (IOM) recommendations for additional self-regulation for food advertising directed to children under age 12. (CARU continues to focus on how foods, and other products, are advertised to children, while CFBAI focuses on what foods are advertised to them.)

The FTC's recommendation emerged from a 2005 workshop and 2006 follow-up report. The IOM's recommendation comes from a report of an expert committee that IOM convened to review research on the relationship of specific causes (e.g., TV ads) and effects on American youth (e.g., food preferences or diet). The IOM concluded that there was not sufficient evidence to find a causal relationship between TV advertising and obesity. The review indicated that advertising, among many other factors, impacts the preferences, purchase requests and short-term consumption of children under age 12, but that insufficient evidence existed linking those indicators to children 12 years and older. Fewer studies were available about the impact of advertising on the food consumption and diet of older children and teens then, and that continues to be the case. Worldwide, regulatory and self-regulatory efforts to improve advertising and food advertising directed to children also mainly focus on children under age 12. For example, broadcast and advertising codes and food advertising self-regulation programs in more than 40 countries generally apply to children under age 12.[51]

A Report on Compliance and Progress During 2014—Executive Summary

In 2014 CFBAI announced new uniform nutrition criteria: "CFBAI participants would be required to meet new, more rigorous uniform nutrition criteria that superseded the company-specific nutrition criteria that had been used previously." The 18 companies that participate and agree to abide by the new standards "represent the majority of the food and beverage ads that aired." CFBAI staff "reviewed more than 4000 food and beverage ads on Children's TV networks and other media in 2014 and hundreds of pages in the detailed self-assessment reports that companies submitted." The independent monitoring of the reports "showed on some occasions foods that did not meet CFBAI's uniform criteria appeared in child-directed programming or in digital media." However, "all issues were resolved" and "we judged the compliance rate to be near 100%."[52]

The 2014 report noted that "more than 50 foods meeting CFBAI's uniform nutrition criteria were added to CFBAI's Product list (this list identifies foods meeting the criteria that the participants may or do advertise to children)." CFBAI also participated significantly in discussion on children's food advertising in public discussions and with government regulators. This included conducting "dozens of one-on-one briefings for legislators, regulators, advocacy groups and companies interested in learning more about CFBAI and food marketing to children issues."[53]

As part of the 2014 report CFBAI provided a review of ads that aired in a 33-hour sample of Nickelodeon programming in 2014 and a 30-hour sample in 2015:

- *Percentage of Food and Beverage Ads.* In 2014 these ads represented just 23% of all the ads, and in 2015 they represented 29% of all the ads.
- *Participants' Share of Food and Beverage Ads.* Ads from CFBAI participants represented 72% and 77% of all the food and beverage ads in 2014 and 2015 respectively.
- *Foods Most Frequently Advertised by the Participants.* Cereals were the most frequently advertised food (48%), followed in approximate equal percentages by yogurts, meals and snacks.
- *Nutrition Highlights.* In 2015, 74% of participant foods contained at least a half-serving of fruit, vegetables, whole grains or dairy, compared to 48% in 2010. These foods were advertised slightly more often than other foods in the sample, representing 82% of the participant ads in the sample.[54]

Children's advertising of food products—an ongoing right versus right ethical dilemma

In this chapter we have reviewed the scientific, legal and ethical issues that determine what we should and can do concerning advertising directed to children 12 and under. Starting with the Children's Advertising Rule in 1978 and moving up through current reports from the Yale Rudd Center and Centers for Disease Control and Prevention (CDC) we have documented the severe health implications of childhood obesity and the urgent mission to reduce the consumption of high sugar and high fat products by children. CDC is concerned that childhood obesity leads to greater health problems in obesity suffered by adults.

A second major finding is that children under the age of 12 do not have the cognitive capacity or experience of adults in understanding the selling intent of advertising. This is the issue focused upon in individual cases brought by the FTC and covered in our outstanding self-regulation initiatives.

A major question discussed is the role of advertising in the high consumption of these products by children. The strong case made by staff in the 1978 report is carried on by the Yale Rudd Center in periodic and comprehensive research. The numbers are impressive.

The legal and ethical questions turn on, as they did in 1978, the remedy to be pursued in reducing the negative health impact of advertising directed to children 12 years and under. In fact, there is also a dispute as to whether advertising causes the consumption. But, assuming advertising plays a role, what to do to reduce the health consequences? The staff in 1978 argued that only a total ban on advertising would present meaningful results. Reviewing subsequent Supreme Court cases, involving the First Amendment Freedom of Speech granted truthful advertising, the case would have to establish (1) the remedy dealt with a substantial consumer injury or public policy (the health consequences of obesity may well qualify). But, then (2) the government would have to establish that the ad ban (or less restrictive remedy) directly advances the government interest. Finally, (3) it would have to be established that the remedy (an ad ban) was the least restrictive remedy imposed.[55]

Finally, is the Federal Trade Commission, the major federal government entity regulating children's advertising, in a position to exercise its "unfairness" authority in banning the advertisements? A strong case could be made from the 1980 Unfairness policy statement that if advertising to children is shown to lead children to consume unhealthy foods, then the commission could use its unfairness authority to stop this "consumer injury." But, as stated in this chapter, Congress prohibited FTC from using its unfairness authority in children's advertising rulemaking proceedings.

It is unlikely that the FTC or another government agency will move to ban ads for high sugar and high fat through an industry rulemaking action. Also, that will not happen under Congress, as it is in Great Britain where government actions are underway to severely restrict the advertising of "junk foods" to children. And, of course, there are those who will argue that an ad ban will not have an impact on reducing childhood obesity.[56]

Absent a legal proceeding and remedy to "right" this ethical dilemma, we turn to the ethical response being made by the advertising industry. We have covered in detail the goals and principles of our industry's self-regulation mission on behalf of children under 12. CARU principles and cases covered demonstrate their focus on the need to insure children understand they are being advertised to and that the claims are true and substantiated. This includes cases dealing with food advertising. Also, the Children's Food and Beverage Advertising Initiative (CFBAI) has enlisted 18 major food and beverage companies (over 50% of the companies advertising to children) in a voluntary program to only advertise the most healthy products to children. In 2014 CFBAI reviewed 4,000 children's food ads and the substantial amount of documents submitted by the participating companies. CARU also is extremely active in its investigations and companies responding show much respect for the mission and staff. While CARU under its Charter has authority to appeal cases to the National Advertising Review Board, which I chair, and can forward investigations to the FTC that are not resolved voluntarily, that is rarely needed.

It is clear that the FTC also respects the industry's self-regulation programs, and in the world of advertising to children counts on the industry to ethically deal with the health and nutrition issues. The Federal Trade Commission has acknowledged the benefits of CFBAI. In 2006, then chair of the FTC, Deborah Platt Majoras, commented:

> I am highly encouraged by the Counsel of Better Business Bureau's initiative on children's food and beverage advertising, and I commend the Council for taking these important steps … This new program … shows real promise, and I hope will encourage more competition in developing and marketing healthier products that are attractive to kids and their parents. The FTC works closely with a number of self-regulatory programs, and will be watching closely to see whether this program results in meaningful improvements in food and beverage advertising to children.[57]

In conclusion, on the one side of the right versus right ethical dilemma we have the consumer injury caused by the overconsumption of high sugar and high fat products being consumed by children. This is of major concern because of the crisis in our country due to childhood obesity. In fact, the government believes this leads to greater problems in adult obesity. According to the Yale Rudd Center Report and the Centers for Disease Control and Prevention, children are exposed to the advertising of high sugar and high fat products in both children's and adult television programming. Progress has been made through self-regulation and by voluntary action of many food advertisers to modify these commercials during children's programming. The self-regulation efforts of the Children's Food and Beverage Advertising Initiative are directed to program content where children constitute 35% of the audience. Children still are exposed to high sugar and high fat advertising on adult programs on TV and online, including by playing games on commercial websites. In this chapter I have included past legal analysis by the FTC, as well as Supreme Court cases that I believe provide the basis for banning or restricting children's food advertising for high fat and high sugar products. This could include restricting such advertising to after 9 pm, as is being considered in Great Britain.

On the other side of the dilemma, it would be difficult, constitutionally, to ban ads for high fat and high sugar products where the audience is made up of a significant number of adults, who presumably understand the nature of the products' impact on obesity and the purpose of the ads—to sell them these products. Further, as noted, the FTC may be prevented from engaging in a children's advertising rulemaking proceeding by past Congressional action on this issue. The FTC, itself, has shown no indication that it would consider such action at the present time.

While the legal considerations for resolving this dilemma are not positive at this point in history, there still are the ethical considerations. I believe we have a strong personal ethical case for working to reduce the negative health problems, including childhood obesity and its impact on bad health, that can result from the advertising to children of high fat and sugar products. At this point in history, we need to encourage the industry to continue its significant voluntary efforts to advertise fairly to children under the age of 12. At the same time, we should continue to look at all regulatory and self-regulatory options as we *"treat consumers fairly based on the nature of the audience to whom the ads are directed and the nature of the product or service advertised" (IAE Principle 5).*

Questions and reflection

1. How extensive is the advertising addressed to children under the age of 12 and by what methods?
2. In comparison to adults what limitations do children have in regard to understanding advertising content?
3. What does the Federal Trade Commission require in all advertising addressed to children under the age of 12?
4. What commitment has the industry made to treating children fairly in advertising through self-regulation?
5. What are the principles advocated by the Children's Advertising Review Unit (CARU)?
6. What are the six suggestions the President of the Council for Advertising Self-Regulation makes for ethics in advertising to children?
7. From a "right versus right" ethical analysis do you feel it is appropriate to advertise high fat and high sugar products to children? What voluntary actions would you recommend the advertising industry undertake?

Notes

1 "Now on digital, there is the opportunity of more blurring of those lines," November 4, 2012, *Washington Post.*
2 "Cereal FACTS: Evaluating the nutrition quality and marketing of children's cereals," Report from the Yale Rudd Center for Food Policy and Obesity, October 2009, http://www.rwjf.org/en/library/research/2009/10/evaluating-the-nutrition-quality-and-marketing-of-children-s-cer.html.
3 FTC Staff Report on Television Advertising to Children, February, 1978.
4 Lord Annan, Report of the Committee on the Future of Broadcasting 166 (1977).
5 FTC Staff Report, p. 19.
6 FTC Staff Report, p. 20.
7 FTC Staff Report, p. 27.
8 FTC Staff Report, pp. 28–29.
9 FTC Staff Report, p. 10, "young children" defined as below the age of eight.
10 FTC Staff Report, pp. 29–30.
11 FTC Staff Report, p. 11, "older children" defined as old as 11 and as young as eight.
12 FTC Staff Report, pp. 30–31.
13 FTC Staff Report, pp. 31–32.

14 FTC Staff Report, p. 32.
15 FTC Staff Report, p. 34.
16 FTC Staff Report, p. 35.
17 FTC Staff Report, p. 43.
18 FTC Staff Report, p. 44.
19 FTC Staff Report, pp. 45–46.
20 FTC Staff Report, pp. 46–47.
21 FTC Staff Report, p. 47.
22 FTC Staff Report, p. 47.
23 FTC Staff Report, pp. 48–50.
24 FTC Staff Report, pp. 10–12.
25 FTC Improvements Act of 1980, Pub. L. No. 96–252, Sections 11(a)(1), 11(a)(3), 94 Stat. 374 (1980).
26 Report of the American Psychological Association Task Force on Advertising and Children, 2004, https://www.apa.org/pi/families/resources/advertising-children.pdf.
27 Self-Regulatory Program for Children's Advertising, Children's Advertising Review Unit (CARU), Council of Better Business Bureau, www.caru.org. Reprinted with permission of the Council of Better Business Bureaus, Inc., 3033 Wilson Blvd., 6th Floor, Arlington, VA, 22201, www.bbb.org.
28 CARU, Self-Regulatory Program.
29 Lee Peeler, President of Advertising Self-regulatory Council, Remarks at American Academy of Advertising Conference, March 15, 2012.
30 "CARU Recommends Duncan Enterprises Discontinue Certain Claims for 'Glam-It-Up! Iron-on Crystals,'" January 13, 2010, www.asrcreviews.org/caru-recommends-dunca n-enterprises-discontinue-certain-claims-for-%E2%80%98glam-it-up-iron-on-crystals% E2%80%99/.
31 "CARU Finds Telebrands Phantom Saucer Ad Accurately Depicts Toy's Capabilities, Recommends Additional Disclosure," August 20, 2014, http://www.asrcreviews.org/ caru-finds-telebrands-phantom-saucer-ad-accurately-depicts-toys-capabilities-recomm ends-additional-disclosure/.
32 Yale Rudd Center Report, "Cereal Facts," November 26, 2009.
33 "A Spoonful of Progress in a bowl full of unhealthy marketing to children," Yale Rudd Center for Food Policy & Obesity, 2012, http://www.cerealfacts.org/media/ cereal_facts_report_summary_2012_7.12.pdf.
34 "Childhood Obesity Causes & Consequences," Centers for Disease Control and Prevention (CDC), Division of Nutrition, Physical Activity, and Obesity, 2012, https:// www.cdc.gov/obesity/.
35 Farley, Thomas, "The Problem With Focusing on Childhood Obesity," New York Times, December 18, 2015, www.mobile.nytimes.com.
36 Sweeny, Mark, "MPs call for junk food ad ban during shows such as The X Factor," The Guardian, November 30, 2015, www.theguardian.com.
37 Sweeny, Mark, "MPs call for junk food ad ban."
38 CDC, "Childhood Obesity Causes & Consequences."
39 FTC Staff Report on Television Advertising to Children, February 1978, pp. 27–30.
40 FTC Staff Report, pp. 10–11.
41 FTC Staff Report and Recommendation, "That the Commission Terminate Proceedings for the Promulgation of a Trade Regulation Rule on Children's Advertising," TRR No. 215–60, March 31, 1981.
42 FTC Policy Statement on Unfairness, December 17, 1980, https://www.ftc.gov/p ublic-statements/1980/12/ftc-policy-statement-unfairness.
43 FTC Policy Statement on Unfairness.
44 Central Hudson, 477 U.S. 566.
45 CDC, "Childhood Obesity Causes & Consequences," pp. 138–140.

46 Beales, Howard, "Advertising to Kids and the FTC: A Regulatory Retrospective That Advises the Present," pp. 19–23, 2004, https://www.ftc.gov/public-statements/2004/03/advertising-kids-and-ftc-regulatory-retrospective-advises-present.

47 Beales, "Advertising to Kids."

48 Beales, "Advertising to Kids."

49 CARU, IHOP press release, September 12, 2012, www.asrcreviews.org/caru-recomm ends-ihop-modify-ihop-com-website-to-better-disclose-advertising-within-game/.

50 Children's Food and Beverage Advertising Initiative (CFBAI), www.bbb.org/council/the-national-partner-program/national-advertising-review-services/childrens-food-and-bev erage-advertising-initiative/.

51 CFBAI's Category-Specific Uniform Nutrition Criteria, June 2013, www.bbb.org. Reprinted with permission of the Council of Better Business Bureaus, Inc., 3033 Wilson Blvd., 6th Floor, Arlington, VA 22201.

52 The Food and Beverage Initiative in Action—A Report on Compliance and Progress During 2014, December 2015, www.bbb.org. Reprinted with permission of the Council of Better Business Bureaus, Inc., 3033 Wilson Blvd., 6th Floor, Arlington, VA 22201.

53 CFBAI, The Food and Beverage Initiative in Action.

54 CFBAI, The Food and Beverage Initiative in Action.

55 Central Hudson, 477 U.S. 557 (1980).

56 Beales, "Advertising to Kids," pp. 148–149.

57 Statement of Federal Trade Commission Chair Deborah Platt Majoras on the Council of Better Business Bureau's Children's Food and Advertising Initiative, November 14, 2006.

4

"NATIVE ADVERTISING"

Transparency of advertising content

> Advertisers should clearly distinguish advertising, public relations and corporate communications from news and editorial content and entertainment, both online and offline.
>
> *IAE Principle 3*

This chapter addresses an ongoing ethical dilemma where the line is being blurred between commercial content on the one hand and news/editorial or entertainment on the other. This practice—called "advertorial" in traditional print media and "infomercials" in TV—occurs today as part of a new online advertising practice called "native advertising," that is one of the hottest new forms of marketing. As I write this chapter the FTC has just published a comprehensive "Guide for Business" on Native Advertising that we shall consider in detail.

There are some who argue that this blurring is not a problem and that consumers don't care. In my view, if consumers are unaware that the "news" or "entertainment" they are watching, listening to, or reading is paid for advertising, they are being misled and treated unethically. First, consumers could attach more credibility to the content if they believe it to be written as a news story. Second, they will not have their minds set in what I would call a "business mode" to evaluate the content/claim, as they would if recognizing it as a paid for, persuasive ad.

Consumers care about how ads are addressed to them. They rely upon the information in ads for purchase decisions, but they will reject advertising information when they learn it was disguised as editorial or entertainment. After reviewing current instances of blurring in traditional media, we will focus on the new challenges presented by Native Advertising, as well as the opportunities that flow from effective disclosure as to its ad content.

Most recently, the FTC charged home security company ADT with misrepresenting that paid endorsements from safety and technology experts were independent reviews. The complaint charges that ADT paid spokespersons to demonstrate and review the ADT Pulse, which is a home security system, on NBC's *Today* show, and on 40 other television and radio programs nationwide, as well as posted blogs and material online. ADT set up the interviews for the endorsers—often providing reporters and news anchors with suggested interview questions and background videos—leaving the consumer to believe they were impartial, expert reviews of the product.

"It's hard for consumers to make good buying decisions when they think they're getting independent expert advice as part of an impartial news segment and have no way of knowing they are actually watching a sales pitch," said Jessica Rich, Director of the Federal Trade Commission's Bureau of Consumer Protection. "When a paid endorser appears in a news or talk show segment with the host of that program, the relationship with the advertiser must be clearly disclosed."[1]

The blurring of the line between advertising and news and entertainment is occurring in both print and online. An online illustration is an apparent news story that actually was a series of public relations pieces for the Central Municipal Water District in California. They were in the form of positive news stories promoting the water district, which is a private business entity, written by a journalist named Mike Adams. When a reporter from the *Los Angeles Times* tried to find Mike Adams, he couldn't because he did not exist. He had been created by the PR firm as part of the paid campaign. This unethical practice also occurs on television stations across the nation when newscasts include favorable discussions about products and services that while in the form of news and analysis actually are paid for advertisements unknown by the viewing audience.[2]

The Federal Trade Commission also has shut down fake news sites that the Commission charged are made to look like legitimate news organizations. They "use the logos of legitimate news organizations or sound alike names and web addresses ... Nearly everything about these sites is fake. The websites—owned by marketers—are a tool to entice people to click on links to the sellers' sites for (diet) supplements." The FTC states you may be on a fake site if "the reporter claims a dramatic weight loss with little or no change in diet or exercise routine."[3]

The line also is blurred between advertising and entertainment. Cardo Systems, the manufacturer of wireless bluetooth headsets, ran a video on YouTube showing individuals "using their cell phones to pop popcorn kernels in close proximity." The industry's self-regulatory unit—the National Advertising Division—concluded that while Cardo never mentioned its name or product, this was, in fact, an ad claiming that cell phones emit heat and radiation, and it is dangerous to users without a separate head-set. Cardo agreed to modify the video making clear it is an advertisement for wireless bluetooth headsets. Millions have viewed the properly disclosed ad.[4]

It is important that advertising agencies and public relations firms have clear standards in regard to disclosing content so they and their clients do not run into legal actions by the Federal Trade Commission. Industry trade associations have published guidelines and the FTC has adopted extensive disclosure guidelines, which we will cover later in this chapter.

Native Advertising challenges and opportunities

One of MillwardBrown's 2015 Digital 8 Media Predictions, authored by Jon Salm, "predicts that native advertising—online ads created to blend in with a publishing platform's format—will be huge in 2015." It is expected that $21 billion will be spent on this format in 2018, but as Jon notes without research a lot of that money will go to waste.[5]

A starting definition for "native advertising" for me came from Stuart Elliott in a 2013 *New York Times* article: "Digital pitches styled to look like editorial content of the publications in which they run."[6] In working with advertising students at Michigan State University in April, 2014, this definition was agreed upon: "Native advertisements are in formats that are natural parts of the media environment in which they are run. Native advertising is the activity of producing, buying and selling native ads."[7]

As to the importance of Native Advertising, I turn again to Stuart Elliott for his viewpoint in his last *New York Times* article:

> Ads as "content": The interweaving of ad matter into editorial content has accelerated, spawning an industry within an industry that describes itself with terms like content marketing, branded content, sponsored content and native advertising. Whatever the phrasing, the practice represents a bold attempt to further blur the line between editorial material and paid peddling. Are consumers who are now willing to opt in for ads they deem entertaining or informative—witness the millions of "likes" for brand fan pages on Facebook and other social media platforms—going to take that in stride, or will the worth of editorial content be diminished, threatening its value?[8]

The Michigan State University students in their review of native advertising concluded that its purpose for the advertiser is "to catch the attention of consumers who may be uninterested in or resistant to conventional ads." For the consumer, it is "to receive advertisements that are more interesting."[9]

The problem associated with Native Advertising is the failure to disclose clearly and conspicuously that the content is paid advertising. In the MSU student review the problems found included: (1) the word "sponsored" used without disclosing the name of the sponsor; (2) very small, unnoticeable, or quickly disappearing disclosures; and (3) the use of ambiguous terms, such as "with" the named company.[10]

The disclosure issue has gotten wide attention by industry and government. The FTC held a hearing in late 2013. "The only consensus among the panelists and speakers was that transparency and disclosure are important, but finding a single solution (whether it be through labels, or color borders or other treatment) seemed elusive. Among the big questions raised: Do publishers need to disclose that the content was also created by or for the advertiser? What is the best language to use? How much graphic separation should there be between native ads and editorial?"[11]

Two years later the FTC responded with a comprehensive package of legal principles and illustrations showing how it expected the industry to conduct Native Advertising. "Marketers and publishers are using innovative methods to create, format, and deliver digital advertising. One form is 'native advertising,' content that bears a similarity to the news, feature articles, product reviews, entertainment and other material that surrounds it online. But as native advertising evolves, are consumers able to differentiate advertising from other content?"[12]

In the introduction to the guide the FTC emphasizes that it is the agency's job to ensure that long-standing consumer protection principles apply in the digital marketplace, including in Native Advertising. Absent the lack of industry agreement the FTC found in its 2013 hearings, this guide is seen as day to day help from the FTC staff as industry produces Native Advertising campaigns. Clearly, the FTC wants and expects these guidelines to be used and followed. We will review them in detail. The first part of the Guide summarizes the consumer protection principles upon which the FTC advice is based. The second part gives explicit examples of when businesses should disclose the content as advertising. The third part provides very specific staff guidance on how to make clear and conspicuous disclosures when using native advertising. Here follows the FTC guide.

Native Advertising: A Guide for Business, FTC, December, 2015[13]

I Established Principles that Support the FTC's Approach to Native Advertising

Under the FTC Act, an act or practice is deceptive if there is a material misrepresentation or omission of information that is likely to mislead the consumer acting reasonably in the circumstances. A misrepresentation is material if it is likely to affect consumers' choices or conduct regarding an advertised product or the advertising for the product.

In evaluating whether an ad is deceptive, the FTC considers the net impression the ad conveys to consumers. Because ads can communicate information through a variety of means—text, images, sounds, etc.—the FTC will look to the overall context of the interaction, not just to elements of the ad in isolation. Put another way, both what the ad says and the format it uses to convey that information will be relevant. Any clarifying information necessary to prevent deception must be disclosed clearly and prominently to overcome any misleading impression.

A basic truth-in-advertising principle is that it's deceptive to mislead consumers about the commercial nature of content. Advertisements or promotional messages are deceptive if they convey to consumers expressly or by implication that they're independent, impartial, or from a source other than the sponsoring advertiser—in other words, that they're something other than ads. Why would it be material to consumers to know the source of the information? Because knowing that something is an ad likely will affect whether consumers choose to interact with it and the weight or credibility consumers give the information it conveys.

Over the years, the FTC has brought many cases challenging the format of ads as deceptive. For example, the Commission has taken action against ads that deceptively mimicked the format of news programming or otherwise misrepresented their source. Other cases focused on misleading "door openers"—promotions with a format that deceived consumers about the nature of the transaction—for example, telemarketers who misleadingly suggested they were calling on behalf of a consumer's credit card company or bank. (The Commission has held that when the first contact between a seller and a buyer occurs through a deceptive practice, the law may be violated even if the consumer later finds out the truth.) Or, as the FTC Endorsement Guides establish, advertisers' use of third-party endorsements may be deceptive if there is an undisclosed material connection between the advertiser and the endorser—one that might materially affect the weight or credibility of the endorsement. The FTC considers misleadingly formatted ads to be deceptive regardless of whether the underlying product claims that are conveyed to consumers are truthful.

The particular forms native advertising takes in the digital marketplace may be new, but the FTC's Enforcement Policy Statement makes clear that the FTC applies the same truth-in-advertising principles it has used for decades to evaluate whether the format of an ad is deceptive. In the context of native advertising, if the source of the content is clear, consumers can make informed decisions about whether to interact with the ad and the weight to give the information conveyed in the ad. However, an ad is deceptive if it promotes the benefits and attributes of goods and services, but is not readily identifiable to consumers as an ad. Thus as the Policy Statement explains, the FTC will find an ad's format deceptive if the ad materially misleads consumers about its commercial nature, including through an express or implied misrepresentation that it comes from a party other than the sponsoring advertiser.

What do businesses need to know to ensure that the format of native advertising is not deceptive? The enforcement Policy Statement explains the law in detail, but it boils down to this:

1. From the FTC's perspective, the watchword is transparency. An advertisement or promotional message shouldn't suggest or imply to consumers that it's anything other than an ad.
2. Some native ads may be so clearly commercial in nature that they are unlikely to mislead consumers even without a specific disclosure. In other instances, a disclosure may be necessary to ensure that consumers understand that the content is advertising.
3. If a disclosure is necessary to prevent deception, the disclosure must be clear and prominent.

II Examples of When Businesses Should Disclose That Content Is Native Advertising

In digital media, native ads often resemble the design, style, and functionality of the media in which they are disseminated. Ads may appear on a page next to non-advertising content. Examples include news or content aggregator sites, social media platforms, or messaging apps. (The Enforcement Policy Statement refers to a page like that as a "publisher site.") In other instances, ads are embedded in entertainment programming, such as professionally produced and user-generated videos on social media. Still other examples include native advertising in email, infographics, images, animations, and video games.

When a native ad appears on the main page of a publisher's site or is republished in other media, it commonly consists of a headline, often combined with a thumbnail image and a short description, which, if clicked or tapped, leads to additional advertising content. Under FTC law, advertisers cannot use "deceptive door openers" to induce consumers to view advertising content. Thus, advertisers are responsible for ensuring that native ads are identifiable as advertising before consumers arrive at the main advertising page. In addition, no matter how consumers arrive at advertising content, it must not mislead them about its commercial nature.

In assessing whether a native ad presented on the main page of a publisher site is recognizable as advertising to consumers, advertisers should consider the ad as a whole, and not just focus on individual phrases, statements, or visual elements. Factors to weigh include an ad's overall appearance; the similarity of its written, spoken, or visual style or subject matter to non-advertising content on the publisher site on which it appears; and the degree to which it is distinguishable from other content on the publisher site. The same assessment applies to any click- or tap-into page—the page on which the complete ad appears.

Example

A kitchen cabinet company paid an online lifestyle magazine, *Styling Home*, to create and publish an article entitled, "10 Must-Haves for a Great Kitchen." The article, which displays a series of images depicting well-designed kitchens, appears in the same layout as other articles on the *Styling Home* site. Most of the images in the article depict and promote the sponsoring advertiser's products. Thus, the article is an advertisement. The ad's format, however, is likely to mislead consumers to believe it is an ordinary *Styling Home* article and reflects the independent views of the *Styling Home* writer, and not those of the sponsoring advertiser. Therefore, a clear and prominent disclosure of the article's commercial nature is necessary.

The more a native ad is similar in format and topic to content on the publisher's site, the more likely that a disclosure will be necessary to prevent deception. Furthermore, because consumers can navigate to the advertising without first going to the publisher site, a disclosure just on the publisher's site may not be sufficient. In that instance, disclosures are needed both on the publisher's site and the click- or tap-into page on which the complete ad appears, unless the click-onto page is obviously an ad.

Example

Fitness Life publishes an article entitled "The 20 Most Beautiful Places to Vacation." No sponsoring advertiser paid *Fitness Life* to publish the article. However, a resort hotel pays *Fitness Life* to display a photo of its beach resort as the twenty-first image displayed in the article. The photo has the same look and feel as the images featured in the article. There is no need to disclose to consumers on the *Fitness Life* main page that the article is accompanied by advertising. However, because the photo appears to be part of the article rather than an advertisement, a clear and prominent disclosure of the photo's paid nature on the click-into page is likely necessary.

The digital marketplace offers alternative ways for advertisers to disseminate content to consumers, including things like news feeds and content recommendation widgets. The same principles of transparency and disclosures apply.

Example

Newsby is an online magazine featuring stories about health, technology, science, and business. A headline published in *Newsby*'s feed reads, "Making Cleaning Fun: How Technology Has Changed Housekeeping," with the subheading, "Vacuum Cleaners are as popular today as when first introduced in the 1800s." The text and an accompanying image are formatted like those of the other articles in *Newsby*'s feed and, if tapped, lead to an infographic with facts about vacuum cleaners, including a list of the "coolest innovations." One of the listed innovations is "Dirt Pulverizer" technology, which purportedly not only picks up dirt, but also cleans the air. Appliance company Machine-Clean Vacuums, which is the exclusive seller of "Dirt Pulverizer" vacuums, paid *Newsby* to create and publish the article on its site. When viewed in the feed of *Newsby*'s site, consumers are likely to interpret the Machine-Clean Vacuums ad as an independent story impartially reporting on information relating to vacuum cleaners, and not an ad developed and published on behalf of a sponsoring advertiser. Thus, effective disclosures informing consumers of the ad's commercial nature—both in the site's feed and on the click-into infographic—are necessary to prevent deception.

Native ads also can be integrated into content, including entertainment programming and video games. In some instances, consumers are likely to understand that a sponsoring advertiser paid for the product integration. In other instances, a disclosure may be necessary to avoid deceiving consumers.

Example A

A video game immerses a player in a virtual world. While exploring part of the virtual world, a player sees billboards advertising actual products. The marketers of the advertised products paid the game designers to include the ads in the game. That billboards are advertisements is apparent to consumers. To the extent that the billboards are for actual products, consumers are likely to attribute the ads to the sponsoring advertisers and no disclosure is necessary. However, the sponsoring advertisers would be liable for any deceptive product claims on the billboards.

Example B

The same virtual world game in the above example integrates branded products in other ways; for example, game characters wear a specific sunglasses brand, drink a particular brand of beverage, and patronize a particular donut shop. The sponsoring advertisers paid the game developer to include their branded products in the game. However, the game conveys no objective claims about the various branded products. Even though consumers may not realize that the sponsored advertisers paid for their branded products to appear, disclosure of this paid product placement is not necessary to prevent consumer deception because whether the branded products appear in the game because of payment by the sponsoring advertiser or because of the video game developer's creative judgment is not likely to be material to consumers.

Example C

A game app tests players' skills to survive in the wilderness and offers a choice of supplies and equipment in each game phase. When players tap to make a choice, a box appears containing a selection of items—for example, a flashlight, a rope, and a hatchet. Each item is accompanied by a short message—for example, the phrase "Light your path" with the flashlight. Among the items players can select is a bar of soap identified by brand name with the text "Clean Up." If tapped, the soap icon takes the player out of the game and into the soap manufacturer's branded game app. Based on consumers' customary use of the game and the similarity of the soap to other items players can select in the game, consumers might not recognize the icon as an ad before tapping and leaving the game. Because the in-app ad's format misleads consumers in this respect, a clear and prominent disclosure informing them of the icon's commercial nature is necessary before consumers tap on it.

Example D

On its website, a home improvement TV show features "do it yourself" videos hosted by an expert builder who provides advice on home projects. A stain manufacturer, ZYX Paints, pays the show to produce and publish on the home improvement show's site a video on building a wood deck. In the video, the show's expert builder uses a ZYX Paints stain and recommends it to protect and maintain the deck. The ad's look and feel closely resembles other videos posted on the home improvement show's site, which customarily are unpaid. In this situation, consumers are likely to perceive the video as independent content reflecting the impartial opinion of the expert builder host or the show's writers, and would not likely attribute it to the sponsoring advertiser. An effective disclosure informing consumers of the video's commercial nature before they play it is necessary to prevent consumer deception.

In digital media, consumers can encounter native ads in a wide variety of settings, including in social media and email. In some cases, advertisers also facilitate the republication or "sharing" of native ads by others, for example, by including social media plugins. In evaluating whether consumers are likely to understand a native ad is advertising, it is important that advertisers consider the particular circumstances in which native ads are presented to consumers. These circumstances include consumers' ordinary expectations based on their prior experience with the media in which the ads appear, as well as how they consume content in that media.

Example

Gormella uploads humorous videos to her dedicated channel on a popular video-sharing platform and has cultivated a significant social media following. Among her videos is one she created for a snack food company to promote its new cracker, Salt-Zs. The video, "Crackering Up in My Local Supermarket," includes a thumbnail image of Gormella laughing in a grocery store aisle. In the video, Gormella starts out in the supermarket aisle and is magically transported to various locales where she talks to people about Salt-Zs. Once consumers view the video, they are likely to identify it as an advertisement and understand that the sponsoring advertiser paid Gormella to promote and endorse its branded product. Nevertheless, before watching the video, consumers likely would not expect it to be advertising, given their experience with other videos she had posted. Thus, the video's commercial nature should be clearly and prominently disclosed before consumers view it.

Yet another setting in which consumers may come upon native ads is in non-paid search engine results. Advertisers should take steps to ensure that any non-paid search listings for a native ad do not suggest or imply to consumers that it is something other than an ad.

Example

A text link and thumbnail image for the same ZYX Paints video described in Example D appears in the non-paid search results returned in response to consumers' queries using a search engine. The textual link to the video reads, "Building a Deck: 5 Steps for Success" and includes the name of the home improvement show, but does not mention ZYX Paints. In this example, based on consumers' customary experience using search engines, they ordinarily would associate a video presented in this manner with the home improvement program and not with a sponsoring advertiser. The advertiser should ensure that any link or other visual element, for example, webpage snippets, images, or graphics, intended to appear in non-paid search results, effectively disclose its commercial nature.

III How to Make Clear and Prominent Disclosures in Native Advertising

Disclosures that are necessary to avoid misleading consumers must be presented clearly and prominently. Whether a disclosure of a native ad's commercial nature meets this standard will be measured by its performance—that is, do consumers recognize the native ad as an ad? Only disclosures that consumers notice, process, and understand can be effective. Inadequate disclosures can't change the net impression created and won't stop consumers from being deceived that advertising or promotional messages are something other than ads.

The FTC staff business guidance document *.com Disclosures: How to Make Effective Disclosures in Digital Advertising* explains what advertisers should do to ensure disclosures in digital advertising are clear and prominent. In general, disclosures should be:

in clear and unambiguous language;
as close as possible to the native ads to which they relate;
in a font and color that's easy to read;
in a shade that stands out against the background;
for video ads, on the screen long enough to be noticed, read, and understood; and
for audio disclosures, read at a cadence that's easy for consumers to follow and in words consumers will understand.

Disclosures must be clear and prominent on all devices and platforms that consumers may use to view native ads. In assessing effectiveness, disclosures should be considered from the perspective of a reasonable consumer. When ads are targeted to a specific audience, the relevant perspective is that of a reasonable or ordinary member of the targeted group. Advertisers should improve their disclosures if there are indications that a significant minority of reasonable consumers do not notice, process, or comprehend them.

Advertisers have flexibility as to how to identify native ads as ads, so long as consumers notice and process the disclosures and comprehend what they mean. Some native ads use text labels or company logos combined with other visual cues, such as background shading, outlines, or borders. Multimedia ads, such as online videos, may use graphics, video or audio disclosures, or some combination thereof. The following discussion describes additional information that advertisers should consider to make clear and prominent disclosures in native advertising on the main page of a publisher site and on the click- or tap-into page on which a complete ad appears.

A Proximity and placement

Place disclosures on the main page of a publisher site where consumers will notice them and easily identify the content to which the disclosure applies.

Advertisers should assume that consumers don't look at everything on a publisher site. In deciding which content items to read or watch, consumers' attention is likely to be drawn to certain focal points on a screen. The disclosure that an ad is commercial content should appear near the ad's focal point. When browsing the main page of news or content aggregator sites, consumers typically look at story headlines on the site. Placing disclosures near a native ad's headline increases the likelihood consumers will see them.

Place disclosures in front of or above the headline of the native ad.

The location and spacing of a disclosure in relation to the native ad it clarifies also matters. If a publisher site is read left to right, consumers are less likely to notice disclosures positioned to the right of the native ads to which they relate. In addition, if native ads are inserted into a vertical stream of content items, placing a disclosure below a native ad increases the risk that consumers will click on the ad without seeing the disclosure. Consumers are most likely to notice and understand disclosures that are placed immediately in front of or above a native ad's headline.

If a native ad's focal point is an image or graphic, a disclosure might need to appear directly on the focal point itself.

Sometimes a focal point on a publisher site is something other than a headline or other written text—for example, images or graphics. Disclosures placed near focal points that are images, graphics, or other visually strong elements might not be sufficiently noticeable to consumers and disclosures might need to be placed on the focal points themselves. For example, in deciding which videos to watch on a video-sharing channel, consumers might pay little attention to written descriptions and instead look at thumbnail images of the videos. Under those circumstances, a disclosure placed directly on the thumbnail image itself is most likely to be effective.

A single disclosure that relates to more than one native ad should be accompanied by visual cues that make it clear the disclosure applies to each ad in the grouping.

Some disclosures may relate to more than one content item, such as with content recommendation widgets included on a publisher site. If a grouping of content items contains a mix of advertising and non-advertising content, a single disclosure should not be used because consumers are not likely to know to which content items the disclosure relates. In those circumstances, native ads should be individually labeled to make clear which content items are ads. In addition, if a single disclosure is used to differentiate more than one native ad as advertising, other visual cues are necessary to make it obvious to consumers that the disclosure relates to each of the native ads in the grouping, such as through background shading that has a clear outline or a distinct border that sets off the native ads from other content items on a site.

Disclosures should remain when native ads are republished by others.

Advertisers should maintain disclosures when native ads are republished by others in non-paid search results, social media, email, or other media. In non-paid search results, consumers are more likely to notice a disclosure if it's placed at the beginning of the title tag for a native ad's search listing. Similarly, URL links for posting or sharing in social media or email should include a disclosure at the beginning of the native ad's URL. In some circumstances, native ads for republishing in other media may include other distracting elements such as web-page snippets, images, or graphics. In placing disclosures, advertisers also should consider how these additional visual elements might influence where consumers look before they click on native ads.

Once consumers arrive on the click- or tap-into page where the complete native ad appears, disclosures should be placed as close as possible to where they will look first.

Because consumers can navigate to native ads in different ways, a clear and prominent disclosure also should be presented on the click- or tap-into page on which a complete native ad appears. A disclosure is more likely to be seen if it's placed where consumers ordinarily start looking on a page. For articles, consumers typically look first at the headline and then browse the content. Disclosures therefore should be placed as close as possible to the headline. In placing disclosures, advertisers also should avoid putting them far above or to the right of the headline, where consumers are unlikely to notice them.

In multimedia ads, a disclosure should be delivered to consumers before they receive the advertising message to which it relates.

With multimedia ads, disclosures generally should be made in the ad itself and shortly before consumers receive an advertising message. Delivering disclosures during or after an advertising message increases the risk consumers will miss the necessary disclosure. But making disclosures too early can be problematic, too. Some native ads may be only a small part of larger programming—for example, a video vignette or video game. In that case, a disclosure at the beginning of programming may not effectively communicate to consumers that the later content is an advertising message. In those circumstances, disclosures should be delivered as close as possible to the advertising messages they cover.

B Prominence

Advertising disclosures should stand out so consumers can easily read or hear them.

Advertising disclosures should stand out. Disclosures should be large and visible enough for consumers to readily notice them. Therefore, advertisers should take into account the size and configuration of the device screens consumers will typically use to view their content. Text labels should be in a font size and color that consumers can easily read on the screen. To be readable, text color should contrast strongly with the background. Using lighter font colors with a dark background makes it less likely consumers will read the text of a disclosure.

Any background shading used to differentiate native ads from non-advertising content should be sufficiently saturated for consumers to notice it. Advertisers also should consider using visual cues in addition to background shading, such as a prominent border that sets off native ads from surrounding content, in case consumers cannot see color differences.

Multimedia ads that deliver an audio message may require an audio disclosure. Audio disclosures should be in a sufficient volume and cadence for ordinary consumers to hear and comprehend them. In addition, visual disclosures in multi-media ads should be displayed on the screen long enough for ordinary consumers to notice, read, and comprehend them.

C Clarity of meaning

Disclosures must be understandable.

Disclosures are not effective unless consumers understand them to mean that native ads are commercial advertising. Disclosures should be in plain language that is as straightforward as possible. An advertiser also should make disclosures in the same language as the predominant language in which the ad is presented. Advertisers should avoid using:

- technical or industry jargon;
- different terminology to mean the same thing in different places on a publisher site;
- the same terminology to mean different things on a publisher site;
- terms that customarily have different meanings to consumers in other situations;
- unfamiliar icons or abbreviations; or
- company logos or brand names unaccompanied by a clear text disclosure.

Terms likely to be understood include "Ad," "Advertisement," "Paid Advertisement," "Sponsored Advertising Content," or some variation thereof. Advertisers should not use terms such as "Promoted" or "Promoted Stories," which in this context are at best ambiguous and potentially could mislead consumers that advertising content is endorsed by a publisher site.

Furthermore, depending on the context, consumers reasonably may interpret other terms, such as "Presented by [X]" "Brought to You by [X]," "Promoted by [X]," or "Sponsored by [X]" to mean that a sponsoring advertiser funded or "underwrote" but did not create or influence the content.

In addition, terms might not be sufficiently clear to consumers if used on a publisher site that also uses different terms to label ads. Using consistent terminology to identify ads on the same publisher site decreases the likelihood that consumers will misunderstand a native ad's disclosure. Moreover, company logos and names on their own are not likely to be adequate to signal that content is commercial advertising.

A final note: The FTC's Enforcement Policy Statement on Deceptively Formatted Advertisements doesn't apply just to advertisers. In appropriate circumstances, the FTC has taken action against other parties who helped create deceptive advertising content—for example, ad agencies and operators of affiliate advertising networks. Everyone who participates directly or indirectly in creating or presenting native ads should make sure that ads don't mislead consumers about their commercial nature. Marketers who use native advertising have a particular interest in ensuring that anyone participating in the promotion of their products is familiar with the basic-truth-in-advertising principle that an ad should be identifiable as an ad to consumers.[14]

This chapter has included a complete version of the FTC guiding principles for native advertising, because the FTC has purposefully provided complete "how to" guidelines concerning how to use native advertising legally and ethically. This includes illustrations of content that it considers to be advertising, as well as how to make "clear and prominent" disclosures that the content is advertising. It is clear to me that the FTC expects the ad industry to read, follow and utilize this guidance. In fact, the Commission has just issued its first consent order since publishing its guidelines with Lord & Taylor for lack of transparency in its native advertising in a fashion magazine and on social media.

Lord & Taylor posted a photo of a dress from its Design Lab collection along with a company-edited caption on its Instagram account and ran an article about the dress collection online. However the Instagram post and article didn't disclose they were paid advertisements. According to the FTC's complaint Lord & Taylor gifted its dress to 50 fashion influencers who were paid $1,000 to $4,000 to post on Instagram a photo of themselves wearing the dress. While they did mention Lord & Taylor's Instagram account and the hashtag #DesignLab in the photo caption, they were not required to state that they had been compensated. The complaint states that the campaign reached 11.4 million users and resulted in 328,000 brand engagements. "Lord & Taylor needs to be straight with consumers in its online marketing campaigns," said Jessica Rich, director of the FTC's Bureau of Consumer Protection, in a statement. "Consumers have the right to know when they're looking at paid advertising."[15]

The Internet Advertising Bureau (IAB) has issued the following in its Native Advertising Handbook:

Regardless of native advertising unit type, the IAB advocates that, for paid native ad units, clarity and prominence of the disclosure is paramount. The disclosure must:

- Use language that conveys that the advertising has been paid for, thus making it an advertising unit even if that unit does not contain traditional promotional advertising messages.
- Be large and visible enough for a consumer to notice it in the context of a given page and/or relative to the device that the ad is being viewed on.

Simply put: "Regardless of context, a reasonable consumer should be able to distinguish between what is paid advertising vs. what is publisher editorial content."[16]

Native Advertising guidance from National Advertising Division

In 2014, the National Advertising Division reached a voluntary settlement with Taboola, LLC to modify its native advertising "recommendation widget" to better assure that consumers understand that clicking on links provided by Taboola will take them to "sponsored content." The investigation and resolution provides valuable guidance to help insure that native advertising is conducted ethically and legally.

Taboola's native advertising disclosures were challenged by Congoo, LLC, a competitor. NAD noted, the companies "compete for the same space on publisher websites but describe their business models differently." Congoo says it links consumers to advertisements and calls the links in its space "ad-plus-text" units. Taboola described its business model as linking consumers to "content you may like" and calls its link a "recommendation widget."

Quoting from the NAD report, "Both parties customize their space to the site on which it appears so that links on the host site look 'native' to the space, but link consumers either to further content on the host site or on a third-party site. When a consumer clicks on a sponsored link on Taboola or Congoo's service, both the host site and the 'widget' provider earn revenue."

As to the adequacy of Taboola's disclosure regarding ad content, NAD referred to the Federal Trade Commission's guidance to online advertisers encouraging companies to "consider several factors to ensure that any labels and visual cues used are sufficiently noticeable and understandable to consumers."

NAD found that "Taboola's disclosures are in a less visible, lighter typeface and smaller font than other text in the widget. Further, the disclosure sits in the upper right-hand corner of the widget, an area that the FTC has said consumers are less likely to notice and read." NAD rejected the challenger's argument that Taboola needed to use the word "advertisement" to inform consumers that its links are sponsored.

NAD was reluctant to require the use of "advertisement" or mandate specific words to use for disclosure in the absence of consumer-perception evidence demonstrating that specific disclosure words are necessary. NAD recommended, "that the advertiser modify its disclosures to increase the visibility of the 'Sponsored Content' or 'Promoted Content' disclosures in terms of font size, font color and boldness, as well as its placement on the page, to make clear that the linked content is sponsored." Taboola, "with the goal of supporting advertising self-regulation," agreed to modify its disclosures.[17]

According to the IAB Native Advertising Playbook, disclosure tags that are being used include: "Sponsored by"; "Sponsored"; "Presented by"; "Promoted by"; "Ad"; and "Advertisement". The IAB Playbook recommends that disclosure tags be large and visible enough for consumers to notice and located near the search result where consumers will see them.[18]

With the publication of the FTC guides on Native Advertising, the industry has very specific "rules" and illustrations as to how to disclose ad content. For instance, referring to the IAB statement, above, that companies are using such phrases as "Presented by" and "Promoted by," the quoted FTC guides urge:

> Advertisers should not use terms such as 'Promoted' or 'Promoted Stories,' which in this context are at best ambiguous and potentially could mislead consumers that advertising content is endorsed by a publisher site. Furthermore, depending on the context, consumers reasonably may interpret other terms, such as 'Presented by (X),' 'Brought To You by (X),' 'Promoted by (X),' or 'Sponsored by (X)' to mean that a sponsoring advertiser funded or 'underwrote' but did not create or influence the content." On the affirmative side, FTC counsels: "Terms likely to be understood include 'Ad,' 'Advertisement,' 'Paid Advertisement,' 'Sponsored Advertising Content,' or some variation thereof.[19]

It is also significant and helpful that the FTC includes descriptions and examples of the many different ways Native Advertising content is being described to consumers as part of original content on publishers' sites. Clearly, the FTC has taken the time to educate the industry as to the importance it sees in assuring that the public is not misled by thinking it is viewing editorial content, and thus giving it more credibility. We can be certain that the FTC expects its guides to be studied and applied.

This was the point made by FTC Commissioner Julie Brill at an AdExchanger conference in New York in January 2016. In referring to the FTC guidelines on Native Advertising, she stated, "No matter the media or format, advertising messages should be easily identifiable to consumers as advertising." She concluded that is not always the case today where some publishers and advertisers take effort to hide labels indicating that sponsored content is paid for by a brand, making people click or hover over these messages to find out. Native ads "cannot function as a workaround that tricks consumers," she said. "It's in everybody's interest to ensure that consumers understand" that advertisers are the ones paying for sponsored content. Such transparency is "key to preserving consumer trust."[20]

The FTC guides were received by the industry with mixed responses. The Interactive Advertising Bureau (IAB) VP of Public Policy Brad Weltman stated, "While guidance serves great benefit to industry, it must also be technically feasible, creatively relevant, and not stifle innovation. To that end, we have reservations about some elements of the Commission's guidance." Specifically, IAB singled out as being "overly prescriptive" the FTC's concern with use of terms such as "partner content" and "promoted post."[21]

Digital publishers took a positive stance. "We've reviewed the guidelines and will be following them appropriately," a Mashable spokesman said. "We have no initial concerns with the disclosure and labeling requirements, and support any efforts that add clarity for our community." Mashable participated in the December 2013 FTC workshop on native advertising that contributed in part to the guidelines.[22]

"*HuffPost* believes it is good that the FTC has released guidelines because there is a lot of inconsistency in the market about native ads," Mary Gail Pezzimenti, VP of content creation at *Huffington Post*, said in an email provided by a spokeswoman. "The key for us now, and always has been, that you must be utterly transparent and authentic with native advertising. We make sure that the reader/audience knows that the content is sponsored by the advertiser through various attributions that are consistent from native ad to native ad."[23]

Very significantly, the Federal Trade Commission makes it clear that its native advertising guides apply not just to the advertiser, but to those business units that help create the ad:

> In appropriate circumstances the FTC has taken action against other parties who helped create deceptive content—for example, ad agencies and operators of affiliate advertising networks. Everyone who participates directly or indirectly in creating or presenting native ads should make sure that ads don't mislead consumers about their commercial nature. Marketers who use native advertising have a particular interest in ensuring that anyone participating in the promotion of their products is familiar with the basic-truth-in-advertising principle that an ad should be identifiable as an ad to consumers.[24]

Underlying the need for advertisers and online publishers to ethically disclose clearly and prominently that their paid content is advertising, is the new and growing power consumers have to block ad content. With Apple's move late in 2015 to allow ad blocking applications in the U.S. 16% of all internet users are blocking advertisements. About $22 billion in global ad revenue was blocked in 2015.[25]

The new software emphasizes the advantage gained by treating consumers fairly in our advertising and marketing. Consumers do not want to be misled concerning the content they are seeking and relying upon in digital communications. When they learn that what they believed to be original or editorial content is actually paid advertising they can now go beyond rejecting that particular ad to simply downloading an app that will block all ads on that site. Of course, this is also a problem for the website because it relies on advertising to fund its editorial.

On the other hand, if the advertiser and the site have treated them fairly, they can keep receiving advertising. In fact, the consumer can reward those advertisers and publishers that treat them fairly by "whitelisting" the site to continue to receive ads from them. Joe Zawadzki, chairman of a company that helps brands get their ads on mobile devices, was quoted as saying, "The call to arms to advertiser and publishers is to make the (advertising) experience a better one. Make it a faster one. Make it one with more relevant advertising that actually works."[26]

Referring to the Millwardbrown prediction—at the beginning of this chapter—regarding native advertising, the author Jon Salm states: "The key for advertisers will be to partner with the best publishers, and the key for publishers will be to follow the native golden rules—confidently identify native ads as sponsored content, match the site's editorial tone, and create content that resonates with the audience."[27]

Questions and reflection

1. The author provides definitions for "Native Advertising," including from the Federal Trade Commission. What is your definition?
2. What is the commercial value of providing attractive ads in the context of the surrounding "original" content in online digital publications?
3. Why is it important that the consumer understands "Native Advertising" is paid content and not editorial?
4. The author points out that the Federal Trade Commission has voiced concerns about the lack of adequate advertising disclosures and has issued precise guidelines it expects to be followed for avoiding deception in the use of "Native Advertising." What are its concerns regarding the industry's current use of phrases such as "presented by," "promoted by," "brought to you by," and "sponsored by"?
5. What terms in addition to "Advertisement" does the FTC say are likely to communicate to the consumer that the content is advertising?
6. What are the points the FTC lists that advertisers should follow to make sure disclosures are clear and prominent in digital communication?
7. What were the major problems the FTC found in the Lord & Taylor promotion of its dress by fashion influencers on Instagram?
8. What advantage does ad blocking software give to the advertiser and publisher that treat consumers ethically in their use of "Native Advertising"?

Notes

1 "Home Security Company ADT Settles FTC Charges that Endorsements Deceived Consumer," FTC Press Release, March 6, 2014, https://www.ftc.gov/news-events/p ress-releases/2014/03/home-security-company-adt-settles-ftc-charges-endorsements.

2 Allen, Sam, "There seemed to be no doubt Mike Adams was a productive journalist, even if his beat was a bit obscure, the Central Municipal Water District," *The Los Angeles Times*, November 8, 2011.

3 "Fake News Sites Promote Acai Supplements," July 2012, https://www.consumer.ftc. gov/articles/0299-fake-news-sites-promote-acai-supplements.

4 "NAD Reviews Viral-Video Advertising," November 17, 2008, http://www.asrcre views.org/nad-reviews-viral-video-advertising/.

5 Salm, Jon, "Getting Native Advertising Right," January 2015, www.millwardbrown. com/global-navigation/blogs/posts/mb-blog/2015/01/26/getting-native-advertising-right.

6 Elliott, Stuart, "Digital pitches styled to look like editorial content of the publications in which they run," *New York Times*, December 13, 2013.

7 Department of Communications + PR, Michigan State University, Native Advertising Class, April 2014.

8 Elliott, Stuart, "The Top 5 Changes on Madison Avenue Over the Last 25 Years," December 18, 2014, *New York Times*.

9 MSU Native Advertising Class.

10 MSU Native Advertising Class.

11 Bachman, Katy, "Native Advertising Workshop Leaves FTC Perplexed," December 4, 2013, http://www.adweek.com/news/advertising-branding/native-ad-workshop-lea ves-ftc-perplexed-154303.

12 FTC, Native Advertising: A Guide for Business, December 2015, https://www.ftc. gov/tips-advice/business-center/guidance/native-advertising-guide-businesses.

13 FTC, Native Advertising: A Guide for Business.

14 FTC, Native Advertising: A Guide for Business.

15 Iadena, Nathalie, "Lord & Taylor Reaches Settlement with FTC Over Native Ad Disclosures," *The Wall Street Journal*, March 15, 2016, www.wsj.com.

16 Internet Advertising Bureau (IAB) Native Advertising Playbook. www.iab.com/wp -content/uploads/2015/06/IAB-Native-Advertising-Playbook2.pdf.

17 "NAD Reviews Taboola's Native Ad Widget, Recommends Clear Disclosures," May 20, 2014, http://www.asrcreviews.org/nad-reviews-taboolas-native-ad-widge t-recommends-clearer-disclosures/.

18 IAB Native Advertising Playbook.

19 FTC, Native Advertising: A Guide for Business.

20 Shields, Mark, "FTC Commissioner Urges Ad Industry to Let Consumers Opt Out of Tracking—Julie Brill also warns publishers and advertisers to make sure native ads are clearly labeled," January 21, 2016, *The Wall Street Journal*, www.wsj.com.

21 Barr, Jeremy, "The IAB is 'Concerned' About the FTC's New Native Advertising Rules, But Publishers Play It Cool," *Advertising Age*, December 29, 2015, www.adage. com.

22 Barr, "The IAB is 'Concerned'."

23 Barr, "The IAB is 'Concerned'."

24 FTC, Native Advertising: A Guide for Business.

25 Gillies, Trent, "Advertisers Sweat as Ad Blockers Proliferate," October 25, 2015, http://www.cnbc.com/2015/10/23/advertisers-sweat-as-ad-blockers-proliferate.html.

26 Gillies, "Advertisers Sweat as Ad Blockers Proliferate."

27 Salm, "Getting Native Advertising Right."

5

"BEHAVIORAL ADVERTISING"

Protecting consumer privacy

> Advertisers should never compromise consumers' personal privacy in marketing communications, and their choices as to whether to participate in providing their identity should be transparent and easily made.
>
> *IAE Principle 6*

Ethics requires that we honor consumers' privacy in the marketing of our products and services. The major area of concern, currently, is the practice of behavioral advertising, also called interest based advertising, where their preferences are collected—often without their knowledge—for targeting particular advertisements to them. Also, patients' privacy needs to be protected in the marketing of drugs and medical procedures. We begin with behavioral advertising, better described as behavioral "targeting."

Ads are targeted to consumers via their computers according to the interests they express in online activities, such as search queries, ads they click on, information they share on social sites, products they put in online shopping carts, and comments they make in their emails. In addition "data brokers" are now collecting information from many other sources, including facial recognition technology (FRT) and other private sources, including "personally identifiable information" (PII), and putting the information together for business purposes.

Collecting this data allows companies to direct more specific ads to consumers. This cuts down on advertising costs—and also elevates the effectiveness to consumers in getting more relevant ads. Yet, research shows that consumers fear that behavioral targeting infringes on their personal privacy. Also, consumers often are not aware that commercial information is being collected. A PEW research study found that 74% say it is "very important" to them that they be in control of who can get information about them; and 91% of consumers felt they were not in control of their private information. Some 86% have taken steps to mask their digital footprints, but many would like to do more.[1]

A more recent survey confirms consumer reluctance in regard to companies using their data. A survey reported by Fortune/Reuters found that "three-quarters of mobile phone users don't trust brands with their personal information, and more than half say their trust has been worn down over the past few years. Only 14% said they'd be prepared to share location and interaction data, and 30% said they weren't willing to share any personal data at all."[2]

Is it legal to collect this data from consumers not providing their consent? Is it ethical to do so and use it in marketing communications?

The collection of personally identifiable information (PII) without consent is illegal under federal and state laws. This includes social security numbers, bank account information, credit card accounts and medical information. Also, as shall be discussed, the collection of information from children online is highly regulated by the government under the Children's Online Privacy Protection Act (COPPA). And the federal government under HIPAA rules protects the identity of health information.

But, the government has not ruled it illegal to collect information online from consumers regarding their brand and product preferences. This includes when they express those preferences on social sites, emails, search inquiries or products they buy online. Attempts to prohibit this collection through "Do Not Track" legislation have been unsuccessful and with the technology now available it would be impossible to enforce such a mandate.

The "right versus right" ethics test

The ethics of behavioral advertising turns on whether the consumer has knowledge of the collection and has given permission for the collection. Applying the "right versus right" ethics test, it is right for advertisers to make it easier for consumers to get commercial information about products and services in which they are interested. It is also right that their private information is not sold or used without their permission. The manner in which data collection disclosures are made and consumer permission obtained (opt-in/opt-out) will determine how this ethical dilemma is resolved in an individual case.

As Jef Richards, Chair of the Department of Advertising and PR at Michigan State University puts it, "The economic promise is big, but the privacy peril is at least equally enormous." He cites the opinion of Polonetsky and Tene: "Finding the right balance between privacy risks and big data rewards may very well be the biggest public policy challenge of our time."[3]

Professor Richards describes two major ethical dilemmas concerning the collection of information from consumers in behavioral marketing. First, he notes:

> Even the most ethical companies can keep promises made in user agreements if they keep control of the data. But, it has become common practice to sell,

lease, or otherwise share data. And that data may be shared again and again, so the person/company holding it may not even know of its origin, let alone terms of the agreement.

Another problem is the reliance on "opt-out" rather than "opt-in" as a common default. This approach says, in effect, "You've given us permission to collect your information unless you tell us to stop." Only if you "opt-out" will collection stop, and the typical approach to recording your opt-out is to put a "cookie" on your computer. But cookies are not persistent, they will be deleted or become unreadable over time. If you choose to block cookies to protect your privacy, you wipe out your opt-out cookies. And some sites use Flash cookies, which can sidestep privacy settings on web browsers or even surreptitiously restore deleted HTML cookies.[4]

The federal government, including the Federal Trade Commission and Federal Communication Commission, has been heavily involved in the ethical dilemmas and legal breaches concerned with behavioral advertising. The FTC has held hearings and it stated as a baseline principle: "Companies should promote consumer privacy throughout their organizations and at every stage of the development of their products and services."[5]

Early in its review, the FTC favored a "Do Not Track" Congressional Law allowing consumers to opt-out of having their data collected, but dropped that approach and it now endorses self-regulation.[6]

The FTC remains vigilant in regard to how the industry is performing its responsibilities in data tracking and allowing consumer choice in its application. In January 2016, FTC Commissioner Julie Brill chided the industry for tracking consumers across many devices without giving any information as to how they are being tracked. Speaking at an AdExchanger conference in New York, the Commissioner discussed how the FTC is investigating the growth of advertisers and publishers targeting the same persons across their laptop, phone and tablet. The FTC looked at the top 20 websites in five different content categories and found many using "cross-tracking" mechanisms, but few were disclosing this or making it easy for consumers to opt-out. The Commission found that cross-device targeting "is harder to detect and harder for consumers to control. It's not clear consumers are meaningfully informed about cross-device tracking."[7]

Commissioner Brill reminded her audience, "The ad tech industry—you—should be mindful the Federal Trade Commission has pushed for more consumer control over third-party data for at least 15 years. And yet, here we are in 2016 and consumers still do not have adequate means to opt out to data collection." She challenged the ad tech industry to take care of this problem or risk more and more consumers avoiding digital advertising through ad blocking technology. "It's really somewhat surprising to me that the ad tech industry hasn't been more motivated to offer consumers better tools to protect their privacy," she said. "It's always been the case that consumers could take matters into their own hands. And that is what precisely appears to be happening."[8]

In addition to urging the industry to engage in ethical self-regulation of providing consumers with information on the collection of data—and providing opt-out choices—the FTC has brought legal cases when that data has not been protected. One such significant case was against the social network Myspace where the Commission elaborated about the charges and order on the FTC website:

> Have you reviewed your company's privacy policy lately? The FTC's proposed settlement with social network Myspace serves as a timely reminder to make sure what you tell people about your privacy practices lines up with what actually happens in the day-to-day operation of your business. While you're at it, double-check to make sure you're giving customers the straight story about third-party access to their information. The Myspace case is the latest in the FTC's line of law enforcement actions challenging what the agency says are false promises made to consumers about how companies use—and more importantly, how they promise not to use—people's personal information. One particular FTC concern in this case is that the information Myspace shared with advertisers gave advertisers access to users' full names, in violation of the company's privacy promises. When it comes to personally identifiable information (PII), a person's name is about as personally identifiable as it gets. Some background on what the FTC says was going on: Like other social network sites, Myspace users can create and customize personal online profiles. To register, people have to give their full name, email address, birth date, and gender. Then there's optional info Myspace collects, like a user's picture, relationship status, sexual orientation, hobbies, etc. Myspace assigns a unique identifier—called a Friend ID—to each profile that's created.
>
> Myspace promised users it wouldn't share their personally identifiable information in a way that was inconsistent with the reason people provided the info, without first notifying them and getting their approval. The company also said that information used to customize ads wouldn't identify people to third parties and that Myspace wouldn't share browsing activity that wasn't anonymous.
>
> But according to a lawsuit filed by the FTC, Myspace provided advertisers with the "Friend ID" of users who were viewing particular pages on the site. Once advertisers had the Friend ID, they could put two and two together to access lots of other personal information—including users' full names. That meant that the company's promises about notice, permission, and anonymous data were false and misleading. To settle the FTC's charges, Myspace has agreed to change its practices to protect users' privacy in the future. Part I of the proposed order prohibits Myspace from misrepresenting the privacy and confidentiality of any "covered information." The order defines that phrase broadly as information from or about an individual consumer

including, but not limited to, a first and last name; home or other physical address, including street name and city or town; email address or other online contact information, like an instant messaging user identifier or screen name; mobile or other phone number; photos and videos; IP address, User ID, device ID, or other persistent identifier; list of contacts; or physical location. That provision also makes it illegal for Myspace to misrepresent its adherence to any privacy, security, or other compliance program. That includes the US-EU Safe Harbor Framework. (In addition to violating its own privacy promises, Myspace's claim that it complied with the Safe Harbor Principles was also false, said the FTC.)

Under Part II of the order, Myspace has to implement a comprehensive privacy program designed to address privacy risks related to the development and management of existing product and services and new ones, and to protect the privacy and confidentiality of covered information. The order spells out the required features of the program. Specifically, Myspace will:

- designate the person responsible for the program;
- identify reasonably foreseeable material risks—from inside the company and out—that could result in the unauthorized collection or disclosure of covered information;
- assess the sufficiency of safeguards in place to control those risks;
- establish and maintain reasonable controls and procedures to address the risks identified through the privacy risk assessment;
- regularly test the effectiveness of the safeguards;
- take reasonable steps to ensure that service providers protect the privacy of covered information they get from Myspace, including putting privacy provisions in their contracts; and
- adjust its privacy program in light of testing, changes to how it does business, and any other circumstance Myspace has reason to know may have a material impact on the program's effectiveness.

Part III puts in place a feature common in recent FTC orders: a requirement that every other year for the next 20 years, Myspace will have its privacy program evaluated by a qualified, objective, independent professional. That person will have to certify that Myspace provides protections that meet or go beyond the protections required by the order.[9]

The Federal Communications Commission also has federal authority over digital data collection and consumer privacy security. The FTC and FCC work together with the FCC having focused on crafting rules for the agency, and the FTC bringing law enforcement actions under its Section 5 authority to prohibit unfair and deceptive practices.

According to a *Washington Post* article:

> The relationship between the two agencies grew more complicated this year when the FCC began regulating Internet providers like traditional telephone companies, a decision that opened broadband firms, such as Verizon and Comcast, to potential new privacy obligations. And the FCC has recently stepped up its enforcement of data security issues, going after telecom and cable companies for breaches of personal information for the first time. This year the agency's Enforcement Bureau has collected roughly $30 million in fines for such cases.[10]

The FTC and FCC now have entered into a "Consumer Protection Memorandum of Understanding" that commits them to work together on protecting consumer privacy and data security. The agreement provides that the agencies express their belief that the Authorities they have as written provide both agencies with the ability to go after carrier and "non-carrier" activities of Internet service providers. The agreement provides, in part:

> Therefore, it is hereby agreed that:
> The FCC and the FTC will continue to work together to protect consumers from acts and practices that are deceptive, unfair, unjust and/or unreasonable including through:
>
> - coordination on agency initiatives where one agency's action will have a significant effect on the other agency's authority or programs,
> - consultation on investigations or actions that implicate the jurisdiction of the other agency,
> - regular coordination meetings to review current marketplace practices and each agency's work on matters of common interest that impact consumers,
> - regular meetings at which the agencies will exchange their respective learning about the evolution of communications markets,
> - sharing of relevant investigative techniques and tools, intelligence, technical and legal experience, and best practices in response to reasonable requests for such assistance, and
> - collaboration on consumer and industry outreach and education efforts, as appropriate.[11]

Now, according to the *Post* article:

> The Federal Communications Commission has hired Jonathan Mayer, a rising star in privacy circles, to serve as its technical lead for investigations into telephone, television and Internet service providers. Mayer is not your

average bureaucrat: He's a privacy practitioner with a track record of shining light on questionable corporate behavior. And his hiring is a sign that the FCC hopes to bring an increasing aggressive approach to protecting consumers' personal privacy to the next level."[12]

Again, according to the *Post* article, it was Mayer, as a computer scientist and lawyer, who was one of the minds behind browser technology called "Do Not Track," to give consumers more control and power over company tracking. "In 2012, Mayer spotted Google bypassing the privacy settings of Apple's Safari browser, effectively letting them better track the online activities of millions of people. The search giant later agreed to pay $22.5 million to settle FTC charges related to the practice."[13]

Continuing to view the right versus right issues in this ethical dilemma we need to look at what the industry can—and is willing to—do to enhance consumer choice and privacy in data collection. It is argued that collecting consumer data on product and services preferences can be useful to consumers in receiving relevant brand information. Also, research shows that consumers are willing to share data in return for benefits, such as discount offers. Pew Research Center reported that 47% of consumers think it's acceptable for grocery retailers to track their shopping behaviors and sell the data to other companies in return for discount offers. About one-third found it not acceptable. The percentage of consumers who wouldn't accept offers was higher for those over 50 (39%) than for consumers aged 18–49 (27%).[14]

Consumer knowledge of their data being collected, and their ultimate choice in whether to permit it, is critical in resolving the right versus right ethical dilemma. The FTC and FCC are pushing hard to enable and insure consumers have this choice. And, from a positive perspective, the industry also is working to make this happen.

Advertising industry members, working together under the Digital Advertising Alliance (DAA), are backing a new voluntary online initiative, "AdChoices," that provides consumers with the ability to learn what information is being collected and to click on a web page to opt-out. A blue triangle icon appears on the ad and, if clicked, takes users to a web page where they can opt-out of having personally identifiable information collected.

The Digital Advertising Alliance provides information on the web as to the purpose of this service and how to use it:

WHAT DOES THE ADCHOICES ICON DO?

The AdChoices Icon (also known as the "Advertising Option Icon") is a sign for consumer information and control for interest-based advertising (which is also referred to as "online behavioral advertising"). When you see the AdChoices Icon on a Web page or near a Web banner it lets you know that information used to infer your interests is being gathered or used to improve the ads you see. By clicking on the AdChoices Icon, you learn about how interest-based ads are delivered to you. More importantly, the AdChoices Icon gives you the ability to control whether you receive interest-based advertising and from which companies.

WHERE DO YOU FIND THIS ICON?

The AdChoices Icon usually appears at or near the corner of online banner ads that you receive as you travel the Web. You may also see the AdChoices Icon displayed on the bottom of Web pages where information about your visits to the Web site may be gathered for the purpose of delivering ads based on your interests.

WHAT IS "INTEREST-BASED ADVERTISING"?

Just what it says: advertising that is delivered to you based on your likely interests. This type of advertising tries to make the ads you see more relevant based on the types of sites that you visit on the Web. With interest-based advertising, you receive ads and offers for products and services that are more likely to be useful to you. For example, a sporting goods manufacturer might work with an advertising network that collects and uses interest-based information to deliver ads to the browsers of users that have recently visited sports-related sites. Or an airline might direct ads to users who recently visited travel-themed Web sites.

HOW IS INFORMATION ABOUT WEB BROWSING USED FOR THIS TYPE OF ADVERTISING?

When you visit particular Web sites and see particular ads online, information is gathered and stored in your browser with the help of small text files called "Web-cookies." By using this information, advertising services providers can attempt to predict your likely interests and to determine which ads may be most relevant to serve you next.

DOES INTEREST-BASED ADVERTISING USE MY PERSONAL INFORMATION?

Interest-based advertising doesn't depend on information that may be personally identifiable to you, such as your e-mail address, your phone number, photographs, etc.

CAN I OPT OUT OF INTEREST-BASED ADVERTISING?

Yes. The AdChoices program is all about giving you information and control so that you can make informed choices about the interest-based advertising you receive online. The AdChoices icon—whether in an advertisement or on Web pages—gives you access to consumer choice mechanisms where you may, at any time opt out of the interest-based advertising that you receive from participating companies.

HOW DOES INTEREST-BASED ADVERTISING BENEFIT ME AS A CONSUMER?

Better ads and offers. With interest-based advertising, you get ads that are more interesting, relevant, and useful to you. Those relevant ads improve the online experience and help users find the things that interest them more easily. There is another benefit for you as well: free or lower-cost products and services. Interest-based advertising supports the Internet itself. Today's Web sites and online services rely on this type of advertising for revenue so that they can offer a richer array of products and services for lower costs or entirely for free. Every time you check the latest breaking news, use e-mail, view weather forecasts, track your favorite stocks or sports team scores, or share photographs and videos, you are seeing the consumer benefits of interest-based advertising at work.

WHAT ORGANIZATION OVERSEES THE ADCHOICES PROGRAM?

The AdChoices program was created and is managed exclusively by the Digital Advertising Alliance (DAA). The DAA is a consortium of the leading national advertising and marketing associations, which have joined together to help ensure the responsible use of consumer information in interest-based advertising. Today, many hundreds of advertising and marketing companies participate in the DAA AdChoices program, and billions of AdChoices Icons are served across the Internet each week.[15]

In my view, this voluntary industry approach, conducted by the Digital Advertising Alliance, can meet the guidance promoted by the Institute for Advertising Ethics, assuming consumers understand and can readily find the disclaimer, and of course, the company abides by the consumer's choice. IAE Principle 6 provides: "Advertisers should never compromise consumers' personal privacy in marketing communications, and their choices as to whether to participate in providing their identity should be transparent and easily made."

With respect to collecting information from children, in 2013, the FTC put a new rule into effect to enforce the Children's Online Privacy Protection Act (COPPA). It provides that companies cannot utilize behavioral advertising, i.e., collect images, audio or personal identifiers, of or on children under 13 without obtaining parental consent—and companies are also liable if third parties operating on their sites collect such data.

The call for enhanced industry ethics for behavioral advertising from federal and state authorities is far from over. According to "AAF Government Report" (January 16, 2015), President Obama has renewed his call for a Consumer Privacy Bill of Rights, which he first made in 2012. "American consumers can't wait any longer for clear rules of the road that ensure their personal information is safe online," said President Obama. "As the Internet evolves, consumer trust is essential for the continued growth of the digital economy. That's why an online privacy Bill of Rights is so important."[16]

The Bill of Rights is not legislation, but a set of principles focusing on individual control, transparency, respect for context, security, access and accuracy, focused collection, and accountability. The principles also call for strong enforcement by the Federal Trade Commission. Behavior advertising is here to stay. Companies will continue to collect information from consumers, including preferences they express online, that are useful to other consumers in their product and service choices.

It is critical that consumers know they can opt out of data collection and that they know how to do so. Both the industry and the government are now focusing on effective consumer education programs. This includes giving consumers knowledge of "cross-device tracking" and effective choices as to how to opt out. Much discussion is underway in industry and government conferences, including how to display the AdChoices icon on mobile devices. "When people are surprised, that can have negative consequences on trust, a brand and enforcement," FTC Commissioner Terrell McSweeney said at a DAA conference in New York City. "I think the consumer education piece is critical."[17]

New ethical principles for protecting patient privacy in marketing

Our ad industry should take note of the ethical standards being advanced for protecting the privacy of patients when marketing client case studies. The National Association of Addiction Treatment Providers (NAATP) recognizes that successful case studies are one of the proven tools for encouraging addiction treatment, but require consideration to ensure patient privacy and to safeguard long-term recovery.[18]

The NAATP revised code of ethics deals with the practice of misleading and deceptive marketing tactics, including those that could reveal a client's identity. The principles include "hold sacred the shared value of our patients' right of privacy." A treatment provider may not reveal clients' identities "in the form of photographic images, video images, media coverage, nor in marketing testimonials at any time during the client's engagement in treatment." Even after the treatment has concluded, treatment centers are urged to use caution in seeking permission to use testimonials, and some recommend against seeking and using testimonials from young clients not in a position to give informed consent to use their stories.

Certainly, those in our industry creating and disseminating marketing materials based on patients' successful medical treatment should adhere to these ethical standards. In fact, the federal government has rules and regulations protecting patients' identities and health information (HIPPA).

The ethics behind the NAATP principles relate and apply directly to Principle 6 of the Institute for Advertising Ethics: "Advertisers should never compromise consumers' personal privacy in marketing communications, and their choices as to whether to participate in providing their identity should be transparent and easily made." The IAE principle relates to marketing instances when we are using personal identifiers of the consumer, including photos, names and addresses. Also, consumers should be aware that their interest in products and services is being collected online and be given the choice of opting out.

A member of the NAATP ethics committee, Bob Ferguson, was quoted as saying: "You want to apply the principles of common sense, fair play and the golden rule." As our Institute urges: "Do the Right Thing for the Consumer."

Questions and reflection

1. What occurs when the advertising industry conducts "behavioral advertising" or as it is also known, "interest-based advertising"?
2. IAE Principle 6 urges consumer privacy and choice. From a right versus right ethical test what are the advantages to consumers of behavioral advertising/tracking? What are the concerns as to how it is implemented?
3. Under the law is it legal to collect Personally Identifiable Information (PII)? What are examples of PII?
4. What does the government require for collecting PII information from children 12 and under?
5. What is "cross-device tracking" and what are the government concerns regarding its use?
6. If a website does not follow its promise to protect the information it collects what action can the government take?
7. The industry has established a new voluntary program with guidelines for collecting online information and providing consumer choice to participate called AdChoice. Under its principles, how do those collecting inform consumers and what choices are provided?
8. What are the law and industry guidelines for protecting patients' names and medical information?

Notes

1 Rainie, Lee, "The state of privacy in America: What we learned," *FactTank*, Pew Research Center, January 20, 2016, http://www.pewresearch.org/fact-tank/2016/01/20/the-state-of-privacy-in-america/.
2 "Survey: 30% of consumers don't want to give brands any personal data," *Fortune/Reuters*, February 22, 2016, http://fortune.com/2016/02/22/mobile-ads-safety/.
3 Richards, J.I., and Fernandez, L. (2014), "Private Information in the Age of Online Behavioral Advertising," Presented at the Australian Association of Social Marketing 2014 International Social Marketing Conference, Melbourne, Australia (July 17).
4 Richards, "Private Information in the Age of Online Behavioral Advertising," p. 9.
5 Shields, Mark, "FTC Commissioner Urges Ad Industry to Let Consumers Opt Out of Tracking," *The Wall Street Journal*, January 21, 2016, www.wsj.com.
6 Shields, "FTC Commissioner Urges Ad Industry."
7 Shields, "FTC Commissioner Urges Ad Industry."
8 Shields, "FTC Commissioner Urges Ad Industry."
9 Fair, Leslie, "Federal Trade Commission's MySpace case," May 2012, www.ftc.gov.

10 Peterson, Andrea and Fung, Brian, "With this Hire the FCC could get tougher on privacy and security," November 24, 2015, *The Washington Post*.
11 FCC-FTC Consumer Memorandum of Understanding, www.ftc.gov.
12 Peterson and Fung, "With this Hire the FCC could get tougher."
13 Peterson and Fung, "With this Hire the FCC could get tougher."
14 Kaye, Kate, "Less Than Half of Consumers Are OK with Swapping Data for Deals," *Advertising Age*, January 15, 2016, www.adage.com.
15 Reprinted with Permission from Digital Advertising Alliance, www.youradchoices. com and www.aboutads.info 2016. The alliance consists of the major national advertising and marketing associations including the 4A's, Association of National Advertisers, American Advertising Federation, Direct Marketing Association, Interactive Advertising Bureau and Network Advertising Initiative.
16 "Consumer Privacy Bill of Rights, White House," AAF Government Relations Report, January 16, 2015, www.aaf.org.
17 Sluis, Sarah, "Digital Advertising Alliance Turns Attention to Opt-Outs For Cross-Device Tech," June 2, 2015, www.adexchanger.com.
18 Miller, Julie, Editor in Chief, "Legal, ethical rules apply when marketing client case studies," July 15, 2015, *Behavioral Health Care - Insight for Executives*. http://www.beha vioral.net/article/legal-ethical-rules-apply-when-marketing-client-case-study.

6

THE ETHICS OF MULTICULTURAL ADVERTISING AND DIVERSITY

Legal and ethical challenges regarding advertising directed to multicultural consumers arose in the late 1990s. First, the government became concerned that minority media was not being used to reach these audiences. Second, from a positive perspective, clients were becoming aware that effective advertising depended upon reaching African-American, Hispanic, Asian American, and other multicultural audiences through understanding their cultural beliefs and feelings. Yet, with the exception of several outstanding minority agencies, the advertising industry employed relatively few multicultural professionals.

The American Advertising Federation, for which I served as president and CEO, saw these challenges as opportunities. AAF began a strong diversity and inclusivity mission that has grown over the past twenty years. It began with educating the industry as to the importance of creating and disseminating advertising that was based on the cultural beliefs and values of the particular multicultural audience, and then recruiting and building a strong professional multicultural workforce to conduct the advertising.

Success of the mission centered on creating a new way of thinking in the advertising community. Up to this point the industry had believed it could reach all consumers with a general advertising message. Once clients came to understand that their central marketing theme would better attract these audiences through understanding their cultural thinking and feeling, they wanted to hire multicultural professionals to help do it. Today, promoting diversity and inclusivity in our industry and society, including portraying fair and realistic images, remains a mission supported by both business and personal ethics.

Our multicultural initiatives—now under the banner "Mosaic"—are based on both legal and ethical grounding. As shall be discussed, we successfully worked with the government in response to their concern that minority broadcasters were being discriminated against. Also, the ad industry was not effectively recruiting multicultural professionals. While I never personally was aware of racial discrimination in my many encounters with clients, agencies and media companies, I kept hearing from executives that they wanted to have a more diverse workforce but couldn't find the candidates.

Recognizing that our multicultural heritage is one of America's greatest strengths, AAF determined to "do the right thing" through a mission of diversity and inclusivity. First, we surrounded ourselves with expert multicultural professionals. Then, together, we provided the industry with reasons why inclusivity is critical, how to achieve it through developing multicultural principles, and then we provided the industry with multicultural candidates.

Mosaic Principles

In 1999, the Federal Communications Commission (FCC) raised concerns that minority media outlets were not being used to reach multicultural audiences. In other words, the FCC did not see the advertising industry as targeting multicultural consumers unfairly, but rather that multicultural businesses were being excluded from targeting those audiences. And that exclusion was considered unacceptable. For the industry this was both a challenge and an opportunity.

FCC Chairman William Kennard called for an industry code of conduct in response to alleged findings of discrimination in ad rates paid to minority broadcasters. Vice President Gore also called on the industry to investigate its practices with regard to minority advertising agencies and minority-owned and formatted media. In response, AAF and thirty-eight advertisers, general and minority agencies, and minority owned and formatted media companies worked for a year to develop voluntary guidelines to encourage greater diversity in advertising and more investment in multicultural marketing.

The initial principles and practices focus on a commitment to take advantage of growth opportunities in multicultural markets by promoting inclusiveness and fairness. This includes minority employment and career advancement, and compensation for creative services and media buys. The principles and practices also include a focus on accountability and results of employment and ad spending to measure investment in multicultural marketing and workforce diversity. Over forty companies and agencies committed to adopting these principles, including Procter & Gamble, Coca-Cola, Johnson and Johnson, Verizon Communications, and Kraft General Foods.

Marking the first time that a president had issued an executive order that addresses advertising, President Clinton issued a directive that required government departments and agencies to take an aggressive role in ensuring substantial minority procurement in government advertising contracts. The executive order also directs each government agency and department to ensure that payment for federal advertising is commensurate with fair market rates in those relevant markets. In addition, it calls on agencies to ensure that the creation, placement and transmission of federal advertising fully reflects the nation's diversity, with special attention given to media that reach specific ethnic and racial audiences.

The executive order was complimentary to AAF's principles and practices. Indeed, when signing his order, attended by industry representatives and myself, President Clinton stated: "I want to commend the American Advertising Federation for responding to the Vice President's challenge and for working with interested parties to develop the Principles for Effective Advertising in the American Multicultural Marketplace, a strategic plan for boosting minority representation in the advertising industry."

Today, the AAF's Mosaic Council promotes the Mosaic Principles that they created to offer clients, agencies, media and independent contractors recommendations needed to institute common diversity practices:

- We must recruit for America. The future of the industry is reliant on a workforce that reflects the diversity of demographics, lifestyle, experience and mindset of America today and tomorrow. Actionable Practice: Require a diverse slate of candidates.
- We must recognize the diversity of talent within the industry. Actionable Practices: Increase multicultural talent nominations for award programs; and Partner with corporate communications to pitch multicultural talent.
- We must provide greater access to development and leadership opportunities. Actionable Practices: Conduct formal training programs (i.e. leadership, management and job-specific skills); and Promote diverse attendance at industry events to represent the organization.
- We must encourage the industry to portray realistic images of multicultural youth and communities. Actionable Practices: Make conscious decisions to produce and disseminate advertising messages that portray many facets of multicultural life; and Challenge creative teams to present ideas that do not reiterate common stereotypes.[1]

The Mosaic Counsel is the industry's preeminent think tank on diversity and inclusion. It meets regularly to discuss recommended implementation of the Mosaic Principles and to suggest actionable practices, such as the ones included above under the four principles. The fourth principle, above, was developed to deal with an important ethical dilemma—how multicultural communities are depicted in advertising and media—and will be discussed later in this chapter.

The Counsel also oversees the annual production of AAF's diversity and inclusivity programs, including Mosaic Career Fairs; Diversity Achievement Mosaic Awards; Thought Leadership; and Most Promising Multicultural Students (MPMS), to which we will turn next.

Most Promising Multicultural Students Program (MPMS)

Since 1996, the AAF's Most Promising Multicultural Students program has connected the best multicultural college students in the country with an advertising industry seeking multicultural talent. Each February the 50 Most Promising Multicultural Students come to New York City where they are introduced to the industry—and the industry is introduced to them. Over three days they are mentored by advertising professionals, attend workshops on résumé writing and portfolio building, visit major agencies and media companies and meet with recruiters.

These multicultural students are among the best advertising students in the United States, and the criteria for their selection is rigorous. Just to be considered, they must have a 3.2 cumulative GPA, write an essay and be nominated by a professor or senior-level industry professional. A panel of respected advertising executives then reviews the applications. The chosen students represent the future of a more inclusive industry and AAF's commitment to building it.

The program began as a response to repeated requests from agency executives who believed in hiring a diverse workforce, but were having trouble finding multicultural entry-level candidates. This presented us with the opportunity to practice enhanced ethics from both a business case and personal case. The business case, based upon AAF's Mosaic Principles, was that the industry needed multicultural professionals to effectively create and disseminate advertisements to multicultural audiences. The personal case was based upon the ethical principles of equality and inclusivity in reaching out and building an industry composed of all races and ethnicities.

The AAF mission always has been to connect all parts of the industry—agencies, clients, media companies and academia. So we utilized our own diverse connections and recruited top minority agencies and media companies into the AAF membership to provide insight and infrastructure. That included Tom Burrell and Burrell Communications; Byron Lewis and Uniworld; Hector Orci and La Agencia; Sam Chisholm of the Chisholm Group; and Don Coleman of Don Coleman Advertising.

This taskforce also included Eddie Arnold and the Nielsen Company and Clarence Smith of *Essence* magazine. With their help, on what became the Mosaic Council, we held a luncheon for the inaugural class of the Most Promising Multicultural Students.

We received immediate and overwhelming support from a number of major marketers, including Bob Wehling and Procter & Gamble; Evelyn Ogilvy and Verizon; and Andrea Alstrup and Johnson & Johnson; as well as general market agencies, including David Bell, then with FCB; Ken Kaess of DDB; Ed Wax of Saatchi & Saatchi; and Carla Michelotti and Don Richards from Leo Burnett. Louis Car from *BET* and Rance Crain from *Advertising Age* represented the media. For a year, with this group, we developed principles and practices on how to effectively market to multicultural audiences and recruit and hire multicultural talent, to build off of the success of that first MPMS program.

We had one benchmark for evaluating the program after the first year: Did the students get hired? And the answer was an overwhelming, "Yes." We built it ... and the industry came. Now, 20 years later, the program continues to be so successful because it draws a truly diverse class of students each year from campuses throughout the country, utilizing the network AAF has in place with its over two hundred college chapters.

The success of MPMS is documented by research showing the high retention rates and success of the participants. Ten years into the program we contacted 75 percent of MPMS alumni: more than two-thirds were still in the industry. Very few programs can claim such a success rate. And these alumni continue to move up the corporate ladder. Tiffany R. Warren is one such example. She was a charter member, coming from Bentley College, and is now Senior Vice President, Chief Diversity Officer, Omnicom Group, Inc. And she remains committed to the AAF ethical diversity and inclusivity mission and has served as Chair, Mosaic Council.

The Mosaic Counsel has enhanced its multicultural student recruiting by conducting annual Mosaic Career Fairs so that even more students and recruiters can connect. Also, the American Advertising Federation and AAF District 2 developed and brought together the Diversity Achievement Mosaic Awards held annually to honor outstanding multicultural advertising and media usage, as well as professionals who lead the way in diversity and inclusion.

The winning entries demonstrate both the commitment of advertisers, agencies, media and individual professionals, and how to best advertise to our multicultural audiences in America. In 2014, the 4A's Multicultural Advertising Intern Program (MAIP) was honored for the 10-week summer program it initiated in 1993. And, minority students in their last year of college are included in the program with a two-day workshop conducted at and by Starcom Mediavest Group where they are immersed in media training and case studies.

Depiction of multicultural youth and communities in advertising/media

Mosaic Principle 4 provides: "We must encourage the industry to portray realistic images of multicultural youth and communities." This positive goal is essential for dispelling the stereotypes that are too often presented in news and entertainment. Also, it is essential in building an inclusive culture in America that we show the full range of roles played by those in the multicultural community.

Actionable practices include challenging agency creative teams to portray the many facets of multicultural life and to avoid reiterating common stereotypes. Also, consistent with building inclusive professional staffs to learn how to effectively market to multicultural audiences, we seek the opinion of multicultural professionals and consumers regarding valid images that resonate.[2]

In reality, multicultural people are not being portrayed fairly. In fact, African-American men and women are being portrayed negatively on television, and in particular, on Reality Television programming. Specific illustrations were presented on September 30, 2015, by a panel of ad professionals and educators during Advertising Week New York.

In TV programming of *Love & Hip Hop*, *Real Housewives of Atlanta*, *Sorority Sisters*, and *Apprentice*, African-American women were portrayed as aggressive and overtly sexually focused on "getting and keeping a man," African-American men as aggressive and dangerous.[3]

Concern was expressed by the panelists that the unfair and negative portrayals are resulting in negative consequences for people of color in our country. Panel members believed that depictions of African-Americans as aggressive lead to violent encounters with both armed police officers and individual gun owners; Trayvon Martin, Michael Brown and Eric Garner are illustrations. The unfair depictions can result in apathy from Americans as to the increasing violence we witness in our communities. Especially for our citizens, who do not have the opportunity to interact with people of color, the "reality" show depictions may influence them to condone over-response by police officials and gun owners.

There also was concern as to how these unfair depictions are affecting our multicultural youth. Instead of encouraging them to strive to grow through education and hard work, as many advocate in the white community, our multicultural youth may be discouraged and led in wrong directions by Reality TV programming. It was understood by the panel that whites are also shown in negative roles, but in the majority of instances on TV, entertainment and news, whites are shown in positive depictions. Panelists urged the same realistic depictions of people of color.[4]

My experience as a mentor for young men of color has a bearing on my concerns as to how our youth of color are depicted. Over the past ten years I have mentored over twenty young African-American and Hispanic youth in the Washington, DC, area. My job is to encourage them to develop a plan for their immediate futures, including finishing high school, getting a job and looking forward to a future of personal growth and responsibility.

The mentoring and friendship that I have had with a young African-American man, ironically named "Wally," over the past eight years has proven to me how we can come together across racial and generational lines to connect in both business and recreation. Two essential ingredients include understanding each other's cultural values and building trust through honesty and consistency. Both relate directly to the fair depiction of people of color in our American society.

It has been important for me to understand the different cultural values we hold, and just as importantly, those that we share. By understanding—and respecting—the values that Wally holds, I believe I can interact more effectively with him. At the same time, I can help him to learn the rules in America that govern business and job hiring, as well as the rules that can make for success in education. This idea is based upon the book, *A Framework for Understanding Poverty* by Ruby K. Payne, PhD. The book describes the rules for three classifications of people: those in "poverty" (generational or situational caused by death of a family member, loss of job, etc.); those in the "middle class"; and those with "wealth." Dr. Payne's key findings are that "An Individual brings with him/her the hidden rules of the class in which he/she was raised. Schools and businesses operate from middle class norms and use the hidden rules of the middle class. The rules are not directly taught in schools or businesses." Dr. Payne emphasizes that in teaching students we must understand their hidden rules and teach them the middle class rules that will make them successful in school and business. Importantly, in doing so we should not denigrate their cultural rules.[5]

From the time we have been together, I know we share the value of working hard to improve our own economic status and to support our families. An important area we have focused on in our mentoring relationship has been in getting and holding a job in a very difficult economy. This has included help in writing a résumé, coaching for job interviews and counseling in building positive relationships with one's boss and superiors.

Opportunities can come to us that we do not control, but when "jumped on" can provide professional growth. Such an opportunity came about for Wally when I was on a school trip assisting my wife Jean with her students. While on the bus, I received a call from Wally in which he said he would not graduate from high school because of book fees he owed. My passionate response was, "You will graduate! We will take care of this, and I will come down to the school tomorrow to help you take care of it."

Another of the adults assisting with the trip overheard the phone conversation and asked me about my mentoring role. He said he was impressed with our mentoring relationship and when I told him that Wally was interested in becoming a plumber's assistant, he said that his wife's cousin ran a plumbing business in Clinton, Maryland. The next day, his wife told Jean at school that she would recommend that her cousin interview Wally and consider him for a job.

This was a wonderful teaching moment on the power of "networking" in the business world. It resulted in Wally getting the job, working with a partner with twenty years of plumbing experience, and working hard to develop his own professional skills. As testimony to his hard work, when he was laid off because of a decline in business, the owner provided a recommendation to another plumbing company where Wally landed the job.

Trust is the basic component of all of our relationships in life, including both personal and business. As I build a relationship I try to always be mindful of how my attitude and actions impact trust building, but I also have to be honest and admit that oftentimes I do not trust another person. And it causes me to want to "control" the situation.

Wally—for his own reasons—also holds back in his trust of others. Several times during our mentoring relationship I have talked with him about where we stand in trusting one another. It was early on when he looked at me and said, "I don't trust anybody. That's just the way it is." Well, he was being honest. But, I think we are both growing in trust as our stories reveal.

It is hard to trust when you have been let down so many times. Trust is hard to come by when you have been abandoned as a child or live in a neighborhood where "I have to watch my back at school and on the way home."[6]

In order to begin to build trust we must be consistent in our actions with others. Don Lowe, our Director of Mentoring, called each mentor to insure that he or she was coming each week to be with our mentees. He did not want us to disappoint the mentee, who would ask, "Is my mentor coming in today?"

Trust is built most importantly when we respond to "emergency" situations. Most often the request comes by text. "Hey, Mr. Snyder, it's an emergency. Give me a call back ASAP!" And, when it is really an emergency, Wally even makes a phone call, something he rarely does because of his preference for text messaging. One evening I received an emergency call when Wally asked if I could take him to the emergency room because he was having headaches from a boxing hit and feared he had a concussion. "Yes," I said and drove to his home and then to the hospital for a late night visit, returning home after midnight.

Trust also has been strengthened when my wife Jean and I have worked with Wally on special projects, as when we facilitated his selling of candy packages to our church members. This was to earn money for his high school so that he could attend his prom. He came to church with us and with Jean's accounting help and training, delivered the products that our members had paid him for in advance.

The building of trust, especially with those who have suffered losses or have little reason to be trustful, is an ongoing mission that can be damaged by any failure to do what we promised. We just have to be consistent in our reactions. I have found my reward in seeing a young man gradually gaining trust—and the strength and happiness that flow from it. It gives me peace and hope. My concern is that "reality" shows depicting people of color in unfair and inappropriate ways will undermine the guidance and trust that is critical for their success and growth.

My counseling was and is based upon the guidance and teaching I received in a small, post WWII Iowa community where the belief was "you will do better than we did." The challenge in my mentoring was encouraging the youth to believe that they would do better than the older people in the community who were stifled by poverty and lack of employment opportunities. It doesn't help that youth of color were, and are being, depicted as violent, on drugs and dangerous to their fellow citizens. The "reality" show depictions discourage them from believing in their futures.

And these so-called "reality shows" do not depict reality as it often exists in our country. There are countless ethical stories of how people actually are helping one another in positive encounters. Also, we are connecting over racial, generational and cultural lines to interact in our daily lives. I include here a story by my mentee Wally that has true "reality show" content:

I began to look for a used car on Craigslist.com. My search for a used car was very successful. I had called and emailed a lot of owners of used Buick LeSabra asking for more information about the cars and trying to come to an agreement on a price. While doing so I came across a burgundy Buick LeSabra with low miles and for a good price which was within my budget and a number was posted to call, so I called the number and an older lady answered the phone.

I could tell immediately by her tone of voice and proper speaking that she was an older woman of white race. She answered the phone very pleasant and soft spoken and I began to inquire about the Buick that was posted online and introduced myself. Then she started to explain to me that she couldn't drive the car anymore because of her age, and that she needed money to afford a power chair, and afterwards she told me that she owned the car for a long time and it had been driven by her very seldom and lightly and went on to express that she never had a problem with it and it had very low miles and overall was a good car. I was impressed with the information she had given me and she preferred to come take a test drive of the car the same day, but I explained to her that I would only be available Christmas Eve, and she agreed to that date and then gave me the address.

So, the next day came which was Christmas Eve and me and my two cousins took an hour road trip to Ashburn, Virginia. Just as soon as we arrive in Ashburn we got pulled over in a townhome complex looking for the address I was given to come see the car. The officer got out of his car and asked for all of our IDs, and he asked where were we headed, and we replied we were looking for this address and kindly the officer told us to follow him to the address.

When we got there I got up to the door and this, old white lady peeks out the window and began to walk over to the door and her first words were you're here to see the car, and I said yes I am and Happy Christmas Eve, and she replied why thank you young man and we began a conversation about things that a young black guy as myself I wouldn't think I could relate to an older white woman, and vice versa. For example, she had Redskin cups and ornaments all over her home. So I asked, was she a big Redskin's fan and she said Hell yes I am and then I begun laughing and told her I was too. Then, she told me she had been to their practice field right there in Ashburn and I knew then that I had found a spark within our conversation that made me and her feel comfortable.

So, we got to her garage and she walked me around her car and instructed me to get in it and take her for a spin around the block, so I did. I was impressed by how well it rode and how up kept the inside was. We got back to her home from the test drive and I knew for a fact that I couldn't leave without this car. So, I got out of the car and quickly walked around the passenger side to open the door for her and she said, "How sweet, and young man only if I was twenty years younger," so I instantly laughed and while laughing she said I'm finally getting rid of my Lady today. So, I asked her how much was she expecting for the car, and she said $2,000.

I told her I only had $2,000 but I didn't want to spend it all on the car and not have any gas to make it home so she said you know young man now days it's hard to come across people that was honest as you just were so you know what give me everything you have and I gave her $2,000, and she handed me back $500 of it. That made me very happy to know that I had a new car and $500 to my name. So, I thanked her so much and told her how much I appreciated her kindness to me and that she will be blessed one day.

From then on I realized that no matter what race or age difference or sex you can get along with each other, and by knowing that, it has changed my outlook on people of different race and age groups and has also changed my ability and wiliness to adapt to different cultures, different people, and different ways of living. So no matter what the circumstances are, we all can get along.[7]

"Do the Right Thing"

Our advertising industry has an ethical obligation to encourage and achieve the fair portrayal of multicultural groups. While these unfair depictions may not violate laws, ethics rises above the law. Stereotyping members of a race or sexual orientation in negative and violent depictions is unethical. Following our ethical definition of "Doing the Right Thing" our programming should reflect the values of America: equality and inclusiveness of our citizens, and fairness and objectivity in their treatment.

First, our industry must insure that our advertisements fairly portray multicultural groups. As discussed in the Ad Week panel we have positive illustrations that advertising is responding. TV ads with Misty Copeland for Under Armor, Goldie Blox, and Dove—Real Beauty Sketches were cited as examples.[8]

Also, a biracial family Cheerios ad made its 2014 Super Bowl debut. An earlier version was subjected to comments online using "angry, overtly racist language," according to Stuart Elliott in the *New York Times*. General Mills stuck with the ad and Camille Gibson, General Mills Vice President of Marketing, said, "The big game provided another opportunity to tell another story about family love."[9]

And, the *Washington Post* reported that during 2015, advertisers embraced gay families "with open arms." Allstate joined in with its "Here's to firsts" campaign "featuring two dads with a cute-as-a-button baby girl. The insurance company joins other major brands—including Campbell's Soup, Chevrolet, Hallmark, Honey Maid, Ikea, Kohl's, Maytag and Tylenol—that have come on board with

LGBT-inclusive commercials and social media campaigns in the past year." Stuart Elliott is quoted: "Marketers have been moving for many years toward including more lesbian and gay consumers in ads, part of a trend reflecting the changing demographics of the American public."[10]

Our advertising community also has an ethical obligation to work toward the fairer portrayal of people of color on TV programming and news. In particular, advertisers and professionals in the television industry must face the ethical dilemmas that arise when deciding to sponsor or produce and air programming centered on multicultural characters.

There is both a business case and a personal case for doing the right thing in the portrayal of multicultural audiences. The business case is based upon the concerns that multicultural (and white) consumers can express to advertisers and television networks. A powerful illustration is the boycott and removal from the air of *Sorority Sisters*.

Black sorority members successfully protested against the VH1 production of *Sorority Sisters*. Greek life social media users "slammed" VH1 and the show producer for airing a show they claimed misrepresents sorority life. One particular Greek member, Reynoir Lewis went as far as creating a petition drive to stop the airing of the Scott-Young produced show. Lewis headlined the petition: "Stop the spread of ignorance and stereotyping of our beloved Black Greek letter organizations. Our founders amongst EVERY organization worked extremely hard to allow us to unite and flourish not only on college campuses, but as a people well beyond our college days, and Mona Scott-Young now threatens to demolish those aims and goals we all abide by." The protesters used online services, including Facebook and Twitter, to obtain petition signatures. While VH1 initially refused to back down and did air the premier episode, the network ultimately pulled the programming.[11]

The business case is more difficult when the audience to whom the reality TV is directed do not ask for fairer depictions. This presents an ethical dilemma for the advertiser, network and producer. On the one hand they can argue, "We are giving the audience what it wants." But, on the other hand, the programming damages equality, fairness and relations in society, as well as the confidence of young people of color.

The personal case for doing the right thing can be powerful in effecting change in the way multicultural groups are depicted. It is based on "feelings" and impacted by the heart, instead of the brain. As ethicist Greg Annear puts it, the personal case is based upon "an ethics of achievement."[12] While feelings are difficult to measure, they are powerful in affecting behavior.

I recall a discussion on my ethics work with a lawyer friend in which he questioned "why" it was important. At first, I made the business case—that consumers care and will reward companies for high ethics and may even pay more for an ethically produced product. He continued in a "cross examination" mode, "So what's in it for me?" I responded that he would do better if his company did better with the consumer. Still pressing me, I responded: "You need to feel better about what you are doing at work!" "Yes," he replied, "so I can sleep at night."

The "Sleep-Test" is actually an ethical descriptor for resolving ethical dilemmas through personal decision-making. Ethicist Joseph Badaracco documents the attractions. First, "It encourages people to ground decisions in their core intuitions, passions and commitment, rather than in principles and calculations." Second, "It helps people feel better about themselves and about human nature, because it supposes that morally good actions are natural and comfortable, that we can trust our instincts, and that we will somehow know or sense what is right and wrong." Third, "Scientists may ... be able to pinpoint the location of moral instincts in the human brain." (Research, reported in *Scientific American* magazine, found that acts of doing good caused healthy growth in specific areas of the brain.) "The fourth reason for the power and appeal of sleep-test ethics is cultural." "Trust thyself," "Do your own thing," "Just do it" are expressions for Americans' need to express themselves as individuals.[13]

The personal case is very important to success in achieving this ethical mandate. Our advertising professionals, as well as producers and writers of programming, should want to do the right thing to portray our multicultural community fairly and positively. And, they will want to take a positive approach in encouraging our society to see the multicultural community not in a limited, negative, often frightening way, but in the many positive roles played in everyday life. Importantly, they can counter negative and unfair viewpoints.

Just as in urging the business case for "doing the right thing" in fairly depicting the multicultural community, we need to reinforce in our professionals the personal case to do so. This includes building the case for "doing the right thing." A number of initiatives have been undertaken.

In 2015, Starbucks launched an inclusivity initiative wherein its baristas had the option to hand out coffee cups on which they had written "Race Together" and start a discussion about race relations. CEO Howard Schultz initiated the action in a video addressing Starbucks's nearly 200,000 workers, 40% of whom are members of a racial minority. Starbucks terminated the barista campaign quickly because of consumer and employee concerns, but plans to continue with other aspects of the "Race Together" campaign, including special insert sections with *USA TODAY* with the goal of fostering discussion and exchange of ideas. Schultz was quoted as saying, "An issue as tough as racial and ethnic inequality requires risk-taking and tough-minded action. And let me reassure you that our conviction and commitment to the notion of equality and opportunity for all has never been stronger."[14]

The oil giant BP launched a public relations campaign aimed at combating racism. While the tag line, "BP: Black People" caused confusion and offense to some among the public, and brought a change to the campaign, the company maintained its stance on the importance of the topic. Company spokesperson

Fern Mulberry said: "I've been asked if BP now stands for Black People. BP does not stand for Black People. Let me rephrase that. We stand for, we *support* Black People. And White People. We like both very much. Do we like one more than the other? No. The important thing here is that our marketing team and partners in PR and advertising felt it was high time to rebrand the B and P so that consumers and lawmakers would see how much we care about people talking about racism."[15]

In the spring of 2015, the American Advertising Federation and Zeta Phi Beta Sorority through its GET ENGAGED social action initiative, co-sponsored "Reality TV: Realistic, Stereotypical, Helpful or Harmful?"—a series of "watch parties" in ten markets across the nation focused on the impact of media images. During the Watch Parties, participants examined the state of African-American images in media, their effects on public perception and policy, and the role that people of good will can play in driving change. The groups consisted of TV and film producers, entertainment attorneys, college professors and students, reality show participants and producers, as well as advertising professionals.

The AAF and Zeta produced a white paper on what has been learned regarding the unfair depictions of African-Americans in reality TV programming and presented findings aimed at "creating more balanced images of African-American women in the media protecting African-American youth from the harmful images, and educating the general public and advertising/media industry about the impact of stereotypes":

> **Seek Multicultural Expertise.** Advertisers have the ability to flex their "client muscle" and ask to integrate multicultural expertise from the television networks and media planning and buying teams. This will prevent their brands from supporting programing that negatively impacts their standing with African-American viewers. Additionally, these teams should consciously and actively seek the input of multicultural consumers to better understand which images resonate, and how best to portray multicultural people holistically in various life situations without erasing the unique aspects of their distinct cultures.
>
> **Mentor Television-Writing Talent.** Diverse casts ruled television in 2014 and 2015, from *How to Get Away with Murder* and *Empire*, to *Jane the Virgin* and *Fresh Off the Boat*. Viewers have an interest in watching more diverse stories on television. Following the HBO Access Writing Fellowship model, advertisers could partner with networks to offer classes and access to mentors, executives and show runners with the intent to help multicultural writers develop and workshop their show.
>
> **Amplify Your Voice, and Vote with Your Eyeballs.** Be a vocal and visible supporter of reality television programs and/or online web series that promote positive images of African-American women and girls. When damaging images arise (whether related to ethnicity, gender, age, lifestyle,

ability), viewers of all backgrounds must be vocal and "put their money where their mouth is" by not watching these shows (driving down the ratings), and making the networks and advertisers aware of their concerns. Remember that a television show only stays on air as long as there are advertisers willing to support it. There is also shared onus on advertising and media professionals to carefully evaluate new programs during the annual television "upfront" meetings. Don't be afraid to ask the hard questions and raise red flags before committing advertising dollars.

Support the Healthy Media For Youth Act. This bill, originally introduced in the House of Representatives in 2010, seeks to research the impact of the images of girls and women in the media, establish a national task force, and provide grants for media literacy and youth empowerment programs. Notably, issues pertinent to African-American girls and women were not addressed in the original bill, and should be incorporated before reintroducing.

Promote Media Literacy in Schools. As elementary, middle and high school students study economics, consumerism, and the Internet/social media, media literacy should be taught to further critical thinking skills. This will prepare students to scrutinize messaging presented in the media, online and offline. Cross-functional teams of educators, advertising and media professionals, social workers and counselors should be established to work with students inside and outside the classroom. Parents must also be educated on the impact that harmful, stereotypical reality television programing can have on children.[16]

The suggestions included holding the television networks accountable, as was accomplished in the *Sorority Sisters* boycott of VH1 network, after making the case on the negative impact of reality TV on the multicultural community and its youth; counter reality TV images with TV campaigns on the negative impact; create a curriculum that can be used by educators and churches to combat the negative impact (Atlanta Watch Party, April 16, 2015.) Other recommendations are to use Twitter and Facebook to make voices heard in opposition to the reality shows (Boston Watch Party, April 16, 2015). An idea coming from a Watch party on a college campus recommended focusing on advertisers by encouraging them to sponsor shows that give more positive images, and then to support those companies that do so (University of Virginia/Charlottesville, April 23, 2015).

The New York Ad Week panel also introduced and discussed the key findings from testing conducted by the Center for Social Inclusion (CSI) as to how to effectively communicate about race: (1) Describe the problem and present messages in emotional terms; (2) Explain why this is not just a problem for African-Americans, but why it is an issue affecting the entire country; (3) Discredit the race wedge lodged by conservatives to encourage individuals of other races to feel that this isn't their problem; and (4) Redefine who the victims are and who the enemies are.[17]

These recommendations support and undergird, making the successful ethical case for the depiction of multicultural groups in a fair manner. They provide the emotional and concrete arguments for "Doing the Right Thing" so as to reflect the values of America: equality and inclusiveness of our citizens, and fairness and objectivity in their treatment.

Questions and reflection

1. What was the "new way of thinking" that the American Advertising Federation developed in the 1990s for advertising to multicultural audiences?
2. The AAF's Mosaic Council has developed four principles for ethically dealing with multicultural audiences in advertising and marketing. What are those principles? List an "actionable practice" for each principle.
3. What are the negative consequences resulting from the unfair depiction of multicultural groups, including youth, in programming or advertising?
4. How can we in the advertising community come to understand the cultural values held by all of our consumers, including those in the multicultural community, and build trust with them?
5. "Doing the Right Thing" in ending the unfair depiction of multicultural people includes making positive portrayals and opposing ones that are unfair. What are positive illustrations made by advertisers? Describe an effective action taken to oppose unfair depictions.
6. Summarize the effective actions that can be learned from the "watch parties" held to counter unfair depictions.
7. The author includes a "business case" and "personal case" for ethically opposing the unfair depiction of multicultural audiences. Summarize each and discuss which you feel is most effective in "doing the right thing."

Notes

1 AAF Mosaic Center & Education, Mosaic Principles and Actionable Practices, http:// www.aaf.org/imis/_PDF/AAF%20Website%20Content/886_MosaicCenter/Mosaic_ MosaicPrinciples.pdf.
2 AAF, Mosaic Principles and Actionable Practices.
3 "Images, Ethics & Power," New York Advertising Week Panel, September 30, 2015.
4 "Images, Ethics & Power" Panel.
5 Payne, Ruby K., PhD, *A Framework for Understanding Poverty*, Highlands, TX: aha! Process, Inc., 1996, p. 3.
6 Zabriskie, Phil, "The Will and the Wire," January 29, 2012, *Washington Post Magazine*.
7 Adams, Wally and Snyder, Wally, *Hey, It's Black Wally and White Wally!*, Washington, DC: Opus Books, www.politics-prose.com.
8 "Images, Ethics & Power" Panel.
9 Elliott, Stuart, "An American Family Returns to the Table," January 28, 2014, *New York Times*, www.mobile.nytimes.com.
10 Petrow, Steve, "Advertisers warmly embrace gay families," December 14, 2015, *Washington Post*.

11 Jules, Anny, "New 'Sorority Sisters' VH1 Show: Black Sororities Boycott Network for Premiering Controversial Reality TV Show," *Latin Post*, December 16, 2014, www.latinpost.com/articles/27949/20141216/new-sorority-sisters-vh1-show-black-sororit ies-boycott-network-for-premiering-controversial-reality-tv-show.htm.

12 Ahner, Gene, *Business Ethics, Making a Life, Not Just a Living*, Maryknoll, NY: Orbis Books, 2007, p. 90.

13 Badaracco, Joseph, *Defining Moments, When Managers Must Choose between Right and Right*, Boston, MA: Harvard Business School Press, 1997, pp. 48–50.

14 Wahba, Phil, "Starbucks says oops: No more 'Race Together' on coffee cups," March 22, 2015, *Fortune Magazine*, www.fortune.com.

15 Kenny, John, "What if Starbucks' 'Race Together' had caught on in Corporate America?" March 30, 2015, *Los Angeles Times*, www.latimes.com.

16 "Reality TV—Entertaining … But No Laughing Matter," American Advertising Federation, http://www.aaf.org/imis/_PDF/AAF%20Website%20Content/000_Resea rch/Research_Whitepaper_WatchParty.pdf.

17 "Images, Ethics & Power" Panel.

7

ETHICAL DILEMMAS WE FACE IN OUR BUSINESS TRANSACTIONS

In addition to ad claims and copy, we face ethical dilemmas in our business transactions with our clients, as well as sub-contractors and partners, and with and between our own professional employees. These range from promises of what we can do for our clients to how we price our services. How we treat our clients and professionals, and how they are treated by our clients and agencies, also present ethical dilemmas. And, then there is how—and if—our professional employees exercise their ethics in their assignments and personal dealings in the business. This can include ethical conflicts in our business relationships because of the personal relationships we hold with the same individuals.

We can take lessons and guidance from others facing ethical dilemmas in the world of business. In this chapter and the next we consider actual ethical dilemmas that have been faced by professionals in the business of advertising. These range from choices made by the CEOs of the company down to professionals working during their first year in the business. Also, there are the experiences of those working for managers that have faced tough choices. The decision made by a manager will have major ramifications for those reporting to him or her, and in many instances for the reputation and wellbeing of the company. Whatever the ethical decision, I am told it goes through the company in minutes. Because of their importance, ethical dilemmas must be considered and managed with care, especially when they involve "right versus right" decisions. Rushwood Kidder, quoted earlier, urges, "You've got to think about it, reason it through, get the mind in gear and grapple with tough issues. In other words, you've got to be mentally engaged."[1]

Solving ethical dilemmas is not just cerebral, but usually evokes strong personal and moral thinking. Joseph Badaracco, in his book on ethics, *Defining Moments*, puts it this way—right versus right decisions illustrate the problem of the "urgent, complicated, and sometimes painful issue of personal integrity and moral identity."[2]

Badaracco urges that "right versus right" choices are best understood as "defining moments." The decision can "reveal a manager's basic values, and in some cases, those of the organization."[3]

We now address ethical dilemmas in our businesses that include right versus right decision-making. They are ones we have discussed in our Institute for Advertising Ethics Certificate sessions where we include the professional views expressed. Also, we will be discussing personal ethical stories, including my own.

Conflicts in business caused by personal relationships

This is the first of our ethical stories told by advertising professionals (in this case without the storyteller's name and company by request) that include the importance of the ethical dilemma to the storyteller and how the situation could be resolved. In his own words:

> The story involves the mixture of friendship and business—and the need to be aware. A few years ago a good friend of mine invited me to join him at his home in a very desirable mountain golf location. This friend also owned an advertising agency that worked for my company. We had been friends long before I joined my company and his agency had served the company long before I joined it. Multiple decades in fact. The agency's role was a small one in my company and I was only indirectly involved as his agency served a different business unit.
>
> The weekend trip to the cabin and golf was spectacular. We had a great time and never talked business beyond cursory mention of someone we both knew and their career news, gossip, etc.
>
> Unbeknownst to me however, the agency's business had been subjected to an RFP (request for proposal), his direct clients were a new group of people and the decision was going to be communicated on Monday morning after we all got back to work. The agency was going to lose the business and clearly the decision had been made prior to the weekend to facilitate Monday morning communication.
>
> A couple things:
>
> 1. Even with the long and strong outside the company friendship, the existence of an active RFP made the weekend awkward and inappropriate. Very bad timing.
> 2. My friend may have reasonably assumed I was aware of the RFP.
>
> While the agency's business was a very small part of my company's advertising activity it represented about 30% of the agency's business. I was not aware of how big my company's business was for them. Longstanding and with many long term staffers on the business at the agency.

The lesson—I clearly should have checked and made myself aware of any goings-on with the agency before spending significant social time together. Just to be safe. Even if not a part of the team I managed. Additionally, I probably should have had a better understanding of my company's business within the agency.

So … maybe not ethics per se. In fact no intentional breach of any ethics. But certainly could appear to be inappropriate. Maybe even more so if they had kept the business. The lesson—be aware of what's going on. Appearances count.

Misrepresentation of agency services to client

Building trust with our clients is critical to our business success and to retaining and growing the business partnership. In fact, achieving a partnership is very difficult in the current competitive marketplace of working with clients. Data shows that the average time a chief marketing officer stays with a client is less than two years. Thus, the agency will find itself working with many critical contacts with the client, and in order to retain the business will have to present its work in a highly creative, competitive and, I would argue, ethical manner.

What should the agency do, then, when it learns that its professionals have misrepresented, i.e., lied, as to new services that the agency can and will provide to the client? More specifically, let us address what the agency leadership should do when it learns that one of its young professionals has lied to the client, and the chief marketing officer has told the agency it wants and expects the new services?

There are two ethical dilemmas to be dealt with. First, what and who will address this problem with the client? Second, what do we do with respect to the young professional who lied to the client?

With respect to the first dilemma we face a right versus right test. On the one hand we could attempt to provide the new service and avoid any discussion as to the misrepresentation. But, this will cost us time, talent and additional expenses we may not be prepared to deal with and provide.

If we determine that we cannot do the new service, then we must tell the chief marketing officer about the misrepresentation and face the difficult consequences. Who will be sent over to "brief" the client? What will be the message? In our discussion groups with professionals and students the choice overwhelmingly is to tell the client of the misrepresentation. Some groups have suggested that the young professional should make the admission and apology. But, he or she will have little credibility, because of the misrepresentation. Therefore, most in the discussion groups believe that a senior agency official, such as the executive account representative, or even the president of the agency, must make the trip to the client. The question is who will be most trusted by the client?

The next ethical dilemma is what does the agency do with regard to the young professional who lied to the client? Again, we face a right versus right ethical dilemma. Many in my discussion groups take the approach of retaining the employee, even keeping him or her on the account, and taking remedial action to strengthen his or her personal ethics. However, the continued involvement may not be acceptable to the client. Most importantly, the action taken by the agency will be witnessed by the firm's other professionals and will send them a critical message as to the agency's and its leadership's ethical values.

We are told that when a company makes a difficult ethical decision it goes through the company's employees in minutes, no matter whether the company is large or small. "Did you see what they did to him?" Or, "Did you see what they didn't do?" If the young professional's employment is not terminated, the firm's professionals may not believe the ethical values are very important.

One ethical story is on point. A senior ad agency official told of an ethical problem when one of its young professionals obtained competitive information from another agency by misrepresenting who he was in a phone call:

> We had a very young, aggressive professional doing a competitive analysis and he chose on his own, without talking to us, to call the competitor of the client we were doing the work for, as a college student to get information. So, obviously it was over the line. Now we have one person that has made an unethical decision. And so we called the client and told them; we called the competitor and we terminated the employment of the person. We made the decision. We probably could have kept him; it was your first job. But, frankly the lesson of what happened with him resonated so much with the rest of the company that it became an ethical issue that took on a whole different importance. I wrestled with should I give him another chance, but in the end I think we didn't want his ethics in the long term. We didn't put it in his permanent record that he had an ethics violation and my guess is he probably never did it again, but suddenly you're sitting there face to face with that kind of ethics problem.[4]

It is important to note that ethical dilemmas concerning misrepresentations of agency services also involve senior agency and media officials, and sometimes the decisions by the agency itself. As an illustration, I was told by a senior professional at a media buying agency that competitors had "won" travel vacations from publishing companies that had obtained the media business. Unfortunately, unknown to the client, it had been charged more for the media placement to cover the cost of the prize than was offered by other publishers.

This ethical dilemma, fortunately, has been getting much attention and discussion in the industry, including by the American Association of Advertising Agencies (4A's) and the Association of National Advertisers (ANA). The focus has been on the need to develop principles to guide professionals on resolving ethical dilemmas that can arise when purchasing and placing advertising for the client. This includes the necessity for transparency involving the sale and the avoidance of undisclosed rebates to the agency or travel gifts, as discussed above, which could result in the client paying more for the media placement.

The 4A's issued its transparency principles in January 2016 to both emphasize the importance of this ethical business practice and to provide concrete guidance for the industry and its agency members. The scope and purpose of the guides in building client trust, as well as the nine principles reflecting the transparency mandate, are set out as follows:

The 4A's Issues Transparency Guiding Principles of Conduct (Reprinted with permission of 4A's)[5]

Background

The matter of Media Transparency has been a subject of high interest and concern in the media and marketing community and will continue to be so. The 4A's and its members have consistently stated the position that transparency and contract compliance are core principles that must exist between an agency and its clients. Trust is the cornerstone of the agency and client relationship.

Scope

The 4A's working group agreed that transparency covers various subject areas that require extensive collaboration to provide clarity and industry guidance, particularly given the rate of change in the industry. The first priority addresses transparency in the working relationships among clients, agencies and the media, covering the following areas:

- Client
- Agency
- Agency group
- Holding company
- Related companies who may be brought to the media business relationship

The principles cover the business arrangements and agency remuneration practices as well as recommended guidelines for media market participants in the United States. They are intended as principles that should be followed as soon as possible. These principles may evolve over time, particularly as the media and marketing landscape continues to evolve, and, as such, will be revisited. They do not represent mandates—but recommended courses of actions.

The following provides nine individual Transparency Guiding Principles of Conduct.

Transparency Guiding Principles of Conduct 1, 2 and 3 address client/agency-retained relationships for U.S. media planning and buying services:

1. The default principle in all client/agency relationships where the agency is agent and the client is principal is full disclosure and full transparency in media planning and buying, unless there is an exception that the client has agreed to in advance and is covered by a separate agreement. Further, the client/agency agreement should specify that the client is the principal and the agency is the agent:

   - The agent acts according to an agreed-upon scope of authority set out in a client/agency agreement. The principal is bound by what the agent does. The agent is the agency that has been given the authority by the principal, the advertiser-client, to act on its behalf and in its name with third parties, e.g., purchasing media from media owners. The agent acts for the principal with the same authority as if it is the principal. The agency acts on behalf of the client according to the client's stated objectives.
   - The client has full visibility into how/how much the agency and any affiliated/related companies who provide services to the client (including agency group and members of the holding company group) are compensated, and there is full transparency in respect to the cost of media and any other costs or fees passed through to the client. Rebates/non-transparent incentives should be reported and returned to the client.
   - The client pays the agency in sufficient time to permit the agency to meet the client's payment obligations to vendors.
   - The agency endeavors to get the best pricing available in the market, based on factors such as the quantity and type of media being purchased, but does not guarantee pricing.
   - Both agency and client should ensure that their respective personnel understand and are trained to understand the meaning of principal and agent.
   - The majority of client/agency relationships have the agency acting as agent and the client acting as principal. Other models exist where the agency is the principal and these are covered under the second principle.

2. The agency and the client can agree to a fixed price or other pricing arrangements for the agency's other products and services through open and arms-length negotiations. These might include proprietary media (including pre-owned inventory) trading desks, barter, programmatic buying and other future models:

   - The agency should always ensure that the client clearly understands the nature, implications and benefits of any opt-in products and services, including disclosed and non-disclosed models. These should be documented with an opt-in agreement, with a clear explanation of any implications for audit rights, access to the agency's underlying costs and whether the agency is acting for the client as its agent or as principal.

3.   The agency business is governed by contracts with clients. All terms of business between the agency and the client should be documented in a formal written agreements(s), and both parties should comply with the obligations to the other party that are noted in the respective agreement:

- It's incumbent on both clients and agencies to communicate key terms of the contract to those individuals in their respective organizations who will be working on the business and be affected by the contract.
- It's critical that there is a deep understanding of the business model by both clients and agencies and the terms of the contract, particularly for opt-in services. As media becomes more complicated, so do the business models and contract arrangements.

Transparency Guiding Principles of Conduct 4 and 5 below address separate commercial relationships between agencies and media vendors and other suppliers:

1.   The agency (agency group and holding company) may enter into commercial relationships with media vendors and other suppliers on its own account, which are separate and unrelated to the purchase of media as agent for their clients:

- The agency is paid by the media partner for services provided, such as barter, content production or research projects. Where this is the case, the agency may consider such relationships confidential and commercially sensitive.
- The agency should disclose, on a confidential basis to the client, the general barter, content production or research projects. Where this is the case, the agency may consider such relationships confidential and commercially sensitive.
- The agency should disclose, on a confidential basis to the client, the general type of commercial relationships and explain the controls and procedures it has in place to ensure that these relationships are on an arm's-length basis. These commercial relationships reflect services provided by the agency, are kept separate and do not promise or commit to client spending.

- It should be clear that the agency's commercial transactions do not influence communications and media planning and investment recommendations for the client, which should be done on behalf of the client and according to the client's stated objectives.

- If the agency recommends any proprietary media (including pre-owned agency inventory) on a media plan, it should be disclosed as such, and if approved by the client, it should be documented with an opt-in agreement.

2. The agency should disclose and seek the client's acknowledgement of any agency's ownership interest in any entity and details of any of its employees who are directors of any entity that the agency recommends or uses as a provider of products or services to the client. In such cases, when the recommendation is made, the agency should demonstrate that the recommendation is as good as, and preferably better than, other independent alternatives that may be available to the client.

Transparency Guiding Principles 6, 7, 8 and 9 below address client/agency Governance:

1. Rebates and other non-transparent incentives on U.S. media spend are not accepted industry practice in the United States:

- As a best practice, the agency/client agreement should require the agency to report and return to the client any rebates and incentives received by the agency, agency group, holding company or other affiliated companies that are based on either the client's spend alone or on the aggregation of other clients' spend, including the said client's spend.

- Although rebates and non-transparent incentives are acceptable in some other markets outside the U.S., media spend in the U.S. should not contribute in any undisclosed way to rebate payments/arrangements in other markets.

2. Agencies operating in the U.S. should comply with all relevant U.S. laws and regulations, including those that apply as a consequence of the agency's parent company, if any, being publicly listed on a stock exchange:

- Client should ask agency to explain their relevant internal controls, policies and procedures (e.g., gift policies) and agency should comply with such requests.

3. The agency and client should discuss and document appropriate audit rights commensurate with the services and products provided,

recognizing that the agency has confidentiality obligations to its other clients and stakeholders:

- Those agreed audit rights should extend to other members of the agency group that are providing or assisting with the provisions of services to the client under the agency/client agreement. The agency will use reasonable efforts to enforce audit rights on affiliates and subcontractors providing services under the agency/client agreement.
- Audits should be undertaken by reputable auditors that are appropriately certified (i.e., a certified public accounting firm), are independent and unbiased, and who will sign a non-disclosure agreement (NDA) acceptable to the agency.

The NDA will permit verification of findings but restrict the auditor from disclosing the media agency's confidential information to the client and using any information received during the audit other than for the purpose of conducting the audit. The agency shall provide the client and the independent auditor with reasonable assistance.

1. The aforementioned principles will evolve and be applied based on new economic models for buying and selling media that will emerge in the future.

The Association of National Advertisers (ANA) conducted an investigation into the alleged rebates and other non-transparent incentives received by agencies. It found that such practices are "pervasive" and revealed "evidence of a fundamental disconnect in the advertising industry regarding the basic nature of the advertising agency relationship." No specific agencies were named in the study. "The media business system is not transparent and marketers are not getting full disclosure on the information they need to make informed" media decisions, said Bob Liodice, ANA's chief executive. According to the article in *The Wall Street Journal*, "some experts believe the most likely fallout will be that marketers and agencies rework their contracts."[6]

The 4A's principles are designed to provide guidelines for setting up the contractual relationship between the agency and client that will govern the purchase of media time and placement. While not specifying exact contract language the principles make it clear that absolute transparency is mandatory, and that rebates and other non-transparent incentives are not acceptable practice. In fact, according to the guides, the agreement should specify that any such rebates or other non-transparent incentives received by the agency should be reported and turned over to the client (Principle 6). It will be important to consider any and all ethical principles that are developed, including by the Association of National Advertisers or other industry representatives, in this important area of potential ethical disagreement between a client and its agency. The 4A's guidelines make an important contribution to resolving this ethical dilemma.

Ethical dilemmas when the client requests unethical conduct

I have often thought of how a young CEO of a small but growing ad agency would respond to his major client's order to do an unethical activity. On the one hand, it is "right" to tell him no, but on the other hand you might argue that it is "right" to obey and keep most of your agency professionals employed by not losing the account. But, if the young CEO exercises the unethical decision, what values does he have left in his agency and how long will his professionals want to be there?

Let us consider an ethical dilemma that our professionals discuss during ad ethics certificate sessions.

Our agency has a major food manufacturer as a client for whom we have been doing television advertising directed to children. Now the chief marketing officer tells us the client wants to advertise online to children (twelve and under) in order to get the name of the candy brand across to them. He tells our creative team he wants the candy brand to be the winning entry in a video game with no reference to the company.

What are the ethical issues and how should we recommend the ad be structured?

First, we need to address the ethical and legal context in our role as agency for the client. We will be responsible to the consumer, parents and children, for the manner in which this ad is crafted. Also, should the Federal Trade Commission find the ad deceives children, our agency will be joined in the enforcement action and final order against the client if it is found the "agency knew or should have known the ad was deceptive."

As documented earlier, in Chapter 3, ads to children must be done in a fair and appropriate manner so that they understand that, in this case, the video game they are playing is an advertisement directed to them. The FTC requires, and our industry's self-regulation body, the Children's Advertising Review Unit (CARU) supports, that advertising directed to children must take into consideration their limited experience and cognitive development.

The challenge in the client's recommendation is encouraging the children to want the candy brand, and by not naming the company, the children will not understand the persuasive content of the game. So, we are facing what can be termed a "right versus wrong" ethical dilemma for which our decision to do the right thing for the consumer should be clear. In fact, if we go along with the wrong decision, the government might very well sue us.

Yet, we still must deal with the client's recommendation, in this case, to engage in unethical, even illegal conduct. The right versus right ethical dilemma could arise that we need to keep the client so that our professionals will keep their jobs. After all, depending on how strongly the client wants the ad, it may seek other agencies to do it.

When I have put this question to advertising professionals I have gotten realistic and fair answers. One told me there are some who will fear that if they are ethical they will not be competitive with those agencies that are not. However, David Bell, Chair Emeritus of the Publics Group, put it positively: "Tell him no, and find a way to do it ethically."

The conversation with the client will be private and internal. The decision should be given to the chief marketing officer after the ad has been effectively and ethically constructed. Also, the conversation should be with those in the agency whom the chief marketing officer trusts the most. This is a difficult conversation, but much easier than after an unethical/illegal ad has been run, and the FTC comes calling on the agency. Agency professionals have told me that this type of situation often requires formal separation from the client.

Working with clients, products, ads with which we disagree

Among our most difficult ethical dilemmas are selecting the jobs we assign our professionals to do, and accepting those that we decide to take on during our professional careers. Here, again, we are often faced with right versus right decisions that will measure and reveal our ethical values and impact our future careers.

We will remember our own difficult decision-making and its influence on our business and personal lives. During my career, tobacco advertising presented one of the most difficult legal and ethical dilemmas for the government and the professional. I began my career with the government on the side of strict regulation of the advertising and marketing of tobacco products. This included the opportunity to serve as junior attorney at the Federal Trade Commission on a case challenging American Brands. Also, as Associate Director for Advertising Practices at the FTC, I oversaw a lawsuit challenging Brown and Williamson for its advertising that promised lower nicotine levels. I remember well the letter from the company's general counsel that he was "shocked and saddened" by our decision to pursue a complaint against his company's advertising.

Tobacco advertising became the advertising that was most highly regulated by the federal government. First, Congress passed legislation prohibiting its advertising on television with the goal of lowering its viewing by youth and children. Next, print advertising required specific rotating health warnings as to the product's severe health consequences.

Because of the extraordinary health consequences of smoking, there was both a strong ethical case for government action as well as a strong personal case for taking action against tobacco advertising. At the time, I wondered how the many attorneys I encountered working on behalf of the product could "sleep at night." Then, that became my dilemma.

After I moved over to the advertising side of the business, first as SVP for government relations, and later as president and CEO of the American Advertising Federation, I faced the ethical dilemma of supporting tobacco advertising. The major initiative became a strongly supported bill in the House of Representatives to only allow black and white print ads showing only the package of cigarettes with no claims, including no taste claims. I worked with attorneys from the tobacco industry, as well as professionals from ad agencies, in preparing testimony in opposition to the bill.

How did I face this work ethically? I now see it as a classic right versus right conflict. On the one hand, the Supreme Court had ruled that the First Amendment to the Constitution protected truthful advertising. Using color in ads and promoting taste in cigarettes, as long as the health warnings were present, did not make the ads deceptive. Also, there was industry concern that if successful in limiting tobacco advertising, the government would make similar no color ads or claims for other adult products, such as alcohol. But, on the other side of the equation, tobacco could be considered a "unique" consumer product in regard to health concerns.

Also, my association was representing the advertising of our members, including tobacco companies, ad agencies and print media. Yet, personally I found myself supporting a product responsible for severe health consequences.

At the time I justified the support of tobacco advertising by my association and personally by limiting our focus to the Constitutional issue of supporting truthful advertising. In a meeting of lawyers preparing for testimony I made it clear that my organization would not support any other arguments against the bill, including impact on jobs and employment. Still, it was a difficult ethical issue for me, one that I shared with my family, and I was relieved when the issue was no longer pursued in Congress, and the industry in the course of business significantly reduced its advertising in the United States. It presented a defining moment in my career that may well have contributed to my quest for understanding the consequences of resolving ethical dilemmas.

Personal ethical dilemmas also involve the content and themes of the ads, and even public service campaigns, we are requested to create. The following illustration is an actual controversial PSA campaign the state of Georgia began in 2012. I will include the response and feelings given in our ad ethics certificate sessions.

A State of Georgia health agency requested the development of what the agency considered to be a realistic and hard hitting PSA campaign to combat childhood obesity, a health issue that affects 25% of the state's children. Up to this point they had focused on PSA campaigns against unhealthy foods. Now they wanted an aggressive TV, outdoor and print campaign that would show actual overweight children in its fight against obesity. There was opposition, including from children's advocacy groups, who believe this will stigmatize overweight kids, causing them to be mocked by other kids.

What are the ethical issues presented and what should be our final recommendation to the state organization, and to our agency leadership? The agency began by putting together proposed ads. One includes an overweight twelve-year-old African-American boy talking with his overweight mother. The script: "Mama, why am I fat?"

Let us review this ethical dilemma from a right versus right analysis, although there may be some that see it as simply "right versus wrong." There are two very powerful sides. On the one hand, obesity is now seen as a major health crisis in the United States with the need to encourage adults and children to take effective action against it. The crisis in Georgia is seminal with 25% of its youth obese. This will impact their health now and as adults, and the capabilities of the government and private healthcare programs.

Even recognizing the severity and urgency of the situation, most of our discussion groups were reluctant to cast actual overweight children in the PSA campaign. The fear of stigmatizing such children in the real world just seemed too great a consequence. While unfair racial stereotyping could be avoided by using children of all races, the negative results are enormous. Most discussion groups suggested continuing to educate parents and children about the extreme health consequences of over-eating, and continuing to encourage corporate sponsorship of youth sporting and physical education programs to get children to adopt a healthy lifestyle.

Yet, the State of Georgia found that the health and PE programs were not working, and that the state continues with a crisis in which nearly one million of its youth are overweight. The state began the new $25 million campaign, "Stop Sugarcoating It, Georgia," as part of a 5-year anti-obesity effort. The ads are modeled after anti-smoking campaigns intended to shock the audience. "It has to be harsh. If it's not, nobody's going to listen," says Linda Matzigheit, vice president of Children's Healthcare of Atlanta, the pediatric hospital running the campaign. But some question the strategy. According to Rodney Lyn of Georgia State University's Institute of Public Health, "This campaign is more negative than positive."[7]

We turn to the ethical choices our professionals have in working on ad and PR campaigns that trouble them personally. Both the professional and his supervisor face right versus right dilemmas. If the company decides to take on the campaign the supervisor's choices may be limited. He or she simply may not have professional staff available to release the professional from a particular account, and if the professional is taken off the account, is there another campaign for him or her to work on? There is also severe pressure on the professional to take on the campaign because of a fear of job loss.

Difficult or not, as has been noted earlier, the decision will be a defining moment for the company, supervisor/manager, and professional. Taking on the highly sensitive product or campaign will go a long way in defining the ethics and values of the company and manager. In this regard, as noted earlier, your manager, in his/her decisions, sets the company's ethics and values. A pre-set company policy on whether, and under what circumstances, a professional can decide not to work on a particular campaign or product can be helpful.

Still, the professional's decision will be a defining moment in his or her career and will impact the future. This is why these decisions should be made after full consideration and based on how strongly held are the ethical beliefs influencing the decision.

Unethical professional conduct within the client or agency

Major ethical dilemmas often turn on how our professionals treat each other, and clients, and how clients and managers treat them. This goes beyond the important laws that govern sexual advances and personal threats to safety. And, often we are concerned with "right versus wrong" actions. Decisions made will have a pronounced impact on the value system and morale of the professional staff.

An illustrative example told to me by Linda Thomas Brooks, a senior advertising professional, concerned her interview with a major agency. She had done all of her research in advance, and noticed that one of the agency's major clients was no longer with the agency. When she asked an interviewer, "Why?" he told her: "Because of the way the client was treating the agency professionals." As noted earlier, this ethical decision had gone through the agency within minutes. He told her, "The employees were first shocked because of the loss of revenue, but then they applauded."

A president and CEO of an ad agency told me of another powerful incident involving the conduct of a senior manager. The manager continued mistreating employees after complaints and counseling had taken place. When it was clear he might be fired, the cry went up, "Do not fire the manager, because the clients respect his professional abilities and their success." Nevertheless, the president terminated the manager because of the unethical and negative effects on his agency and professionals. And, he reported that there were no negative consequences.

Oftentimes, problems can be overcome by honest counseling with an offending employee and everyone wins. One manager told me of how a situation involving the unethical interactions of a senior professional with company staffers was overcome through a series of difficult discussions that resulted in a last chance, Performance Improvement Agreement (PIA). This occurred because the agency leadership was willing to deal with the situation and hold firm to doing the right thing.

We also end this chapter on a positive note. Ethical dilemmas involving serious professional interactions between clients, and within the business, can be resolved, just as are content and dissemination ethical dilemmas, by companies that recognize the importance of establishing and conducting an internal ethical value mission to "Do the Right Thing." The next chapter helps to explain how that can be accomplished.

Questions and reflection

1. The author cites Joseph Badaraco in his book, *Defining Moments*, as stating that "right versus right" ethical dilemmas often reveal the basic values of a company, manager or professional. Discuss one of the dilemmas presented—or one of your own—that provided such a "defining moment."

2. What was the lesson taken by the professional in his story of the ethical conflict he experienced between business and personal relationships?

3. What are the two primary ethical dilemmas to be resolved when it is learned one of our agency professionals has misrepresented or misled one of our clients?

4. What are the "right versus right" dilemmas in determining whether to conduct unethical business requested by a client? What are ways we could respond ethically?

5. Discuss how you, as an agency professional, would respond to the "right versus right" ethical dilemma presented by the State of Georgia's mission to combat childhood obesity.

6. In the 4A's principles of conduct regarding billing for agency services, including media placement, what role does "transparency" play and what is the position on rebates and other non-transparent incentives?

Notes

1 Kidder, Rushwood, *How Good People Make Tough Choices*, New York: HarperCollins, 1995, p. 13.
2 Badaracco, Joseph, *Defining Moments, When Managers Must Choose between Right and Right*, Boston, MA: Harvard Business School Press, 1997, p. 13.
3 Badaracco, *Defining Moments*, pp. 6–7.
4 David Bell, Chair Emeritus, IPG, AAA Conference, March 15, 2012.
5 "The 4A's Task Force Issues Transparency Guiding Principles of Conduct," January 28, 2016, www.prnewswire.com/news-releases/the-4as-task-force-issues-transparency-gui ding-principles-of-conduct-300211716.html.
6 "Ad Business Full of Nontransparent Practices, Study Finds," Suzanne Vranica, June 7, 2016, www.wsj.com/articles/ad-business-full-of-nonstransparent-practices-study-finds-14653 03654.
7 Lohr, Kathy, January 9, 2012, heard on All Things Considered, "Controversy Swirls Around Harsh Anti-Obesity Ads," *NPR*, http://www.npr.org/programs/all-things-con sidered/2012/01/09/144899755/.

8

INSPIRING AND ACHIEVING ENHANCED ADVERTISING ETHICS

> Advertisers and their agencies, and online and offline media, should discuss privately potential ethical concerns, and members of the team creating ads should be given permission to express internally their ethical concerns.
>
> *IAE Principle 8*

Now that I have covered why ad ethics is important to the consumer and to our professionals, and the ethical dilemmas now being faced, this concluding chapter details how we can inspire and achieve the practice of enhanced ad ethics. In writing it I am indebted to advertising professionals who have explained the inner-workings and pressures found in the competitive businesses that make up the advertising world. This has been important because the role of this book is to serve as both an ethical discussion and a pragmatic guideline as to how to practice and achieve enhanced ethics. I begin with the importance of the business culture.

Creating ethical cultures is everyone's business

First, we need to create ethical cultures within our businesses that will guide and motivate our professionals. As Linda Thomas Brooks puts it: "We should be guiding and motivating industry professionals, and that behavior will have a halo on the consumer reaction to our industry as well."

Turning to our experts in ethics we learn first from Gene Ahner who stresses: "A business organization is more than a group of people who happen to be contractually related to the company. We are, or must become, a community of shared values if we are to succeed."[1]

Rush Kidder, who established the Institute for Global Ethics, put it this way: "It is all about articulating shared values and developing a vision for the future—since that, after all, is how consensus is built and gridlock broken."[2]

It is imperative that our supervisors and managers understand and buy into the company's values. Ethicist Joseph Badaracco urges: "Managers are the ethics teachers in their organizations. Their decisions and actions send continuous cumulative messages to their organizations about how things really work and about how to get ahead."[3]

These business values or credos often come from the founder(s) and executive leaders of the company. A prime example is Leo Burnett, who is often cited in this book on ethics. He set the primary value: "When a man knows deep in his bones what is right, and keeps acting on it, he avoids the trap of compromise—he remains incorruptible." He also urged: "Ethics is at the center of how we express a brand."[4]

The Institute for Advertising Ethics also articulates the values and principles that can assist an advertising firm to establish its cultural vision and heritage. The Preamble to the IAE Principles and Practices for Advertising Ethics states:

> The explosion of new technologies is changing the marketing and advertising landscape both domestically and globally. New media, new ideas, new challenges, new cultural opportunities are swirling around the industry and impacting the way it does business.
>
> The one constant is transparency, and the need to conduct ourselves, our businesses, and our relationships with consumers in a fair, honest, and forthright manner.
>
> This is especially true in today's often hostile environment, with revelations of wrongdoing in particular industries and government programs resulting in an erosion of public confidence and trust in all of our institutions.
>
> It is particularly fitting in such times that we remind ourselves of the ethical behavior that should guide our personal and business conduct.
>
> The eight Principles and Practices presented here are the foundation on which the Institute for Advertising Ethics (IAE) was created. They are based on the premise that all forms of communication, including advertising, should always do what is right for consumers, which in turn is right for business as well. For while we are in an age of unparalleled change, this overriding truth never changes.[5]

Howard Bell, President Emeritus of the American Advertising Federation and Member of the Advertising Hall of Fame, wrote the Preamble. He developed and communicated his high ethical standards during his over twenty years of service as president of AAF, and prior to that as head of the National Association of Broadcasters self-regulation program.

The Preamble serves as an excellent value statement for today's advertising clients, agencies, media and suppliers. It emphasizes the importance and need for enhanced ethics in a time of both opportunity and challenge as we engage in digital communications. At the same time we are experiencing skepticism from the public, as to business and government. The Preamble calls for us to announce to the consuming public that we will be open and honest in all of our business interactions. Transparency in all aspects of our advertising and PR messages has never been more important.

This is a clear statement of the need for enhanced advertising ethics that comes from the top of the organization and down through its managers. The company's values must also show how the firm's professionals are expected to accomplish the goal of enhanced ethics. Adoption and support of the IAE's eight ethical principles can provide the foundation for moving forward on how to do it. The IAE webpage also provides instructions for how the IAE preamble and principles can be simply adopted to help establish a culture of ethical values for the company.

American Advertising Federation Ethics and Principles[6]

The AAF, the advertising industry's trade association representing local advertising federations, college chapters and leading clients, agencies and media companies, has been a source for how to practice and inspire advertising ethics since March of 1984 when it published its ethics and principles. This has been a strong guideline for me, as it represents many of the important cases and findings that the government, including the FTC, promulgated in the 1970s and 1980s as part of the then new consumer protection movement to avoid deception and unfairness in advertising.

- **Truth:** Advertising shall tell the truth, and shall reveal significant facts, the omission of which would mislead the public.
- **Substantiation:** Advertising claims shall be substantiated by evidence in possession of the advertiser and advertising agency prior to making the claims.
- **Comparisons:** Advertising shall refrain from making false, misleading, or unsubstantiated statements or claims about its competitor or his/her products or services.
- **Bait Advertising:** Advertising shall not offer products or services for sale unless such offer constitutes a bona fide effort to sell the advertised products or services and is not a device to switch consumers to other goods or services, usually higher priced.
- **Guarantees and Warranties:** Advertising of guarantees and warranties shall be explicit, with sufficient information to apprise consumers of their principal terms and limitations or, when space and time limitations preclude such disclosures, the advertisement should clearly reveal where the full text of the guarantee or warranty can be examined before purchase.
- **Price Claims:** Advertising shall avoid price claims which are false and misleading, or savings claims which do not offer provable savings.

- **Testimonials:** Advertising containing testimonials shall be limited to those of competent witnesses who are reflecting a real and honest opinion or experience.
- **Taste and Decency:** Advertising shall be free of statements, illustrations or implications which are offensive to good taste or public policy.

Business ethicist Gene Ahner notes the importance of the role professional associations, like the Institute for Advertising Ethics and AAF, perform in enabling professionals to achieve ethical decision-making. "Most professions have developed associations that set standards and provide legitimacy. These associations set principles of ethical conduct that transcend the individual business. In case of conflict, the standards of the profession should prevail over the business expediency of the moment, even though the business is paying the salary. More and more professions identify obligations that come not from a company but from the profession itself."[7] Positive illustrations are the legal profession with the state Bar Codes of Ethics, and journalists with the Journalist Creed.

Fostering an internal process for practicing the company's ethical values

Again, I quote the learning of Linda Thomas Brooks, a successful and recognized leader of our industry: "Just as we plan a successful frequency of our client's ad messages, we need to communicate our ethical messages with frequency as well. It's not enough to say it once or put it in the employee's handbook and consider it done. Our standards need to be reinforced in a systemic way."

Ethicists and theologians would agree. "Reinhold Niebuhr and his colleagues thought that ethical statements were worthless unless they told how to change one's immediate environment for the better or the right thing to do in a real-world situation."[8]

Here are ways that advertising and PR firms are communicating their business values. The Martin Agency publishes its business values in the *Little Red Book* that is distributed to all professionals. Ketchum, as a large public relations organization with many employees, emphasizes the importance of its values system with a video directly from the CEO, teaches all new hires with a webinar in the first three months, and conducts a mandatory quiz annually to check that everyone knows the ethical values. Smaller firms could do the same with live presentations by the executive leadership and one-on-one and small group training. The Ketchum code of business conduct is now presented.

Ketchum Code of Business Conduct

The Ketchum Code of Business Conduct outlines the policies by which all personnel (including employees, independent contractors and freelancers) are expected to conduct business on behalf of Ketchum and its clients, and applies worldwide to Ketchum and its related companies. The Code serves the dual purpose of providing not only guidance in specific situations, but also the principles and values that guide all aspects of employment with Ketchum.

Some highlights:

Truth and Accuracy in Communications—I will present our clients' products, services or positions truthfully and accurately based upon the information made available to me from our clients and I will not knowingly misrepresent them. I am committed to complete transparency of sponsorship in all communications as outlined in the Ketchum Disclosure Guidelines.

Confidential Information—I will keep all proprietary and non-public information concerning our clients' products, strategies, plans and other business information in the utmost confidence and not disclose any proprietary and non-public information to anyone outside of Ketchum without the permission of our clients.

Gifts, Excessive Entertainment and Other Payments—I will extend no cash payments, loans, extravagant gifts, excessive entertainment or other payments to the employees, agents or associates of our clients, and I will honor our clients' policies on gifts and entertainment. I understand that Ketchum defines "extravagant gifts" and excessive entertainment as those that would tend to cause individuals to make or retain business relationships that they may not otherwise make or retain. I will seek the counsel of management when I am in doubt about any specific gift or entertainment.

Employee, Social Media/Blogging—Client information is confidential.

Always act in a professional manner.

You are responsible for anything you do. Think twice.

Pay attention to fact checking, grammar and copyright.

You are always representing Ketchum.[9]

Providing our professionals with our company ethical values is only the first step in assuring that they are understood and practiced on a daily basis. Our principles are necessary and useful, but must be applied daily to right versus right ethical dilemmas. We must establish the expectation that our professionals will engage in ethical decision-making, i.e. they will take the time to discuss and provide their concerns regarding the ad copy and business interactions in which they are involved daily.

In my college classes on ethics, I have asked students to express their ethical concerns about particular ads. For instance, I asked creative classes their views on a print PSA with the good intention of getting young people to vote in the last national election.

Several expressed concern that the ad depicted violence against women and that, therefore, the message would be rejected. As one of the women stated, "I don't care how good the ad message is; I will not pursue it if it contains violence against women." In role-playing I asked if they would express those concerns to me, as their account executive, before I talked with the client. The answer: "Yes, if you give me permission."

What I learned was placed into our final advertising principle 8. It is critical that our professionals know they can express ethical concerns about the ads or client interactions—and that they are expected to do so—or they just might not do so.

In addition, we must give our professionals guidance and support in resolving ethical dilemmas. As ethicist Joseph Badaracco puts it, "Have I orchestrated a process that can make the values I care about become the truth for my organization?" He stresses the importance that an ethical decision works, has cash value, and has been determined through a valid decision-making process.[10]

This process must be practical and doable in a competitive industry such as advertising. Business ethicist Gene Ahner provides an excellent illustration from Texas Instruments, the hi-tech semiconductor design and manufacturing company:

- Is the action legal?
- Does it comply with your best understanding of our values and principles?
- If you do it, will you feel bad?
- How will it look in the newspaper?
- If you know it's wrong, don't do it, period!
- If you're not sure, ask.
- Keep asking until you get an answer.[11]

When the manager and his/her team are faced with the ethical decision-making it is important they understand and accept the ethical value underlying the decision. This includes looking at both sides of the right versus right dilemma and understanding and discussing competing views and interpretations of the situation or problem. This certainly includes the impact the decision will have on the revenues and strength of the company, as well as impact on the professional staff.

The decision by James Burke, Chairman of Johnson & Johnson, to pull all containers of Tylenol from the market in 1982 is highlighted by ethicist Joseph Badaracco as a "defining moment" that "revealed, tested, and renewed the company's commitment to its ethical values and its corporate credo."[12] The action was taken after six people in the Chicago area had died from taking poisoned Tylenol capsules. While the action cost J & J the retail value of $100 million, Burke analyzed both sides of the right versus right ethical dilemma and determined what would be best for consumers, the company and its value system.

Ethicist Badaracco sees Burke's talent as understanding what J & J's action would mean to the consuming public:

> James Burke, with his long and successful experience in marketing relied upon this talent in a crucial early moment of the 1982 Tylenol episode. Some managers at Johnson & Johnson argued that the company faced a "Tylenol problem"—a business problem affecting a single product. Burke's diagnosis was different. He sensed, quite correctly, that the media would run with the story as a "Johnson & Johnson problem," that the government would view it as a public health problem, and that the company's customers would define the problem as simply fear of Johnson & Johnson products.[13]

The ethical manner in which J & J handled the Tylenol crisis thirty-four years ago can be a model for companies and their executives facing ethical/legal challenges today.

While it is best if ethical deliberations take place before a major challenge becomes public, companies can still work to rebuild their reputations through doing the right thing in creating a new culture for their brand and professionals.

Rebuilding consumer trust after the VW emissions cheat device scandal

At this writing the Volkswagen emissions scandal is unprecedented in the scope of the international government investigations and negative consumer reaction. It began on September 18, 2015, when the United States Environmental Protection Agency (EPA) issued Notice of Violation of the Clean Air Act to German automaker Volkswagen Group. The company had programmed their model year 2009 through 2015 turbocharged direct injection (TDI) diesel engine so that U.S. standards for nitrogen oxides emission were met only during laboratory emissions testing. NO emissions during driving were up to 40 times higher. The EPA classified this programming as a defeat device, prohibited by the Clean Air Act. An estimated eleven million cars worldwide, and 500,000 in the United States, included such programming. Volkswagen became the target of regulatory and criminal investigations in the U.S. and Europe, and faces up to $46 billion in potential fines. Its stock plunged in value by a third, and the Group CEO resigned. The company announced it would spend U.S.$7.3 billion on new devices to be refitted in a major recall campaign. An internal memo has surfaced indicating that the company's top executives might have known about the defeat device investigation as early as May 2014.[14]

The ethical and legal scandal continued to grow as U.S. and German regulators spoke in regard to their investigations. It was announced that the EPA had added Porsche to the list of automobiles fitted with devices intended to thwart pollution controls. "Volkswagen has once again failed its obligation to comply with the law that protects clean air for all," Cynthia Giles, the EPA's assistant administrator for enforcement, said at a news conference.[15]

And, the German Federal Motor Transport Authority (K.B.A.) stated that the software used in the EA189, the original diesel engine implicated in the scandal, "is an illegal defeat device according to the K.B.A.'s legal interpretation."[16]

On November 18, 2015, Volkswagen ran a full page ad in the *Washington Post* headlined: "We're working to make things right." The ad reports that "over the past several weeks, we've apologized to you, our loyal customers" about the incident, which the ad terms: "the 2.0L VW diesel *emissions issue*" (emphasis added). The copy goes on: "As we work tirelessly to develop a remedy, we ask for your continued patience." The company then offers its "affected TDI owners" a $500 Volkswagen Visa Card, a $500 Volkswagen Dealership Card, and no-charge 24-hour roadside assistance for three years. The ad concludes with "We sincerely hope you see this as a first step toward *restoring your invaluable trust*" (emphasis added).

This, of course, is the issue that must be resolved: the re-building of consumer trust by the consuming public, and in particular, those VW diesel owners directly affected by what has been termed a willful intent to defeat government clean air emission testing. Shortly after the Volkswagen CEO resigned, the *Washington Post* ran an article quoting a troubled VW diesel owner: "The CEO resigning, it doesn't really impact me. I want to know what they're actually going to do for all of these supposedly clean diesel car owners. I don't want this car. It makes me feel sick that I've been driving this car for about four-and-a-half years and belching all these toxic fumes into the atmosphere."[17]

Volkswagen of America has reported that it is creating an independent claims program for the owners of nearly 600,000 diesel vehicles that emit up to 40 times legally allowable emissions. The deputy administrator of the program said it is too early to say if the program would offer buybacks to vehicle owners, cash, or other specific compensation for mileage or performance harmed by emissions repairs.[18] Volkswagen—as it faces and responds to worldwide government investigations, lawsuits and recalls of millions of diesel cars—must also look to the future. A new leadership attitude must create a new way of thinking in terms of how it interacts with its professionals and, very importantly, consumers from around the world. Certainly, a highly visible credo is required that promises an ethical response to the challenges the company and its professionals will face. Then, VW, following the J & J public model, must build consumer trust through *actions* that demonstrate it is following its credo to "do the right thing" in a competitive marketplace.

The company, as in the case of all companies, must demand that its professionals follow the credo and practice ethics in their right versus right decisions, and enable them to do so by a process that teaches and reinforces decision making when confronting ethical dilemmas. This can include mentoring younger employees by senior professionals who faced, struggled with, and resolved difficult ethical dilemmas.

The mentoring process must be voluntary, both from a standpoint of recruiting senior mentors and encouraging younger professionals to participate. The importance of the one-on-one discussion must be emphasized so that talk will take place in a timely manner amid the high pressure environment found in the ad business. Above all, questions and answers should be kept in private. The important goal in establishing the mentoring process is to create trust so that the company's professionals can learn from the ethical dilemmas experienced from their colleagues.

Ethicist Joseph Badaracco, relying on the teaching of classic ethics, puts it this way:

> Encourage managers to look beyond questions … and search for answers, in the form of rich, detailed stories of actual managers, their dilemmas and choices, and the consequences of their actions. This is a way of under-standing the power of these questions and preparing, as best we can, to answer them well when a right-versus-right conflict arises.[19]

Inspire our professionals with our own ethical stories

When I asked David Bell—in an on camera interview at an American Academy of Advertising Conference—how to inspire advertising professionals, he empha-tically answered that we need to tell them our ethical stories to make them "feel" the importance of ethics, not just provide written rules and regulations. Here is his response:

> I think we have to make the subject of ethics emotional. You know, because when you talk about ethics in a rational fashion everyone just nods. We have to make it a cause that talks about how the crafted practice we choose for our careers rides 100% on that. And if we want to be successful, we want our clients to be successful, we want our work to be successful, it has to start with that, so we need to find a way to make the subject emotional.
>
> One of the things we can do is learn how to teach the creation of ethical cultures. I'm talking about cultures in the agency organization and client organization. I spent quite a few years working with Johnson & Johnson and know they believed (in the) need to teach people how to celebrate those ethical choices that people make when the grey choice would have been so easy to make, and that's how you create a culture. When somebody singles somebody out and says do you know what he did or she did, and everybody hears about it; knows the examples, they are like beacons. People say, "Wow, somebody cares about that." I also think singling that out really makes people care about where they work because there are five things that are more important to people in our industry than money and one of them is "I really feel good about coming to work." How can you not feel good about

coming to work when you work at a place that celebrates people who make hard choices that are the right ones. Sometimes people would say in the agency business that companies are known for the clients they turn down more than the clients they accept, or the things they say no to. So, brainstorming how to make emotional right choices sexy is worth all the time we spend on it. You know the stories are (so) believable. We just simply collect, from all the big time practitioners we know, the stories of those hard choices and just tell these stories.

I'll tell you my favorite about a very big company that shall remain nameless; it was competing with our agency for the same account. And down to two finalists. First they present in the AM, then us in the PM. Big time important client. In fact a highly respected journalistic enterprise, major city newspaper. So this highly respected competitor had made its presentation. Afterward the publisher walked into our office and said, "You have our business." Wait, wait, we have been preparing for weeks our presentation. He said, "Would you like to know why?" I said, "Please." He said, "Your competitor down the street in their presentation made disparaging remarks about your agency and we don't operate that way." Wow! Now take ten of those stories and the glances always come back positive. Look at what happened to Tylenol when they were the first to deal with the crisis right. And look at the companies that haven't dealt with the crisis right. Even knowing that happened. Jim Burke is in the Hall of Fame. Right now. It comes back. The whole thing comes back. People that act like that, get it back.[20]

David Bell's story is a good one for us to think about and discuss. Remember, he is cited at the very beginning of this book for urging, "Trust is the currency of our business—and—Ethics is the engine of Trust." He believes in the importance of enhanced advertising ethics, and his story emphasizes that resolving ethical dilemmas is personal and emotional.

Other prominent advertising professionals have provided their ethical stories that can inspire us to want to "do the right thing" ethically. Tim Love, former Vice Chair of the Omnicom Group of advertising agencies, has provided me with several stories from his 41-year advertising career. The first story details his ethical response to a major dilemma in his first year of practice when working on a major account and client (renamed):

Excite Dishwashing Liquid
    In fall 1972, after just two months in the advertising agency business, with Dancer Fitzgerald Sample in New York. I was assigned to work on the Johnson and Proctor client's Excite dishwashing liquid.
    Excite was a brand that was launched in the late 1960s on a strategy of hand-mildness for a category that was largely hand washing. While the automatic dishwashing machine for the home appliance market was gaining

acceptance, household penetration of dishwashers was still well under 50% in 1970.

The bulk of household dishwashing occasions were by hand, hence the relevancy of a mildness positioning. Other brands, whose mildness positioning garnered substantial share of the market were Ivory Liquid, Palmolive Liquid and Lux.

Excite's product proposition when launched was a technical advantage on skin mildness and safety combined with a noticeable fresh peach scent. The advertising proposition used to launch Excite in the US was "New Excite Dishwashing Liquid for a Peaches and Cream Complexion." This proposition quickly gained a foothold in market with a modest 5% market share by the early 1970s about three years after the national expansion of Excite.

At that point, heightened competitive marketing combined with the difficulty for consumers to experience superior mildness with Excite (versus Ivory and Palmolive) saw an erosion in Excite's market share to 1.5%. At that point, product upgrade news was developed in the form of a more fragrant peach scent for Excite. The new proposition behind the upgrade was "Introducing New Improved Peach Excite for a Peaches and Cream Complexion. New Peach Scent."

This fragrance news lifted interest in Excite temporarily behind the introductory sales promotion and increased media that supported the upgrade. The brand saw its share of market briefly go up to 2% and then drop down below 1% after launch. Clearly we needed to rethink the relevancy of Excite's product positioning and strategy.

Careful and exhaustive market research indicated that the mildness sector of the category was being rendered less relevant by accelerating penetration of dishwashers across the country. While automatic dishwashers did not completely eliminate hand washing, the nature of hand washing was increasingly for tough to clean items that could not be put into the dishwasher. The market in essence shifted. This made all mildness brands, Ivory and Palmolive included, less relevant and opened up market opportunity for brands like Joy ("So clean it shines"), Ajax and, later on in the late 1970s, ushered in P&G's Dawn brand ("Takes grease out of your way.").

The challenge for Excite in 1973 was to restage the brand behind a tougher cleaning formula and to move to a performance-based strategic proposition. At that time, Excite developed a new formula that was designed to deliver superior cleaning on "proteinacious" food stains. The most commonly encountered examples were dried egg yolk, spaghetti sauce, backed on grease from cooked meats, etc. Clearly all the research showed that with increased dishwasher penetration the market opportunity going forward for the hand-washing portion of the market was in cleaning efficacy.

As this new formula for Excite was being qualified in market, it needed new advertising to communicate the advantages of the new formula. This is when I was assigned as assistant account executive on the brand. And, my first assignment was to go into a video laboratory at the agency and develop the most impactful demonstrations and visualizations of New Excite's efficacy I could create.

I spent two intense weeks developing a variety of demonstrations designed to show how well the new Excite cleans, even the toughest of cleaning challenges. I experimented in my own kitchen as well as in the agency's video lab. Finally, after two weeks I was ready to put 10 ideas on video tape for my bosses to see and potentially to show to our client.

There was only one visualization I deemed a potential winner. It was simply showing little bits of white paper floating in a bowl of water and how a drop of Excite dramatically released the surface tension on the water driving the little bits of white paper to the edge of the bowl. This was an old science classroom visual to demonstrate surface tension. Any liquid detergent could do this visualization, but no one had used it up to that time. The other 9 demonstrations we put on video tape were less promising, despite using every kind of proteinacious examples I could find.

The only other demonstration I had that showed potential promise was a process demonstration. Specifically, I allowed dining plates, coated with dried egg yolk, spaghetti sauce and bacon grease to sit in a basin full of Excite and hot water over night. Then, in the morning, I videotaped how easily the matter washed off the plates under the faucet with little hand involvement. Many of the people on the team, all men I might add, were impressed that the New Excite seemed to "make dishwashing easier."

My bosses looked at my demonstration tape and immediately invited me to go to Chicago for my first trip to the client. They wanted me to present my findings.

I was excited and very nervous about making this presentation as I knew it was considered a key building point for the work overall on Excite and to sustain the brand.

The meeting in Chicago was deemed a huge success. The client and agency leaders all coalesced around the idea communicated by the "soaking" demonstration of how Excite makes dishwashing easier.

Off to focus groups with consumers (all female) in Milwaukee with prototype television storyboards, a common qualification and learning stage in the advertising and marketing service business.

This was my first business trip to do focus groups in a 41-year career of focus groups and consumer learning. I was invited to these groups as reward for my hard work in creating the product demonstrations. As the junior agency person on the mission, it was my responsibility to write the summary of learning from the focus groups and provide my written summary to our internal agency management team the day after we returned from Milwaukee back to our offices in New York. This meant I had to handwrite the summary (no iPhone or Blackberry's then) on the plane on the way home and spend the next day fine-tuning the observations and my recommendations.

On the flight home, is when it all hit me. We had developed an advertising proposition for the brand that was relevant, "ease of cleaning," but was based on a process that actually depended on making the dishwashing process more arduous and time-consuming. But, how could I tell my bosses this? It would be career suicide to throw this negative assessment into the mix at this stage with no other directions to pursue.

Too much work and momentum from product development to research and business planning for the new already occurred. I thought to myself:

- I am too new at this and maybe I don't see things correctly.
- It isn't my responsibility to decide this.
- Other wiser people at the client and agency seem very committed to the "ease and convenience" proposition. They all heard women in Milwaukee clearly respond positively to the idea of making dishwashing easier.
- My thoughts will draw criticism and raise questions about my viability for Marketing and Advertising.
- Maybe I am missing something. Maybe I am not any good at this business.

In my heart I too heard those women in Milwaukee say they would like a dishwashing detergent that made dishwashing easier. There was no doubt about that. However, it seemed to me there was an important piece of the puzzle that the women were not articulating. I did not think they would really want to increase the labor and process of dishwashing by allowing the dishes to soak in a sink of Excite and water over night. I could not see them positively engaging in the process, which would call for them to finish the dishes in the morning.

The point is that I just did not really believe they would do this. Therefore, they would ultimately see the "Emperor's new clothes" in the proposition. Instead of making dishwashing easier we were asking them to add steps and process to an already arduous task.

I stayed up all night writing that first consumer insight summary covered in self-doubt. After having the one-page memo (following the classic O&P style of management on paper) typed, it was distributed late morning to the whole internal agency team including my immediate boss, his supervisor and the big boss in charge of the whole account group. I was exhausted.

Then, around 4:00pm, the big boss's assistant came to my cubicle and said sort of menacingly, "Larry wants to see you." That meant now.

I knocked on the doorframe to Larry's office and he motioned for me to come in and sit down in front of his desk. He then reached down under his desk and pushed something which corresponded with his office door automatically shutting. It was going to be a very private discussion.

Larry held up the summary I had written and said he had a couple of things he wanted to talk to me about the memo. I gulped and listened intently for his next words: "Are you saying we are doing something unethical on this business?"

Honesty, that was not something I was thinking. It wasn't a word that may have crossed my mind in all the anxiousness over what I was feeling. "I don't think I said that, no. I don't think that is a word I used in my memo," I blurted out to Larry.

Then, I told him: "I just don't think it will work, is all. I just don't see how we can convince consumers that Excite makes dishwashing easier when they have to adopt a more laborious and time-consuming process to receive that benefit."

Larry said: "Good, that's what I thought you were saying. Good memo." And, that was the end of that story. Also the beginning of the end of Excite.

In the famous ad for Cadillac written in 1914 "The penalty of Leadership," the writer says that "leadership draws the white light of introspection" and "that which deserves to live, lives."[21]

The second Tim Love story occurred twelve years later in his career when he had climbed the agency ladder and now was the top agency executive on major accounts. He sets up the ethical dilemma, which is career threatening, and then the way in which he resolved it along with the personal consequences:

The Penalty of Ethics

There are some disturbing consequences one faces when deciding what is ethical or not in the advertising business. This issue is particularly acute because it coexists with a fundamental premise of democracy—the right to freedom of speech—which is an essential tenet of the advertising and marketing communications industry.

How does one decide whether there is merit in expressing an ethical point of view through our behavior? There are ramifications, risks, indeed penalties that come with making a decision that something is unethical and then publically expressing this opinion. The penalties are something that one must weigh, because ethics are such a personal barometer. Everyone has their own personal barometer of what is truthful, fair and beneficial to humankind. This personal barometer is called one's integrity, being truthful to yourself. This was well articulated by Polonius' last words to his son Laertes in Shakespeare's Hamlet: "This above all, to thine own self be true, and it must follow, as the night the day, thou canst not be false to any man." After devoting 41 years in the profession of advertising and marketing communications, I can say upon reflection that Polonius' advice was one of the most consistent and ever-present factors in my career. The example of an ethical dilemma made so poignant for me occurred in 1987, when I was faced with the prospect of doing something very much against my personal barometer of ethics.

Background

This example occurred in 1987 following the acquisition of Dancer Fitzgerald Sample (DFS) in late 1986. DFS was a large privately owned advertising agency in New York, acquired by a publically held agency network. DFS was the 12th largest agency in the U.S. at the time with the biggest New York office of any agency.

This acquisition was a forerunner in creating a global network for clients who were rapidly advancing their business and brands presence across the planet. It was among the first such "mergers" that precipitated a dramatic consolidation in the advertising agency industry. It became clear that the only way DFS could maintain their most valuable client relationships in the U. S. was to expand their service to meet the needs of their client's brands globally. The problem was how to pay for this increased infrastructure when the shareholders of DFS were principally the employees of the agency in the U.S. The quickest way to raise the capital required was to form a relationship, "merge," with a publically held agency network elsewhere or to have its own IPO. The problem with the latter alternative was that it left the agency unconnected globally facing a long-term scenario of expensive acquisitions country by country. Merging became the quickest way for DFS to protect its relationship with its largest clients. Merging was simply a matter of agreeing to the money and how the resulting entity would be managed.

The most senior management of the agency had more at stake, obviously from a financial standpoint. Yet they were further along their life stage in terms of career, funding their kids' college education and taking care of family needs like aging parents and considering their retirement needs. This had the effect of making them far more favorably inclined to "cash out" and less concerned with management control and talent continuity on their client relationships. Selling the agency could offer them the money to retire comfortably and sooner.

Obviously, the context for younger management like myself was significantly different. While the financial impact was substantial, my generation was still in the "becoming" life stage of personal value creation with our clients, a key factor in a professional services business. And since our professional life stage was still at a relatively early stage, we were far more concerned with the impact of management responsibility change and the attendant effect this would have on our ability to continue to grow our personal value in the merged organization.

This divergence of perspectives became acutely real to me in the spring of 1987. Unbeknownst to me, was the enormous ethical dilemma that this would present to me.

At the time of the announced merger in 1986, I was the youngest member of the DFS New York management board and responsible for several client relationships. My largest role was on a major part of the agency's P&G business, a founding client of DFS in 1923. My other important client management responsibilities were a beverage spirits client, an important public service initiative for the National Counsel for Adoption in Washington D.C., and a start-up client in the rapidly developing frozen entree market. My responsibility on P&G required me to report to a new senior manager who also was in charge of new business development. (I will call him Bill in this case. Not his real name.)

My responsibility for the beverage spirits client required me to report to another Managing Director of the Agency (Fred), who had very little involvement with the client during the winning of the account and ongoing work we were doing for them. The frozen entree client was a close personal friend with the President of DFS (Steve), who asked me to be responsible for the day to day leadership on this new brand. Four client relationships with four different bosses: a prescription for confusion and potential concern over fealty to each manager.

The reporting complexity was further exacerbated when our president asked me to assume responsibility for a fifth client, I will call Client #5. Client #5 had put DFS on warning over complications it encountered with an earlier "merger" with another of its agencies and an issue over client conflict. Client #5's CEO and Chief Marketing Officer had expressed high regard for me to Steve. Steve asked me to help "save" our Client #5 business.

Because client relationships are the most valuable aspect of any professional services business, the "merger" of DFS with their other agency network also posed some significant complications of management leadership between the leaders of the two merged companies. As often happens in a problematic merger, it was decided to have two people sharing the office of CEO of the merged company. In other words, DFS's CEO, Steve, was made joint CEO with the CEO of the merged partner company.

An Ethical Dilemma Presents Itself

On Thursday April 17, 1987, I was in my office at DFS in New York busily preparing for an upcoming meeting with the Board of Directors of our beverage spirits client which was due to take place the following Tuesday April 21st at their headquarters in Louisville, Kentucky. I had been invited by the Chairman of the Board and CEO to present an update to the Board on our work for their brand of vodka, their brand of schnapps and cordials and to give a status report on the launch of a new wine-cooler brand which we handled for them. Around 2:00pm I received a phone call from Steve that he and several other DFS managers were meeting in our main conference room on a new business opportunity. He asked me to put down what I was doing and immediately come to that new business meeting.

As I knocked on the door and walked into the conference room, I could see that the meeting involved about 10 of our most significant DFS leaders. Including Steve and Bill, our new business leader, and the person to whom I was reporting on one of my clients, Fred to whom I reported on our beverage spirits client, the agency's overall Creative Director, our primary Executive Creative Director, our head of research, and another account management leader, Mitch, who like me, ran a significant part of the agency relationships and who often got involved in new business solicitations, called a "pitch."

As I entered the room, Steve jumped up from his seat at the board room table and said: "Get in here, Love. We are preparing a pitch for the Henry Welker Spirits" (a large beverage alcohol company). "Love, we need you to tell us everything you know about the liquor category from your experience," he said.

I have thought long and hard about why I experienced an immediate feeling of alarm and discomfort at that precise moment standing there in front of my colleagues seated at the table. Maybe it was the lack of civility our CEO exhibited towards me in front of everyone, but I don't think so. I knew Steve was just being his usual brash self. No, what jumped up in my stomach was a feeling that I was being asked to do something that was potentially against the best interest of our beverage spirits client. I needed to know more before jumping to that conclusion. It is not unusual for a potential client to seek a meeting with a competitor's agency in order to gain insight and knowledge about their competitor.

I asked Steve, if we knew what Henry Welker Spirits was interested in talking to us about. He said it was for the Henry Welker line of schnapps and cordials. While still standing before the table of participants, I informed Steve that Henry Welker was a direct competitive conflict with our current spirits client. I told him that while the current client was smaller than Henry Welker, it was an important business our client had recently invested heavily in with new marketing and packaging. I stated our solicitation of Henry Welker would be potentially problematic and that our client would not appreciate hearing of our talking to their direct competitor.

I suggested we treat the Henry Welker opportunity carefully and look at the first meeting as a general agency credentials presentation with no information sharing based on experience. I suggested since I would be in a meeting with the current client on the very same day of Henry Welker's visit, that it would be appropriate for Steve to give our current client a "heads-up" call informing them that we would be meeting with Henry Welker the following Tuesday, that we had no idea what they were interested in talking to us about from their portfolio and given the diversity of their portfolio, we decided to take this "familiarization meeting." We simply wanted them to know in advance of the meeting and to assure them that we would in no way jeopardize our existing relationship. We would not include any people currently working on their business in this familiarization meeting. Finally, I added that the beverage alcohol industry was characterized by its competitive nature among distilleries and that our client would be very upset if they were to ever hear about our meeting with their "blood competitor" without the courtesy of a "heads up" from us.

You could have heard a pin drop in the room. People sat there staring at me. For what seemed an eternity. Then Steve asked me how big our current client was in terms of revenue compared to Henry Welker. I told him it was a small fraction of our revenue and small compared to the potential of Henry Welker.

He replied that we should not tell our current client until we knew we had something concrete in our hands from Henry Welker. He suggested we could then go to the client and negotiate an increase in compensation or switch clients to Henry Welker. Our new business leader, Bill, quickly added that current client was less important than the opportunity with Henry Welker and that he believed we could potentially get more business because of the overall size of Henry Welker. He recommended in front of the assembled group of colleagues that we not inform our current client.

At this point my initial reaction of alarm and stomach sickness shifted into a calm, quiet feeling. What came out was from my heart. I said: "This is exactly what is wrong with our industry today. Clients see their agencies increasingly attracted by huge sums of money, where management continuity and trust with client relationships takes a back seat to the financial gains from merging and going public. If it got out that we were soliciting clients who are in direct conflict with existing clients, our fundamental business character would be questioned by all our other clients. We must protect our fundamental character and the hard earned trust we earned in these relationships."

One of the people staring at me from the board room table said: "Hear, hear." I could have kissed him as it shook me into the real time, present, and the challenge I had just expressed to our CEO and the new business leader.

Steve replied that I shouldn't worry about any of that, that I was "way over-reacting" and that he knew what he was doing. He said we would go ahead and pitch Henry Welker and that I would be expected to give the pitch team a complete briefing on the beverage alcohol category the following morning. He dismissed me without further discussion to go back to my office and prepare for the briefing the next morning at 9am sharp.

I have often thought about that long, lonely walk back to my office and the complexity of feelings I had. Overall, I felt sad. Sad that the company I loved had changed so much. Sad and angry that I was being forced to confront my own principles with what my management was telling me to do, with self-doubt and fear. I had a significant home mortgage, a wife and three little children depending on me. They were counting on me to provide for their safety and wellbeing. Yet, I also felt they were expecting me to do the right thing, to be ethically responsible in my behavior.

A very loud alarm was ringing in my head. It was telling me to run as fast as I could away from my company and the whole conundrum over client relationship integrity.

Cooler Heads Prevail

That evening on the way home I stopped off at my former boss and mentor's house. I wanted his advice about my thoughts of resigning from the agency the following morning, instead of giving the orientation. My mentor prevailed in convincing me that a precipitous resignation would feel good for about a half hour and that it really was not the appropriate way to care for my family. He agreed that the situation merited my looking to leave the agency, but to do so in less of the heat of feelings. Importantly, he reminded me that resigning would prevent me from receiving a $300,000 incentive plan the agency had offered me to remain for five years after the merger. This was a lot of money for a kid from Ohio whose father had been a used television repairman and who was already living very close to the edge with a mortgage and three children to educate. He convinced me to do the orientation the next morning but also take steps to begin to look elsewhere for another job.

In thinking about my mentor's advice, I was grateful that his reaction confirmed my professional feelings about the ethical dilemma I perceived. I was also grateful that he could head off my frustration and anger over the dismissive attitude and behavior exhibited by my company's CEO. My mentor's reasoning to protect my family first was very much appreciated. Not surprisingly, when I arrived home, my wife and best friend was terrified that I would quit and urged me to swallow my feelings while beginning to look for a new company to join.

The next day, on Friday, feeling very uncomfortable and oddly sort of unclean, I briefed my DFS colleagues as best I could. I left that evening on the train for our home in Westchester County, New York, feeling sad about the whole affair and wondering what could happen if our current client found out that my company was pitching a competitor at the very same time I was attending their board meeting the following Tuesday in Louisville. I did not sleep much that weekend. I did not feel good about myself or my company, the company I had loved since joining out of graduate school, the company where I flourished for the first 14 years of my professional career. I remember it was Easter weekend. The Easter Egg Hunt we took our kids to only temporarily got my mind off of my sad feelings about what had happened to shake my love and faith in my company. I kept telling myself it was time for me to grow up and that I was investing far too much personal equity in expecting my company, or any company, to be perfect. I kept thinking the age-old rationale—"It's just business."

On Monday morning I caught my usual 6:27am train to Manhattan. My thoughts continued to whine and spin over the dilemma I continued to weigh. It occurred to me that Steve may have simply been defending his CEO stature when I confronted him in front of our colleagues about the issue of conflict of interest. This ethical question was obviously not something he appreciated being raised in front of others, especially since the dual CEO role was heightening competition between CEOs for the eventual, inevitable decision to have one CEO.

That is when I decided I should try to see Steve that morning, privately. I reasoned that he would find my position more agreeable in the privacy of his office and that he would agree with my request that he notify our current client about the visit of Henry Welker to our offices while also reassuring him of our commitment as evidenced by the call. In fact, I believed Steve would appreciate how I was seeing this situation as an opportunity to enhance our relationship with our current client by our transparency.

I did not even know if Steve would be in the office Monday. But as the train sped along to Manhattan that morning, I was suddenly hit with the "what if" question. What if I was able to see Steve and what if he continued to disagree with my perspective?

In advance of this potential outcome, I felt I would need to be prepared to submit my resignation. I could not see any other way to reflect and underscore my feelings. I knew this was a question of ethics for me. I needed to test my commitment to these feelings, even if Steve insisted on his position. I concluded that I should have a letter of resignation on me in case the discussion did not go the way I hoped.

By the time the train got into Grand Central Station I had drafted the handwritten letter. (No computers or smart phones in 1987.) I handed the draft letter to my assistant to type asking her to keep the nature of the letter private between her and me. She brought the typed version into my office in tears. I had not thought about what my departure might mean for her or the other people who reported to me. I assured her I did not think it would come to fruition, but asked her to get me some empty moving boxes in case I had to leave that day. Then I called Steve's office to see if he was in and if he had some time to see me. He was in and he would see me at 11 a.m.

When I went into Steve's office, I closed his office door behind me. I told him I had to discuss the conflict issue with him and that I was sorry I had brought this issue up to him in front of our colleagues. I told him I needed him to hear me out on this as it continued to trouble me, especially since I would be at our client's board meeting the following day. The same time as the Henry Welker visit. I asked him to give our client a heads-up, courtesy call. I told him this would be greatly appreciated and would enable us to talk with Henry Welker with a clear conscience.

Steve, nervously puffing on his cigarette, said to me: "Who are you talking to? Where are you getting these ideas? What the heck are you doing?" These questions hit me hard. I stopped and considered where my feelings were coming from. I said: "It comes from me, Steve. I am weighing this situation personally and believe strongly that we need to do the right thing."

That's when he said: "Look, I know what I am doing. You don't need to worry about this. I have it under control. You are forbidden to talk to the client about this." Forbidden? Forbidden to talk to my client? That had not been my plan. I wanted him to make the courtesy call, as our CEO and as someone in our management besides me who was directly responsible for our client. It would not be right for me to notify the client as it would imply more negative about the agency. To the client, this should not even be an issue which I would entertain—either meeting with a blood competitor or dealing in disloyalty to my company.

That's when I reached into my pocket and pulled out the letter of resignation and put it in front of Steve. I could hardly believe it was happening. The whole thing seemed to evolve in slow motion. I had a weird mixture of humor over the irony of the situation, sadness and self-doubt about whether I was doing the right thing. Steve read the letter and said again, "Who are you talking to? Where are you getting these ideas? Your thinking is way off!" My reply was instantaneous, from my heart and unplanned: "I feel unclean here. It makes me really sad, because I have loved this company. This situation makes me want to go home and take a shower. I would rather flip hamburgers than continue to work here. I am going to clear out my office and leave at 5pm tonight."

Steve paused and reflected a moment. He said: "Well, what if I do call the client. Will that change your feeling?" I said to him: "I think that would be a good idea for you to call them. In fact, our client will thank you for the call. No, it won't change my decision. It should never have come to this to have you see my point of view. I am leaving tonight."

Then, he hit me with some unforeseen consequences. He informed me that with the Client #5 decision being weighed by that client, if I left at that moment, fifteen of my colleagues working under me would lose their jobs.

In hindsight I should have told him this was his problem, not mine. Nonetheless, I could not fight my feelings of responsibility to the fifteen colleagues, especially the account leader who was in hospital recovering from an illness. I could not see how my decision would not impact them, because Steve was assuring me he would make sure that is how they would see it. Knowing the Client #5 decision to retain or fire us was weeks away, I told Steve I would stay until the decision was made. Steve asked me if I would reconsider. I said no. He then told me not to talk to anyone about this and I assured him I wouldn't and went back to my office.

About an hour later Steve returned to my office door to tell me he had called our client and that I was right, they had expressed great appreciation for the call. Steve again asked me if this changed my intentions. I said no.

Five weeks later on a Friday near the end of May, DFS was notified by Client #5 that it would be severing its relationship as of July 1. That Sunday I drove to Manhattan, saddened with tears in my eyes that this whole situation had come down to this ending. It was not a good feeling. It was not the outcome I had wanted when I came to New York out of graduate school to begin my career. It was a sad ending to the joy, appreciation and sense of loyalty I had towards my company for 14 years. I quietly packed up my mementos of the 14 years, including the many letters, awards and keepsakes from my clients and colleagues. The world seemed uncommonly still, the office completely quiet. There was no one else there that Sunday morning. No one to face except myself.

Reflection: The Penalty of Ethics

Over the past 29 years since my decision to abruptly leave DFS, I have had numerous other opportunities to engage in thought over what is or is not ethical behavior. I have reviewed and relived the experience outlined above, questioning over and over why I reacted the way I did. As I said, it was not a happy outcome. When we are part of a situation of events that are not desired, events that are not pleasant, one can hardly absolve themselves from responsibility for the outcome.

Because of this, I have come to believe that ethical decisions boil down to treating others as we ourselves would want to be treated. It is unethical to treat yourself in a way that does not reflect your own beliefs and values over what you deem as healthy for you. Being true to yourself is a key part of one's integrity. Being true in how you treat others against the standard of how you would wish to be treated is the central question of ethics. I did not want to treat our beverage spirit client any different than how I would want to be treated were I them. Further, I could not let my company cause me to do something that was not in keeping with my own character and sense of values.

The penalty of this is the significant derision and self-doubt one can incur when making an ethical decision. It may ultimately have an impact that is broader in effect than yourself, but the essence of the discomfort is personal. "Do unto others as you would have them do unto you" is a simple divining rod for guidance. So simple, yet so difficult to exercise in the context that ethical decisions often emerge in business.

We can have a thousand reasons to look past our integrity in some business situations. We can have a thousand reasons to create advertising messages to attract, delight and engage people on behalf of our clients with little if any sense of responsibility for what is communicated by the advertising. Nonetheless, we only have one reason to keep the issue of ethics high in our mind and in our behavior. This is taking responsibility for doing unto others what you would demand for yourself. Taking care of this principle assures we are not vulnerable to losing ourselves.

The penalty of ethics is the toll it takes on your definition of yourself, on your image to others, the unpopularity, anxiousness and guilt it can cause others to feel, especially when you are dealing in business relationships where so many people are involved. The positive public consequences may remain undisclosed to us for some time. This is why one must seek consequences that are personally consistent with our sense of self-worth and responsibility to ourselves and our family. No one else can see ethical situations exactly the same way you do and you will be greatly disappointed if you expect otherwise.

Afterwords

After resigning from Saatchi DFS, I realized what my mentor had foretold. Making that ethical choice felt good for about a half hour. It was quickly replaced with fear and the uncertainty generated from numerous associates and family members asking me what my reasoning was. No one could quite understand why I would have left such a bright career or a company which so obviously had valued and rewarded me.

Within days I found out my clients and colleagues were genuinely concerned about my health and wellbeing. They had learned of my departure and were told I had surprisingly just up and quit all of a sudden. That I was not happy where the industry was heading with all the consolidation taking place and that I needed some time to get my bearings and sort out some things on my own.

Many of my colleagues knew that I left despite significant financial incentives to stay. The 5-year bonus feature was only one part of the financial consequences of leaving without a new source of remuneration on the horizon. Financial considerations can be cataracts that significantly cloud our vision about ethical considerations.

Another penalty of ethics is facing the innuendo communicated by those who cannot understand your ethics. In my case, clients and colleagues were left to wonder if I had some kind of personal problem. Like "all the above" potential issues of that time, e.g. a marital problem, a drinking or drug issue or an emotional problem like a breakdown.

Since I had not made any concrete next step plans, I decided to go off on my own and start my own agency called Tim Love Advertising. With this chapter, I learned the importance of cash flow, the responsibility of being even more accountable for my creative work. I wrote and art directed the work for Tim Love Advertising. I am proud that the British Knights campaign tripled the client's revenue in 10 months. Proud that my creative featuring rap artist Kool Moe Dee represents one of the first uses of rap in a broad scale, national campaign (it is on YouTube) and that our work for the

National Council for Adoption won an Effie Award for effectiveness while significantly eliminating the stigma around adoption.

While there was great satisfaction in creating a successful agency from scratch, it ultimately helped me to conclude I could create more effectively with broader impact in a larger organization working with diverse people. A dream of mine and my wife's had been to work internationally. My own little agency would not soon lead to international experience. This dream would be more feasible with global clients I would not soon have with my little agency.

DFS did not go anywhere with Henry Welker. Our spirits client eventually discontinued their relationship. Steve was not successful in becoming the CEO over his co-CEO and he eventually left for another job.

My career went on for a span of 41 rewarding years in the advertising agency business. The relationship equities I enjoyed with my clients and colleagues who never lost faith in me continue to this day. And the financial sacrifices I made with my ethical decision in 1987 were a very small price to pay for the self-confidence, esteem and financial rewards that would come to me over the ensuing years.[22]

We will now read and feel the international ethical perspectives of Ahmad Abuljobain, a senior advertising executive, serving automotive and healthcare clients in both the United States and throughout the Arabian Gulf, while working for agencies including Leo Burnett and DMB&B. Ahmad had the opportunity to work closely with Tim Love on international accounts, and he is in a unique position to comment on Tim Love's two ethical dilemmas. As we review his account, we will learn from an international perspective the role and importance of personal ethics in resolving difficult ethical dilemmas and the origin of our ethical beliefs:

Living with the Penalties

I am the slipper child of an old-school Iraqi mother. She threw that damned thing with the painful accuracy of a sniper at every alleged indiscretion. A raised voice, a retort, a partially eaten dinner, a door unopened for a lady, a less than glorious report card, a displeased elder, and so on. By the time I had to earn a living, I was sufficiently conditioned to imagine a slip-on whizzing by at anything remotely questionable. When I joined the advertising industry, I pictured quite a bit of footwear.

Tim's experience juggling the newly merged agency's revenue priorities with an existing client's need-to-know would certainly qualify as a "slipper moment." His inner struggle will resonate with many in the Arab world's advertising ranks; and probably cause a few frowns among those decrying his naivete. There is, after all, a world of difference between the reality of business and the idealism of good conscience; and if finding the right balance, the right rules, was easy, we wouldn't have Volkswagen, Enron, or Arthur Andersen debacles; and Sarbanes-Oxley (SOX) would be more effective. Agencies would be fairly paid, would not fear sudden loss of income, and they'd know how to charge clients without risking lawsuits, settlements and embarrassing headlines.

I was managing director of Leo Burnett's digital operations in the Middle East when SOX came out. I recall the reverberations, and consequent late nights complying with new guidelines. I also remember debating with our Finance Director the effectiveness of such stringent procedures without what should have been concomitant regulation of client behavior. By that time, I had already spent around a decade in advertising, having left behind the more mundane world of think tanks. My first few years in the business felt like a surreal "loss of innocence" from *Lord of the Flies* or *To Kill a Mockingbird*. I was sometimes told to do things I didn't feel were right; and yet not everything was so obviously wrong. Tim correctly notes one's personal barometer, his or her integrity, defines that person's standard of ethics. The challenge comes when the values of our upbringing are put to the test in an opaque world.

Transparency, as Tim advised, is desirable. It can also be good for business—when the client demonstrates equally honorable principles. Such was the case when, for a few years, Tim and I worked at the same agency albeit me as a lowly account manager in Dubai (then New York) and he running the global show for P&G at D'Arcy (before yet another merger into BCom3 then Publicis). Procterians tend to be rigid about their standards; and I enjoyed the simplicity of working on that complex business: difficult and challenging but always straightforward and crystal clear. I cannot ever recall facing an ethics issue working on P&G brands. Perhaps it was the system, the procedures, the people or all the above. Even when they decide to move accounts, the process is a meticulous quantitative and qualitative evaluation.

Yet what do you do if transparency is treated as leverage or drives a kneejerk decision to fire you for the mere possibility of an infidelity? The ramifications can be severe. When a client abruptly goes, so does the revenue that pays for staff and overhead. So when a client *might* go without much ado, it can be difficult for a manager to do the right thing. This reality is far more common than the egalitarian one.

Yet Tim's unclean feelings didn't come about due merely to the issue of transparency; but rather the whole matter of conflict was so brazenly considered. The issues Tim raised were not limited to clarity. The factors to consider were insubordination—a staffer publicly undermining a director; intimidation—an executive berating, even belittling, a colleague; presumption—guessing what clients may infer, want or do, allowing conjecture to influence tactics; and size—limited agency accounts and clients morphed into a Cerberus taking on Medusa or Hydra. The combination made for an emotional roller-coaster, leading to an emotionally-charged result—one that hadn't considered the implications (a distraught assistant, prematurely fired staff, loss of income). Nevertheless, when the dust settled, it is clear that Tim made peace with his choice.

He did not, however, emerge unscathed. Tim's conclusions underlie a painful memory, one where he bore the brunt of his decision largely alone— and which is presumably the point of his piece: "The penalty of ethics is the significant derision and self-doubt … the toll it takes on your definition of yourself … (and) facing the innuendo communicated by those who cannot understand your ethics." He points out a truism that "(N)o one else can see ethical situations exactly the same way you do."

I am therefore reluctant to evaluate the merits or errors of the unfortunate series of events that led to his resolve. (Particularly since, in my culture, critiquing an elder may result in a slipper to the head.) But I can say with certainty that the unenviable position he found himself in is universal. Throughout my advertising career, I saw managers struggle with the same dilemma. In the Middle East, the challenges are greater because client commitment to agencies is fundamentally fickle. True, there are a good many decent, honest people in the business; yet fear of loss or lost opportunities is palpable whichever door you walk through.

There are hundreds of agencies spread across 22 Arab nations serving a population similar in size to that of the United States; yet ad spend is a drop in the ocean in comparison to North American budgets. The competition is ruthless and the regulations are limited. Agencies that serve multinational clients are subject to global alignments; and big, regional accounts are few. The International Advertising Association has a voluntary code of ethics, particularly focused on the pitch process. The subject has been debated by industry leaders for decades because clients small and large often have no qualms about inviting dozens of firms to pitch simply to hear ideas or rattle the incumbent. Once you win an account, it is common to suffer delayed receivables for months on end until you figure out if the problem is administrative or someone vying for an inducement. Some clients unilaterally decide to reduce invoice values (this happened following the global crisis of 2008). Large agencies with well-trained talent are often undercut by cheaper, less qualified operations which even big clients will choose based on price not skill; so they face a choice of compromising proposed rates in favor of padded production invoices and retained volume rebates. The list goes on; and the higher up the management ladder you go, the greater the pressure to massage your values to conform.

That is why to work in advertising can sometimes feel like being in the Light Brigade, famously eulogized in Alfred Tennyson's verse: "Theirs not to make reply. Theirs not to reason why. Theirs but to do and die …" And this path, I believe, is the one Tim did not want to walk—that of blind obedience to a tactician who didn't realize the gravity of a dubious move. Making a decision to break rank will always attract some form of derision. Tim's choice was a brave one; but when you hold on to standards that others deem archaic or impractical there is no avoiding the pain that will come with ensuing recrimination. Such choices will not jolt others into revising their views. If anything, it will make them more committed to them; and some will even find reason to tarnish you for holding on to values they deemed malleable.

Still, living with the penalties of remaining true to your ethics will always be a short-term discomfort. I would much rather suffer the righteous slap of mother's slipper than the questionable tread of a boss's boot any day of the week.[23]

The personal case for enhanced advertising ethics is demonstrated by the ethical stories we have recounted by David Bell, Tim Love and Ahmad Abuljobain. David Bell urges that we tell our ethical stories to our professionals and "make them feel" the importance of what we have done and learned. Tim Love does just that in telling his own very difficult ethical dilemmas, and confirms what his mentor had told him: you may only feel good for about one half hour about doing the right thing. It is important to know that there may well be negative responses to our ethical decisions. The short-term consequences may be difficult for us, yet Ahmad agrees with Tim's ethical actions, and he also prefers suffering those short-term consequences rather than not remaining true to his ethics. It is also encouraging that the international and American ethical responses to knowing the "right" course of action are similar.

I also want to emphasize the importance of knowing the ethical principles and codes of conduct of our businesses. Yes, and being aware of the law and cases that govern our ethical decisions. In this book I have focused on the current ethical dilemmas our professionals are facing every day in their decisions on the content and dissemination of advertising and PR content.

We are reaching a crisis level on the creation of "Native Advertising" with the Federal Trade Commission insisting through law enforcement actions that consumers are not deceived into believing the paid content is original content. Similarly, the FTC and the FCC, as I have documented, are now working together to insure that consumer privacy is protected and consumers are adequately informed regarding behavioral advertising. The lack of transparency has become critical in Native Advertising, collection of consumer information in digital marketing, and in the powerful selling potential of blogs. This is all documented for our professionals to study and know.

Also, this book has focused on the ethical dilemmas incurred in the marketing of specific products and services. The battle continues and is intensifying between the drug companies and the American Medical Association over the direct to the consumer (DTC) advertising of prescription drugs. This advertising is very important to the industry and to the consumer. It is one of the biggest categories of advertising for the ad industry, and truthful medical information is a major source of information for the consumer. But, it must be conducted in a legal and ethical fashion to provide those benefits. The legal and ethical guidelines are presented in this book along with a recommendation for voluntary enforcement of the industry code by a third party entity, such as the Advertising Self-Regulatory Council.

We are just beginning the battle over the advertising of e-cigarettes. Marketing and advertising are well underway and industry associations are growing in the defense of this new industry. Food and Drug Administration-proposed rules and regulations are included in this book.

Finally, I have placed emphasis on the important role of ethics in the advertising to children twelve and under, which is a major and growing category in the United States. The record documents that care must be taken to insure that they understand that the content is advertising, because unlike adults, they lack experiential and cognitive abilities to understand the persuasive nature of ad content.

In all of these areas it is important that our professionals are familiar with the ethical principles, and governmental laws and regulations, governing this advertising. But, while important, that is just the beginning. The ethicists, and advertising professionals, I have quoted all have made it clear that ethical principles are worthless without decision-making and action. In the important areas cited above, the manner in which the ad and PR content is constructed will determine its legality and ethics. And that will be determined by the motivation and beliefs of the professionals assigned to the ads and PR.

Back to David Bell's knowledge and experience. As he urges, our best course of action is to inspire our professionals to "do the right thing" in resolving the ethical dilemmas they face. He is convinced, as am I, that our professionals will be inspired by listening to the ethical stories we encounter in our careers. "Make it emotional!" They "will want to come to work" and will be encouraged to act ethically for the benefit of the client and customer.[24]

We all win by the practice of enhanced advertising ethics. First, we build trust in order to build brand loyalty and corporate trust. Second, we support our professionals who want to "do the right thing" for their businesses and consumers. In closing allow me to quote my second favorite industry icon, Leo Burnett: "Cling like wildcats to the only realities we can swear we have hold of—our own sacred and individual integrities."[25]

Questions and reflection

1. Why is it important for an advertiser, agency, media company, and third party supplier to have a credo or value system for their professionals to practice?
2. What are the values articulated in the Texas Instruments credo?

3. What is the rule expressed for gifts and entertainment in the Ketchum Business Code?
4. In what ways can those values be emphasized by management and passed down to their professionals?
5. Discuss how James Burke and Johnson & Johnson responded to the Tylenol crisis in the 1980s, and how what they did could help Volkswagen rebuild its image and value system after the international charges of equipping their diesel cars with "illegal cheat devices."
6. What does advertising legend David Bell urge us to do to inspire our professionals to want to practice enhanced advertising ethics?
7. Describe the two ethical dilemmas encountered by Tim Love and how they were resolved differently because of his immediate bosses' reactions to the dilemmas. What role did his "mentor" play in his resolving his second story dilemma?
8. Discuss why Ahmad Abuljobain supported Tim Love's quest for transparency with his client; and how he states that clear and transparent rules and discussions with his client P&G eliminated ethical client–agency ethical dilemmas.
9. Tell one of the ethical stories we have discussed, or another that you know, that has made you "feel" the importance of practicing advertising ethics.

Notes

1 Ahner, Gene, *Business Ethics, Making a Life, Not Just a Living*, Maryknoll, NY: Orbis Books, 2007, p. 55.
2 Kidder, Rushwood, *How Good People Make Tough Choices*, New York: HarperCollins, 1995, p. 101.
3 Badaracco, Joseph, *Defining Moments, When Managers Must Choose between Right and Right*, Boston, MA: Harvard Business School Press, 1997, p. 65.
4 *100 Leos—Wit and Wisdom from Leo Burnett*, Chicago, IL: Leo Burnett Company, Inc.
5 "Principles and Practices for Advertising Ethics," Ethics and Principles, Institute for Advertising Ethics, 2011, www.aaf.org/_PDF/AAF%Website%20Content/513_Ethics/IAE_Principles_Practices.pdf.
6 "American Advertising Federation Ethics and Principles," 1984, American Advertising Federation, www.ccny.cuny.edu/sites/default/files/adpr/upload/Advertising-Code-of-Ethics.pdf.
7 Ahner, *Business Ethics*, p. 147.
8 Van Dyke, Peter, *The Story of Dietrich Bonhoeffer*, Uhrichsville, OH: Barbour Publishing, 2001, p. 50.
9 Ketchum Communications Code of Business Conduct, Ketchum, Inc., 1285 Avenue of the Americas, New York, NY 10019 USA.
10 Badaracco, *Defining Moments*, pp. 96–97.
11 Ahner, *Business Ethics*, p. 150.
12 Badaracco, *Defining Moments*, p. 86.
13 Badaracco, *Defining Moments*, p. 93.
14 "2014 VW Memo Warned of Probe," *The Wall Street Journal*, February 16, 2016.
15 "EPA adds Porsche model to list of VW emission cheaters," *The Washington Post*, November 3, 2015. The Federal Trade Commission has now filed a complaint against

Volkswagen, charging deception with the "clean diesel" claims and seeking an injunction and compensation for consumers who bought or leased the vehicles. "FTC sues Volkswagen over 'clean diesel' ads," March 29, 2016, http://www2.smartbrief. com/servlet/ArchiveServlet?issueid=
9E1DBFOO-8C2C-48BC-B8B4-9F7632CB193E&lmid=archives.

16 "Volkswagen's Software Was 'Illegal Defeat Device,' German Regulator Says," *New York Times*, December 2, 2015.
17 "Volkswagen CEO resigns," by Thad Moore, *Washington Post*, September 23, 2015, www.washingtonpost.com/business/economy/volkswagen-ceo-resigns-after-emissions-ch eating-scandal-spreads/2015/09/23/6b09e540-6203-11e5-8e9e-dce8a2a2a679_story.html.
18 "Volkswagen creates U.S. diesel emissions claims program," by David Shepardson, December 18, 20015, www.reuters.com/article/us-volkswagen-emissions-idUSKBNO UO2QW20151218.
19 Badaracco, *Defining Moments*, p. 128.
20 David Bell, AAA Conference, March 15, 2012.
21 "Excite Dishwashing Liquid" by Tim Love, March 2016; the name of the client and product have been changed in this story.
22 "The Penalty of Ethics," by Tim Love, March 2016; some of the names have been changed in this story.
23 "Living with the Penalties," by Ahmad Abuljobain, Managing Director of Consilior, a marketing consultancy based in the United Arab Emirates.
24 David Bell, AAA Conference, March 15, 2012.
25 *100 Leos—Wit and Wisdom from Leo Burnett*, #85.

INDEX

4A's (American Association of Advertising Agencies) 21, 134–5, 139–40

AAF (American Advertising Federation): author's role in xv; Ethics and Principles 148–9; ethics discussions in xvi; and multicultural marketing 42, 115–19, 127
Abuljobain, Ahmad 169, 172
achievement, ethics of 10, 125
ACT (Action for Children's Television) 52–3, 61
AdChoices 109–12
addiction treatment 112
ADT case 19, 85
advergames 70, 76
advertising: competition in 3; FTC standards for claims in 17–19; government regulation of 15; purpose of 5–6, 36
Advertising and Violence: Concepts and Perspectives 42–4
advertising ethics: business case for 6–10; components of 14–15; personal case for 10–11; *see also* enhanced advertising ethics
advertising industry: and childhood obesity 75, 79; client/agent relationship in 139; image of 7–8; importance to economy 6; and multicultural communities 115–18, 124; self-regulation of 20 (*see also* self-regulation)
Advertising Standards Authority (Britain) 22

advertorial 84
affirmative disclosures 35–6, 60–1
African-Americans, depictions of 120, 127–8, 143
Ahner, Gene 5–6, 10, 146, 149, 151
alcoholic beverages: ethical guidelines for 29–31; ethical stories on 161–3; fairness in advertising 15; promoting moderation 47; regulation of advertising 142.n31
ALJ (Administrative Law Judge) 18–19
American Medical Association (AMA): Council of Foods and Nutrition 54; and DTCA 23, 25; prohibitions on advertising xv
ANA (Association of National Advertisers) 21, 114.n15, 134, 139
Apple 4, 100, 109
Arab nations 169, 171
Arthur Andersen 1–2, 170
ASRC (Advertising Self-Regulatory Council) xv, 21, 28–9, 31, 173
asthma, drugs used to treat 24
audit rights 137–9

Badaracco, Joseph 11, 126, 131–2, 147, 151–2, 154
BBDO 11
Beales, Howard 74
Beer Institute Advertising and Marketing Code 29–30
behavioral advertising 103–5, 109–12, 172
being true to yourself 167, 172

Bell, David xv–xvi, 9, 118, 141, 154–5, 172–3
Bell, Howard xv, 20–1, 147
biracial families 13, 124
Black children 69; see also African-Americans
BP 22, 47, 126–7
Brooks, Linda Thomas xv, 144, 146, 149
Brown & Williamson Tobacco Company 37
Burke, James 3, 151–2, 155
Burnett, Leo xv, 9, 11, 118, 147, 169–70, 173
business ethics xiv, 2, 10, 14
business values 147–50, 172

Cameron, Glen 25
Cardo Systems 85
CARU (Children's Advertising Review Unit): age focus of 76–7; Core Principles 64–5; guidelines 65–7, 140; investigations by 68, 75, 79; review of cases 18; and self-regulation 21–2, 28–9, 50; and violence in advertising 44
CBBB (Council of Better Business Bureaus) 21, 75, 80
CDC (Centers for Disease Control and Prevention) 40, 57, 69, 71, 73–4, 78
CDER (Center for Drug Evaluation and Research) 27
Central Hudson case 16, 36, 73–4
Central Municipal Water District 85
cereals, children's 50, 57–8, 68–9, 71, 78, 81; see also sugared products
CFBAI (Children's Food and Beverage Advertising Initiative) 50, 75–80
CHC (Coalition for Healthcare Communication) 26
cheating 3–4, 11
Cheerios 10, 124
child-directed advertising, use of term 76
childhood obesity: and food and beverage advertising 51–2, 68–71, 73–4, 79–81; PSAs on 142–3; and sugared products 57
children: ability to comprehend advertising 52–7, 71, 78; collecting information from 104, 111; and depictions of violence 42–4; disclosures and disclaimers for 67; and DTCA 24, 27; ethical issues in targeting 7–8, 51, 67–8, 140, 173; levels of advertising to 63–4; overweight 142–3 (see also childhood obesity); regulating advertising targeted to 17–18, 21, 50–1; tobacco use by 31, 37, 39; treating fairly xiv, xvi, 15, 58–60, 81; under age 12 76–7

cigarettes: health warnings on 32–5, 37–9; regulations on 31–2; see also e-cigarettes
client/agency relationships 135–9, 160–1, 163
client conflict 161–7
Clinton, Bill 116–17
Code Review Board 30–1
commercial information, as protected speech xv, 5, 16, 35–6, 43, 63, 73
compliance, ethics of 10
Congoo 98
Consumer Information Power 4, 9, 44
consumer injury 32, 72–3, 79–80
consumer privacy xvi; advertising invasive to 8, 103–4; Bill of Rights 111–12; federal authority over 107–9, 172; see also data collection
consumer protection, beginnings of movement xiv, 17
consumer trust see trust-building
content aggregator sites 89, 94
controversial products xv–xvi
cookies 105
COPPA (Children's Online Privacy Protection Act) 104, 111
corrective advertising 19
cross-device tracking 105, 112
CSI (Center for Social Inclusion) 128
CSPI (Center for Science in the Public Interest) 53, 61
CTP (Center for Tobacco Products) 38
cultural values 120–1

data collection: from children 64; federal authority over 107; opt-in/opt-out from 104–6, 109, 112–13
deception: and advertising to children 60, 71; in cigarette advertising 34–6; FTC use of term 18–19, 22–3; and native advertising 87–8, 97; reasonable relation to 48; in trade names 62.n47
dental health 52–4, 57, 73
DFS (Dancer Fitzgerald Sample) 160–1, 164, 167–9
Digital Advertising Alliance (DAA) 109, 111–12, 114.n15
digital footprints 104
digitally altered images 22–3
digital media: alcohol advertising in 30; blocking advertising in 4, 100–1; for children 77; native advertising in 89, 92
disclaimers 18, 36, 67, 111
DISCUS (Distilled Spirits Council of the United States) 30–1

Diversity Achievement Mosaic Awards 117, 119

doing the right thing, as definition of ethics xiv, 3, 14

Dolce and Gabbana 8, 44

Do Not Track laws 104–5, 109

door openers 88–9

DTCA (direct-to-consumer advertising): authority over 18; debate over allowing 23–5, 172–3; ethical standards of 8; professional and industry input 25–8; trust in 7–8, 28–9

e-cigarettes: ethical dilemmas in advertising xvi, 2; fairness in advertising 15, 39–41; regulation of 31, 37–9; sale and marketing of 31, 173

Elliott, Stuart 86, 124–5

emergency situations 122

endorsements: in children's advertising 64; transparency in 19–20, 88

enhanced advertising ethics: arguments for 3–4; and author's background xiv–xv; business and personal cases for 3, 118; qualifications in xvi; stating need for 148

Enron 1–2, 170

entertainment, excessive 150

EPA (Environmental Protection Agency) 152–3

ethical cultures 146–7, 152, 154

ethical decisions: challenges in 14; in companies 131, 134

ethical dilemmas: client requesting unethical conduct 140–1; company guidance in resolving 151; disagreement with clients 141–4; impact on behavior 159–60; misrepresenting agency services 133–4; mixing friendship and business 132–3; personal decision-making on 126, 131–2; in professional conduct 144; stories of resolving *see* ethical stories

ethical principles 118, 139, 148, 172–3

ethical stories xvi–xvii, 122, 132–4, 154–73

ethical values 10, 134, 141, 148–51

ethics, penalty of 159, 167–71

Euro-Pro Operating 22

Excite dishwashing liquid 155–9

expert advice 19–20

Facebook 9, 22, 86, 125, 128

fair balance requirement 27–8

fairness, in advertising ethics 15, 23

fake news sites 85

Family Smoking Prevention and Tobacco Control Act 37–9

FCC (Federal Communications Commission): and advertising to children 18, 52, 58; and consumer data collection 107–9, 172; and multicultural advertising 116

FDA (Food and Drug Administration): and cigarettes 37–8; and DTCA 23–4, 27–9; and e-cigarettes 31, 39–41, 173; and FTC 18

federal advertising, minority placement of 116–17

First Amendment: protection of advertising xv, 5, 15, 72, 79; and tobacco advertising 35–6, 38, 142; and violence in advertising 42–3

food advertising, for children 66–70, 76–9; *see also* sugared products

food industry, and CARU 75

FRT (facial recognition technology) 103

FTC (Federal Trade Commission): on advertising claims xiv–xv, 18–20, 22–3; authority to regulate advertising 15–17, 24, 61–2; and children's advertising 51–2, 60–3, 71, 74, 78, 140–1; and consumer data collection 105–9, 111–12; Enforcement Policy Statement on Deceptively Formatted Advertisements 88, 97; on native advertising 84–9, 97, 99–100, 172; on online advertising 98; process of cases 17–18; and self-regulation 29, 77, 80; and tobacco products 32–7, 59–60, 141; and violence in advertising 43

FTC Act: and regulatory authority 18; Section 5 17, 34, 52, 58, 60, 63, 71, 73, 107

FTC unfairness authority: and advertising to children 16–17, 58–60, 63, 71, 74, 79; policy statement on 72–3

gambling 61

gay families 124–5

General Mills 124

GET ENGAGED initiative 127

gifts 135, 150

Google 4, 109

Gore, Al 116–17

Great Britain *see* United Kingdom

green marketing 9

grey choices 154

Groupon 9, 45

half-truths 15, 18, 64
health information: in cigarette warnings
  32–4, 37; in DTCA 27; protection of
  personal 104, 112
Healthy Media For Youth Act 128
Hot Buttons 7–8
Huffington Post 100

IAB (Internet Advertising Bureau) 97–100
infomercials 84
information: confidential 139, 150; personal
  see PII
Institute for Advertising Ethics (IAE) xvi;
  and behavioral advertising 111
Institute for Advertising Ethics (IAE)
  Principles and Practices for Advertising
  Ethics 3, 5; Preamble 147–8; Principle 1
  1, 6; Principle 2 1, 10; Principle 3 84;
  Principle 5 14, 23, 50, 73; Principle 6
  103, 112; Principle 7 14; Principle 8 146
interest-based advertising see behavioral
  advertising
International Advertising Association 171
Internet providers 107–8
IOM (Institute of Medicine) 77

Johnson & Johnson 3, 118, 151–4
Journalist Creed 6, 149

Kent State University 9, 45
Ketchum 149–50
Kidder, Rushworth 10, 12, 147
Kirkpatrick, Miles 17

language, plain 96
Lord & Taylor 97
Love, Tim xv, 155, 159, 169–72

McNamara, Carter 14
MAIP (Multicultural Advertising Intern
  Program) 119
managers: ethical decision-making by 151;
  misconduct by 144; setting ethical tone
  of companies 11, 131–2, 143–4, 147;
  teaching ethics to 154
Martin Agency 149
Mashable 100
Mayer, Jonathan 108–9
media literacy 128
media transparency 135
mentoring: author's experience of xv–xvi;
  and ethics teaching 153–4, 164, 168,
  172; of multicultural youth 120–3, 127

mergers 160–1, 163–4, 170
misleading impressions 65–6, 88
misrepresentation 14, 87–8, 106–7, 133–4,
  150
Missouri School of Journalism xvi, 6, 25
moral courage 2, 10–11
Mosaic initiatives 115–19
MPAA (Motion Picture Association of
  America) 68
MPMS (Most Promising Multicultural
  Students) 117–19
multicultural expertise 127
multicultural groups, depictions of 117,
  119–20, 124–6, 128–9
multicultural marketing xvi, 10, 41–2,
  115–16, 126–7
multimedia ads 94–6
Myspace 106–7

NAATP (National Association of
  Addiction Treatment Providers) 112–13
NAD (National Advertising Division): legal
  strength of 17; native advertising
  guidance 98–9; review of cases 18; and
  self-regulation 21–2, 28–9
Nader, Ralph xiv, 17
NARB (National Advertising Review
  Board) xv, 18, 21–2, 28, 79
National Advertising Self-Regulation
  Council 67
National Council for Adoption 161, 169
native advertising xvi; consumer attitudes to
  84; disclosures of 89–96, 98–100; FTC
  principles on 87–9; treating consumers
  fairly 100–1; use of term 86
NBER (National Bureau of Economic
  Research) 26
NDA (non-disclosure agreement) 139
networking 121
nicotine 32, 38, 40
Nike, Phil 3–4

Obama, Barack 111
offensive advertising xiv, 4, 15, 41–5, 59–60,
  149
online advertisements see digital media
OPDP (Office of Prescription Drug
  Promotion) 27
opt-in services 137
OTC (over-the-counter) drugs 18, 24, 28

partner content 100
patient privacy 112

Payne, Ruby K. 121
people of color 41–2, 120, 122, 125; *see also* multicultural groups
PETA (People for the Ethical Treatment of Animals) 8
Pfizer case 17
P&G (Procter & Gamble) 156, 161, 170
PhRMA (Pharmaceutical Research and Manufacturers of America) 26–9
PIA (Performance Improvement Agreement) 144
PII (personally identifiable information) 103–4, 106, 108–11
pitch process 162–3, 171
Pitofsky, Bob 17, 20
poverty, understanding 121–2
prescription drugs: direct-to-consumer advertising *see* DTCA; fairness in advertising 15, 23; high prices of 25; and patient privacy 103
price advertising 15–16
price competition 5
prior substantiation doctrine 17, 19
privacy *see* consumer privacy; patient privacy
product innovation 5
product placement 8, 30, 91
professional associations: advertising by members 5, 15–16; and ethical values 149
promoted content 99–100
PSA (public service advertisements) 3, 9, 44–5, 142–3, 150–1
publisher sites 89–90, 94, 96–7, 99

race, effectively communicating about 128
racism 42, 126–7
reality TV 42, 120, 122–3, 125, 127–8
reasonable basis, prior xiv, 17, 22
rebates, undisclosed 135–6, 138–9
recommendation widget 98
regulatory activism 17
remedial options 33–4, 36–7
retroactive premarket review 39
RFP (request for proposal) 132
Rich, Jessica 20, 85, 97
"right versus right" situations 11; in advertising to children 51, 67, 78, 80; and company values 150–1, 153; in consumer privacy 104, 109; and ethical dilemmas 131–3, 140–1, 143
"right versus wrong" situations 140, 143–4
rules, understanding reasons for 2–3

Schultz, Howard 126
search engine results 92
self-doubt 158, 163, 166–7, 171
self-regulation: and alcoholic beverages 31; beginnings of xv; in children's advertising 50–1, 64, 74–8, 80; and cigarettes 33; of consumer data collection 106; in DTCA 28–9; and e-cigarettes 40; and truthful advertising 20–2
sexual orientation 106, 124
side effects 24–7
Sleep-Test 126, 141
smoking, health risks of 32–5; *see also* cigarettes; e-cigarettes
social media: consumer opinions on 9; junk food advertising on 70; regulating advertising on 20; sharing native advertising on 92, 95
Sony case 20
Sorority Sisters 120, 125, 128
Soul Works 11
SOX (Sarbanes-Oxley) 170
sponsored content 86, 98–101
Starbucks 126
stealth marketing 8
stereotyping: in children's advertising 64–5; as ethical issue 8, 127; offensive 15, 41
sugared products: advertising to children 52–4, 57–63, 71; FTC authority to regulate 17; health impacts of 57, 71
Sun Oil Company case 17, 19
Supreme Court: on fairness in advertising 59; on regulation of advertising xv, 5, 15–17, 73–4, 79; on tobacco advertising 36–7, 39, 142

Taboola 98–9
Texas Instruments 151
tobacco 8, 31, 37–40, 51, 141–2; *see also* cigarettes; e-cigarettes
tooth decay *see* dental health
TPSAC (Tobacco Products Scientific Advisory Committee) 38
transparency: of arguments 4; corporate 2, 134–5, 139, 165, 170; in endorsements xvi; in native advertising 87, 89–90, 97, 100, 172; and personal information 111
Transparency Guiding Principles of Conduct 135–8
trust: building 6–11, 120–2, 133, 135, 173; ethics as engine of 9, 155; rebuilding after scandals 152–3

truth: in advertising ethics 14–15; ethics rising above 23
truthful advertising xv, 88, 100, 142
Turlington, Christy 22
Twitter 9, 20, 45, 125, 128
Tylenol crisis 3, 151–2, 155

unfairness, in depicting people of color 41–2, 120, 124, 127; *see also* FTC unfairness authority
United Kingdom, childhood obesity in 70, 79–80
Urban Outfitters 9, 45
USDA (U.S. Department of Agriculture) 54; Dietary Guidelines 66–7
US-EU Safe Harbor Framework 107

vaporizers 39; *see also* e-cigarettes
VH1 network 125, 128
video games 43, 50, 76, 89, 91, 95, 140

video-sharing platforms 92, 94
violence, depictions of 15, 41–3, 151
Virginia Pharmacy Board case 15–16, 35
virtual worlds, advertising in 91
vitamins, advertising to children 62
Volkswagen emissions scandal 3–4, 152–3, 170

Warner-Lambert Listerine case 17, 19
Werbach, Adam 6
whitelisting 4, 101
Williams, Walter 6
women: objectifying 8, 30, 45, 49; violence against 15, 44, 151

Yale Rudd Center for Food Policy and Obesity 57, 68–71, 73–4, 78, 80

Zeta Phi Beta Sorority 127